HURRICANES
OVER BURMA

RAF photo of the author, taken at Agartala, Bengal, 1943

HURRICANES OVER BURMA

Squadron Leader
M.C. "Bush" Cotton, DFC, OAM

Including
The Memoirs of
Wing Commander "Bunny" Stone, DFC

GRUB STREET • LONDON

But there are deeds that should not pass away
And names that must not wither.
(Byron, "Childe Harold")

Published by
Grub Street
The Basement
10 Chivalry Road
London SW11 1HT

Produced and published in Australia by
Crawford House Publishing Pty Ltd
PO Box 1484
Bathurst NSW 2795

British Library Cataloguing-in-Publication Data
A catalogue record is available on request from the British Library.

ISBN 1 898697 40 X

Printed in Hong Kong by Colorcraft Ltd

95 96 97 98 99 00 01 02 03 04   10 9 8 7 6 5 4 3 2 1

CONTENTS

FOREWORD BY
AIR MARSHAL J.W. NEWHAM

About thirty-five years ago I attended an aircrew reunion at Cowra, New South Wales. As a "pipe-opener", we gathered at the airfield to be treated to a dashing and professional glider display flown by one Monty Cotton. Afterwards I noticed how readily he was accepted by that exclusive fraternity whose bond is forged by the thrills and terrors of battle. And when we chatted together later, Monty seemed especially interested in, if not envious of, my then line of business – flying F86 Sabres. He had remained an enthusiast.

In the early 1980s, his brother, Australia's ambassador, was my immediate boss at the Australian Embassy in Washington, DC. Sir Robert was, in his quiet way, very proud of his younger brother. Last year I attended the RAF's 75th Anniversary Memorial Service at Westminster Abbey as guest of the Chief of Air Staff. My son and I were seated in the best seats next to Group Captain Jimmy Elsdon, who later enquired if I knew "Bush" Cotton and related the circumstances of their friendship. Thus I discovered something of Squadron Leader Cotton's exploits and reputation, and of his RAF nickname. *Hurricanes over Burma* is a record of these events.

This edition now embraces, as a separate book within the volume, the memoirs of Bunny Stone, who was CO 17 Squadron when it reformed and shipped to its new operational theatre, Burma. Monty Cotton was his senior flight commander. The Burma coverage of each book is much the same – places, people, events, anecdotes – yet the perspectives differ, making them a matched pair. Importantly, the second book covers the long period Monty spent recovering from his injuries received in air battle.

The war in Burma was little known in Australia – savage campaigns fought in tough, mostly impassable terrain, dreadful and dangerous weather, appalling living conditions and the lowest equipment-supply priority at a time Britain was sorely pressed on a number of fronts. Consistently and unfairly, the proportion of decorations fell below the norm for other theatres too.

Lesser known is the number of RAAF members who were assigned to the theatre. At the peak, around 1 100 served within the RAF, which included about 500 aircrew spread across sixty operational squadrons. It is unfortunate that few books other than the official histories cover these activities, which makes this volume more than valuable. It is a story of extraordinary survival, endurance and ingenuity, spiced with the humour and wonderful harmony and goodwill that can be generated in such adverse circumstances. It is a very personal story, too, of the manifestation of the daydreams of a barefoot lad who ran wild in the outback district of Broken Hill. Although Monty Cotton was blessed with a natural ability for flying, he reached the pinnacle of his dreams, the command of a fighter squadron, by dint of determination and hard work. As he is by inclination a man of the outdoors, a man of action rather than a scholar, it redounds to Monty Cotton's credit that he has placed his memories on record with a selection of his photographs, together with Bunny Stone's memoirs and excellent pen drawings.

Air Marshal J.W. Newham, AC, OA
Chief of Air Staff, RAAF (Retd)

Book 1

HURRICANES OVER BURMA

The Story of an Australian Fighter Pilot in the RAF

Squadron Leader
M.C. "Bush" Cotton, DFC, OAM

Part 1
THE FIRST FORTY

FOREWORD

England was in a bad way in late 1941. I do not know if it is fully realised the tremendous effect that the injection of young and eager blood from the then dominions had upon us in the Fighter Command of the Royal Air Force.

Exhausted by the Battle of Britain, together with the atrocious losses in France in ten days, morale in our service was still at a low ebb.

I had just been privileged to attain command of the well known No. 17 Fighter Squadron, part of the Kenilworth's Wing which consisted of No. 17, No. 3 and No. 615 (Auxiliary Air Force), whose honorary Air Commodore happened to be none other than the late Sir Winston Churchill.

No. 17 Squadron ended up at Catterick in Yorkshire due, I understood, to take our Hurricane 2cs to fight against German tanks in the Caucasus. Having lost some of my best pilots (Norwegians, Poles, Czechs) due to posting, I was relieved when one day a tall burly figure appeared in my office – none other than the present author, one of the first Empire Air Training Scheme pilots to invade this country.

Recently promoted to Flight Lieutenant, from the famous 43 Squadron of the Tangmere Wing, he had already proved himself in action. We looked at each other with a certain wariness; I with tremendous relief, he with that directness of look of a true "Down Under", which one could easily interpret as "My God, a real Pommy", for I had been educated at an ancient public school.

We got on famously together but eventually "Bush", to my sorrow, was wounded over Rangoon in the first Burma campaign. He survived to command the squadron in happier times, when they returned to Burma in the second campaign, which was to lead to victory.

I leave him to finish his fascinating story of a life of great experience and adventure.

Wing Commander C.A.C. Stone, DFC, RAF (retired)
Kingsbridge
South Devon
ENGLAND

PREFACE

Photography has always been one of my hobbies and, in August 1940, when I was selected as one of the first forty airmen to be trained overseas in the Empire Air Training Scheme (EATS), my dad bought me a second-hand Exacta camera to take with me. This camera used Kodak 120 roll film which produced a 60 x 40 millimetre negative and (being a reasonably small unit and having a 12-second to 1,000th-of-a-second focal-plane shutter) it proved to be an ideal camera for a wide range of applications. It also had a delayed-action shutter, which allowed me to get into my own pictures. Later on in the war, when new film became impossible to obtain, I was fortunate in being on fighter squadrons for most of my service, because they had their own photographic section for developing both cinefilm and still photographs and could keep pasting some of their strip film onto my old paper rolls and keep me in business.

At the end of the war I therefore had some hundreds of negatives, only a few of which had been printed or enlarged. Some of these I had sent home and others remained stored in my tin trunk, which followed me around the world and somehow never got lost, or too badly spoiled, by the tropical climates in which I served. For nearly forty years these negatives stayed in the trunk while I was busy in our family sawmill business, which I joined in 1946 at Oberon in New South Wales. A couple of years after I had retired in 1982, I decided to get back into photography and built a well-equipped darkroom in my garage. When I had finished that task I set about enlarging my wartime negatives, also copying some photos taken by others, together with various other memorabilia I had collected in my travels, or that my dad had saved during the war.

In 1986, I was informed by one of my old comrades from the first forty airmen mentioned above that a reunion of the survivors was to be held at Surfers Paradise in Queensland. Not many of us had survived, or had kept in touch after the war due to the fact that we were selected from all over Australia and mainly finished up serving in different squadrons in the Royal Air Force. Therefore I knew that none of them would have seen the photos I took when we were all training together in 1940. This spurred me on to produce an album of some 200 enlargements which I could take to the reunion, where it was most popular and of course led me to doing more enlargements for various old friends and survivors. After that job was over, my children decided that I must write my wartime memoirs and use my photographs therein as the way of bringing more veracity and interest to the account of my experiences.

In our early days at boarding schools, away from the family, we were commanded to write at least one letter a week to those at home. The habit thus formed continued during my early teens and twenties and the wartime ones were saved by my dad, at my request, and some are used within the text to show what my actual thoughts and reactions were at that time. My experiences in the war divide into two distinct phases and they are therefore recorded in two separate parts.

The first part is called "The First Forty". This details my days of growing up at Broken Hill, where I was born, my education at Roseworthy Agricultural College, my days in employment at Berri on the Murray River, my joining and training with the RAAF, my trip overseas with the first forty of the EATS and finally my days flying Hawker Hurricanes with No. 43 Fighter Squadron RAF in 1941 in the United Kingdom.

The second part, called "Seventeen in Burma", is the recounting of the two years and nine months that I spent in the Burma-India theatre, also flying Hurricane fighters, with, and finally commanding, No. 17 Fighter Squadron of the RAF, before returning to Australia after being overseas for more than four years. After my return I spent the rest of the war in a test-flying unit at Laverton in Victoria, which, while it was interesting enough, does not inspire me to recount, as I considered the war was over for me. I took no more photographs, nor did I write many letters home, so most of my recall would be guess work.

A further reason for writing this account is to pay homage to one of the outstanding aircraft of World War II, the Hawker Hurricane. Although, later on in the war, I flew and loved the Spitfire, the Hurricane was a wonderful machine. Rugged, easy to fly and maintain, a superb gun-platform because of its stability and visibility, it could absorb an enormous amount of punishment and abuse, and saved many lives as a result. Another thing that many people do not realise is that it shot down more enemy aircraft during the Battle of Britain than the Spitfire. It was the mainstay of the first Burma campaign as far as the RAF was concerned.

Another motive for writing the book is to leave behind for my children and grandchildren some lessons which life taught me during my wartime experiences. A lot has been said and written about the effect of war on people and the good things that it does for those that survive it without permanent injury.

What tends to be forgotten is that the youth of today have plenty of opportunities to achieve the same sorts of goals, which can be just as exciting as, and certainly less traumatic than, going to war.

> *Yet much remains to conquer still*
> *peace hath her victories, no less renowned than war*
> (Milton, 1608-1674)

M.C.C. Cotton
14 Jenolan Street
Oberon NSW 2787

ACKNOWLEDGEMENTS

The five maps and the excerpts in the text from *Defeat Into Victory* by Sir William Slim (copyright 1950 by Sir William Slim, originally published by Cassell in the United Kingdom) are reproduced with kind permission from his son, the Viscount Slim.

I am grateful to all who have made this book possible, especially for the advice from Tony Crawford, the Managing Director of Crawford House Publishing; Group Captain Donald McClen, former Chief Executive Officer of British Aerospace, Saudi Arabia; Chris Shores, for the extracts in Appendix C, from his book *Aces High*; Dr Roman Judzewitsch, my son-in-law; and Air Marshal Jake Newham, AC, RAAF, retired Chief of Air Staff.

My dear wife Stella has been her usual rock of reliability in offering judgements and suggestions and I lovingly dedicate this book to her.

1 AT BROKEN HILL

My salad days, when I was green in judgement.
(William Shakespeare, *Antony and Cleopatra*)

Apart from being my birth date, 27 March 1917 was notable for a victory by a French general, Joffre, against the Germans in World War I. A later friend of mine born on the same day was given the Christian name Joffre.

Thankfully my parents decided to call me Montague (Monty) after a much-loved uncle, Monty Warren. He was the general manager of the Port Pirie lead and zinc smelter works in South Australia, to which all the ore was sent by rail from our home town of Broken Hill in New South Wales. Broken Hill was one of the richest ore bodies of silver in the world at the turn of the century and, like all mining towns, was a pretty tough place in which to be born. The ribbing with which Joffre and I met over our names during our school days was fairly rugged at first, but as time passed it turned out to be rather fun to have such an exclusive name.

Mind you, when Mum and Dad also tacked on the other names of Charles Carrington, it gave one schoolteacher at an Adelaide school the chance of calling me "M.C. Cubed" or "MC^3". In fact during my stay at this school, there were three Cottons there at the one time. They were referred to as Primus, Secundus and Tertius, and you can guess who finished up as Tertius.

The name Carrington is supposed to be a family name inherited from our English ancestors but I have a suspicion that it, together with a family crest, was acquired by a member of the South Australian branch of the family. I expect that traditions such as this have to start somewhere and it has subsequently meant that all the male descendants of the family carry this name. I must confess that it does not impress me greatly but my dad's father, Robert, was really rapt in the idea of the name and the family crest. This is described in genealogical language as an "Eagle, Holding in its Dexter Claw a Bell". The motto under it in Latin is "*Fidelitas Vincit*" ("Faithfulness Conquers").

He had the crest engraved on his cufflinks, gold watch and chain, sovereign case, notepaper, envelopes and sundry other items of display. He lived by the tenet, "A good name is better than all riches", and was a great admirer of all things English.

One can understand and appreciate this because, during World War I, he was the manager of the National Bank of Australia in London. While there he personally uncovered a network of German-born sympathisers in South Australia who were sending large sums of money to their homeland via Switzerland. As a result he was offered a knighthood by the Brits but declined it saying that the men in the trenches were more deserving of such an honour.

He was offered and accepted the title "Freeman of the City of London", and my brother Bob, being the eldest in the family, inherited the actual certificate. A few years ago Bob was made a knight of the realm for services to his country as a member of the Australian Senate. I often wonder if Grandad knows about this. He would surely approve most heartily.

Life at Broken Hill, however, amid the sons and daughters of miners and the citizens who supported them was not conducive to the parading of one's supposed good breeding. The desert climate was such that for most of the year we did not have to wear shoes. I can still remember developing pads of thick skin, like a

Me at eighteen months old

Right: My father, Hugh Leslie Carrington Cotton, aged thirty-one, with me (right) and my brother Bob (Robert Carrington), aged three

Bottom left: My mother, nee Muriel Florence Pearce, the daughter of a Cornish miner at Broken Hill. She was a lovely lady with a most beautiful soprano voice

Bottom right: Me at age four and a half. Mother made these smocks for us

kangaroo dog, on the bottom of my feet and I could run over gibbers and broken ground as though it were grass turf. After school the order of the day was to see what mayhem could be indulged in. Hunting rabbits with shanghais (slingshots) or BB airguns, swimming in the local waterholes, building bicycle-racing tracks and numerous other strictly outdoor activities was the pattern of our lives.

Life with nature was more important to us than homework and I am not so sure that we suffered from the lack of academic training to the extent that it gave any advantage over us to those who were the experts and prize-takers at the end of the year. A game that we used to play, called "Quonnie on a String" (derived from the English game of "Conkers"), occupied an enormous amount of our time. It was so named because we used the nuts of a native stree called the quandong. One of the nuts was drilled out laboriously with a sharpened nail and threaded on a string.

The game was played by two contestants. One laid his quonnie on a small sandhill and the other lashed at it with his. The changeover from being striker to struck was then made. The one which eventually emerged unbroken was the winner and given a ranking which included all the victories previously acquired by the loser. Some characters tried to cheat by filling their quonnie with molten lead, but were banned for life when found out. In those days one could find these native trees only a few miles from the town but today it would be hard to find one anywhere west of the Darling River, to the South Australian border, because of the depredations caused by the rabbit, drought and overgrazing by the sheep-station owners.

For reasons I have never been able to fathom, my main attention from the earliest times centred upon aeroplanes. I used to spend countless hours out of school in the building and flying of aeroplane models powered by rubber bands, or carving miniature models out of wood. No one else in the family was the least bit interested but this, and a similar fascination with motorbikes and cars, became a part of my dream world.

Being descendants of bankers and business people, and therefore expected to enter refined careers in offices rather than workshops, it was impressed upon us in our early days that we would have to receive an education which the state-run schools in Broken Hill could not provide beyond the primary level; that is, a grounding in the classics as well as the sciences. This would mean being enrolled as boarders in a private school in Adelaide (some 300 miles away from Broken Hill) and the family fortunes were assiduously addressed with this end in view.

My dad was an old scholar of Saint Peter's College in Adelaide, so he and Mother struggled and saved to send their sons there. They felt that the ideals of this school, with its motto of "*Pro Deo et Patria*" ("For God and Country"), was exactly how they wished their boys' education to be oriented.

To qualify as entrants to this exclusive school, the applicants had to sit for an examination, one subject of which was the Church of England religion. We had attended Sunday school in our local church but, being yearners for the great outdoors, there were a number of occasions when my cronies and I would be "absent without leave" and involved in other pursuits such as swimming or football. In fact I came up with a schoolboy howler in the scripture exam by answering the question, "Who were Cain and Abel?" with the statement that, "They were two brothers who murdered each other."

In spite of this I was duly admitted to the St Peter's preparatory school in

1929 and spent the next four years at this college, which I disliked intensely. It was a direct copy of an English public school, with all of the associated stupidities, such as fagging (being a slave of a senior student) and rule by prefects who were also allowed to cane the students. This was always carried out on the backside and it seemed to me to entail a competition by the wielder of the cane to see how many livid bruises he could raise on the subject. Some students said they preferred caning to detentions or impositions. Those of us who disliked the pain and degradation of being thrashed by some slightly older character, for whom we may have had no respect anyway, had no choice.

The school had one saving grace which made my life bearable, and this was the collection of London *Illustrated News* magazines in the library. They were a complete record, back to the turn of the century, and I soon fastened on to the numbers containing all the exploits of the British and Allied fighter-pilot aces of World War I. The deeds and scores of Albert Ball, James McCudden, Mick Mannock, Billy Bishop, Georges Guynemer, Eddie Rickenbacker and a host of others were added to my dream world.

My ambition in life from then on was to become the leader of a Royal Air Force fighter squadron. Of course I could not keep my big mouth shut and disclosed this to all and sundry, including my dad and grandfather, as a result of which the balloon went up with a vengeance. Dad explained to me in a reasonable manner that I should really concentrate first on getting an education that would allow me to pass my Intermediate Exam (today's School Certificate) before thinking about any career.

Grandfather, however, made no bones about his ideas as to what I should be. As he had spent his whole working life in the service of the National Bank he sniffed with disdain at my aims and said: "Young man you should assiduously prepare yourself for achievement to the honoured position of bank clerk." I hesitate to describe what my mental reaction to this was, but it had to do with manure from male cattle. In my day we were taught that adults could do and say no wrong and that obedience to their teachings was of paramount importance. My decision was outwardly to go along with their admonitions but inwardly to take no real notice of them.

The dichotomy of thought which resulted from all of this meant my dislike of school in general, and St Peter's in particular, ended in my failure to pass the Intermediate Certificate exam. Alarm and despondency reigned within the family circle. It was now established beyond much doubt that I was a natural rebel against normal school life and a lover of the great outdoors, guns, aeroplanes and adventure.

Dad decided to get me away from the last three worthless ambitions and hit upon the idea of sending me to Roseworthy Agricultural College. This institution, some 30 miles north of Adelaide, was a government school whose objective was to turn out diplomates in agriculture, oenology and viticulture who might be able to use their knowledge on their own properties, or apply it in business or a job in government service. It had an unfortunate reputation as being something of a home for rebels because, some years previously, the student body had gone on strike about their living conditions. The end result was that the old principal was replaced by a new, younger man, Dr Allan Callaghan, who was attempting to rebuild the reputation and to improve the academic quality of the college.

As a result of my application to be a student, Dad and I duly turned up for an interview with "Doc" Callaghan (as he became fondly known to all) and we apologetically explained that I had not qualified for an Intermediate Certificate (a requirement for enrolment) but that I had passed in English, maths, chemistry and physics. At the time, the college was really scratching for pupils so the Doc brushed aside my failure to pass the "Inter" and smartly enrolled me. Later on in my years at the college (which I came to love), he told me that one day the reputation of the place would be so high that only students who had passed the Leaving Exam (today's university matriculation) would be able to apply for enrolment, and the college would be highly selective as to who would be able to enter. All he said then has come true and the college's reputation today is worldwide and a credit to his hard work and leadership.

I actually enrolled a week or two before the college term started and was put to work picking grapes. In the late summer, at a temperature hovering around the 100° Fahrenheit, it was hot work and, in spite of warnings to not do so, I sampled the grapes in order to slake my thirst. The end result was a craving for water and this, combined with the fact that I had never done any real physical work beforehand, soon reduced me to a trembling wreck. Weighing in at about 126 pounds (57 kilograms) and being a puny 5 feet 6 inches (168 centimetres) tall, I wondered how I was going to survive the year, but I managed to stagger through each day until, at the end of a fortnight, when the term started I began to get used to the hard toil.

Some of the trials that we first-year students had to go through on our initiation ceremonies were running the gauntlet of the second and third-year students armed with pillows, being bodily tipped out of bed while fast asleep at 4 o'clock next morning, and finding, at breakfast time, after lifting the inverted tea cups from their saucers, dead sheep's eyes staring at us when we up-ended them to see why they were upside down. Another test which engendered a lot of interest was a first-year cross-country race, at the start of which contestants were weighed in and bets placed on the outcome. Some of the obstacles which had to be surmounted, such as swimming across a 9-inch deep duck pond, racing up and over a large heap of manure, running across fifty rows of vines in the college vineyard, and various other tests of endurance and fortitude, were all part of the fun.

The earthiness and rustic humour of the life was illustrated in one of my earliest letters home, wherein I reported that there was a brothel in our dormitory and the abortions were emptied by the third-year students – forgetting to explain that a dormitory raid was known as a "brothel" and an "abortion" was a clothes closet. Mother apparently nearly had a fit on reading this and strongly recommended that I be dragged away from the college immediately.

First-year students spent alternate days working in the fields and the classroom. I found that this life suited me admirably. All the mystery of the begetting of life in nature, which was hidden from young people as much as possible in that era, was suddenly stripped away by lessons in animal husbandry and veterinary science, with their associated activities such as leading mares to the stallion and cows to the bulls. Added to this was the discovery that the girls at Gawler (some 10 miles away) were very friendly and were frequent invitees to the college dances and other social events – so different from the total refusal at St Peter's to encourage any fraternising whatsoever with the opposite sex.

Another aspect of college life which appealed to me was the Light Horse troop. Made up entirely of college personnel, it was a fully equipped Vickers machine-gun outfit, being a detached unit of the 48th Battalion in Adelaide.

Students go to their field jobs by farm wagon

One of the first (and hardest) jobs at harvest time is the making of field ensilage

A Clydesdale colt, having been thrown and anaesthetised, is about to have its pockets picked (that is, it is about to be gelded)

Bags of wheat are loaded by hand onto a farm wagon for transport to railhead or storage. Each bag weighs about 160 pounds (72.5 kilograms)

The assistant farm manager was an ex-soldier who had served in Palestine with the Australian Light Horse in World War I, and he made an excellent instructor in riding, armaments and tactics. He soon had us stripping and reassembling machine-gun parts while in darkness under a groundsheet, using only a bullet as the basic tool. He taught us rifle shooting on the college 500-yard rifle range and we often went to competition shoots at Port Adelaide.

The greatest fun in the college troop, however, was tent-pegging with cavalry thrusting swords, and it was a great thrill to gallop flat out down the course and try to spear the 3-inch wide wooden pegs. A near-tragedy occurred once when Bob Hay, a third-year student and dux of the college, went haring down the course and, as he lowered his sword past the horse's head, the fool thing shied off to the left and Bob continued straight on. We looked down the course with horror as he staggered to his feet and seemed to pull the sword out of his body. The sword had slipped from his hand and he had actually fallen on it, but it had only penetrated the front of his tunic, from side to side, without scratching him.

Bob Hay joined the RAAF at the outbreak of war and we met up again at Somers camp in Victoria in No. 1 course of the Empire Air Training Scheme in 1940. He went on to become the bombing leader in the famous 617 Squadron RAF ("the Dambusters") and was finally mortally wounded during a raid over Turin. The recently improved college swimming pool has been named after him in honour of one of Roseworthy's greatest students – he epitomised everything that was finest in the Australian character.

At the end of my first year I had filled out to a weight of 151 pounds (69 kilograms), reached a height of 5 feet $11\frac{1}{2}$ inches (182 centimetres) and was literally a mass of muscle and sinew, able to lump bags of grain (weighing well over 100 pounds) all day, stook hay sheaves, cut and stack silage, milk cows, groom and harness Clydesdale draughthorses, muck out stables, shear sheep and also butcher them. We had to do all of the jobs of farm labouring that were needed on a farm where there were no tractors to carry out most of the tasks. The senior students were able to get the more interesting jobs of ploughing with the eight-horse teams, cutting and binding hay, and stripping wheat – being more occupied in the classroom and laboratory than we were.

In my final year, the Caterpillar Tractor Co. presented the college with an RD6 tractor, which of course virtually revolutionised such jobs as ploughing and cultivating. The diehard "Horse-farmers" instituted a college debate against the "Mechanisers" as to the probability that horses could ever be replaced by machines. In fact they won the debate by using the argument that horses returned their manure to the soil, thus maintaining the humus and increasing fertility, as against the machine which did not. Those of us who were all for mechanisation did not realise that the answer to their case was legume crops grown and ploughed in especially for their ability to increase nitrogen. Otherwise we might have won on the issue of productivity.

Off to play cricket at the town of Gawler, 15 miles away. Our transport is the college drag, drawn by two Clydesdale farm horses

One other aspect of life at Roseworthy that was somewhat unique was the leg-pulling that went on. Nowhere was this more practised than on those who took themselves too seriously. One case that fixed itself in my memory, perhaps because I was a party to it, concerned a chap who considered himself a real expert in track-and-field sports. He went into a long training routine in preparation for the annual sports day, certain that he was going to win the championship ribbon, plus various cups and medals, and never hesitated to let everybody know about it.

Some of us convinced him that, to have a maximum of energy and stamina for all the events he was going to win, he must ensure that he eliminated any involuntary ejaculation of his semen; that is, "wet dreams". We believed that dreaming occurred when one rolled over onto one's back, so we recommended to him that he sleep with a special device, made from half a tennis ball fastened to his back, which would wake him up when he turned over, thus preventing him from any dreaming at all.

This he did and on the day of the sports was all fully charged up and raring to go. However he was so keyed up before the events that he decided to relax with a short nap on the bench in the change room and, not to be repressed, nature sprung upon him the father (mother?) of all wet dreams half an hour before the start. Of course he did not achieve half the goals he coveted and blamed it all upon the fickle god Pan. We all nearly passed out with mirth and were bemused at how little control does the mind have over matter when nature dictates the rules.

Life at the college became so much of an enjoyment to me that I always regretted having to spend all the long holidays at Christmas time at Broken Hill, even if it did mean I could renew acquaintance with old (actually, young) girlfriends. When the college announced that some three weeks of military manoeuvres would take place in the Barossa area during January 1936, I immediately applied to join in.

We firstly had to collect enough horses on hire from the local farmers and get them to the military barracks and parade ground at Gawler. Having done this, we were instructed in how military horses were to be tethered and handled in order to turn them into true Light Horse remounts. We set out two long rope lines through rings on pegs driven firmly into the ground at 20-foot intervals. They were laid parallel to each other and about 12 feet apart. Each horse was then fitted with a headstall which had a ring on the bottom strap, through which a strong tether was tied to the front rope. The nearside rear leg was then fitted with a single hobble around the pastern, to which a rope was attached, and this in turn fastened to the back rope. Thus we had a neat line of horses exactly the right distance apart from each other and securely tethered fore and aft. This was the objective, but most of the untrained nags had different ideas and the first one to feel the restraint and object to it, by madly lunging backwards and forwards, started a complete riot, in which the others joined with great gusto. But the crafty military had, over the centuries, designed their equipment with all this in mind; nothing gave way and no animal got loose. Being reasonably sensible, once they found that it was no use kicking against fate, the horses never again rebelled against the restraint.

Having got them used to being obedient in the horse lines, our next job was to get them to stand in troop formation while we mounted, and after that to stand still until given the order, "Forward march". We troopers were all equipped with rifles, which had to be placed into a leather holster on the offside of the horse as we swung our right leg over the saddle. The first attempt to do this started a few riots among the more fractious nags. The sight of a trooper halfway over his horse with a rifle clutched in one hand while his horse gyrated under him until he fell off was always a source of great mirth until it happened to oneself. Finally, after much coaxing and swearing (I rapidly learned where the expression "swears like a trooper" came from) we managed to get the troop all headed in the one direction. Within a few days, horses and men looked very professional, and behaved that way.

Before the camp started I had been up to Broken Hill and, at the request of our troop, had shot some emus and collected the plumes therefrom, on a friend's station property . We were adorned with nice large bunches of these traditional Light Horse feathers in our hats and were much envied by the blokes who joined us from the city with the regulation small plume in theirs.

Nevertheless we all got on well together and the city troop set off to act out their role as the enemy for the next two weeks.

It fascinated me to see how the army had designed all our equipment and horse-drawn transport to enable us to be totally self-sufficient no matter where we were; with the exception of long-term supplies of food for man and beast. I guess that in real action in a strange land they simply took what the country would provide if they could not purchase it.

We set off in reconnaissance formation to locate the enemy – "somewhere in the Barossa Valley" – as instructed by the headquarters staff who were running the "war" from Adelaide. The Barossa Valley was the traditional area for the growing of vines and the production of some of Australia's most beautiful wines, so we knew we would not die of thirst. We had scouts riding ahead for some distance as the troop came behind with packhorses loaded with the Vickers machine-guns, tripods and ammunition. Horse-drawn tenders with our food, tents and other gear brought up in the rear. Every day at about lunchtime a strange coincidence took place, in that the main body of the troop always seemed to arrive at a village or a crossroads where stood a hotel or village inn. Having halted for a moment, we were suddenly confronted by the forward scouts galloping back to say that they had sighted the enemy over a distant ridge some miles ahead. Nobody seemed to be too put out by the news and dismounted to partake of liquid refreshments for men and horses. Only the horses drank the water.

Suitably reinforced, we would be on our way again to see if we could intercept the enemy, discover his location and strength, and annihilate him, or have to sneak away undetected. The experiences we had were thoroughly enjoyable. They included firing our machine-guns at targets both by day and by night, map-reading, also by day and night, and generally being instructed in every phase of cavalry warfare, most of which would prove to be quite valueless in the true conflict yet to come. What it did do for us, of course, was to make us more self-reliant, and it taught us the value of teamwork, besides the useful techniques of reading a compass and taking advantage of ground for concealment.

It also recalled to my mind the stories I had read about how pilots were chosen for serving in the Air Force in World War I. Apparently one of the attributes that was highly significant was whether or not they were good horsemen. For the life of me I could never fathom out how this could determine that they might make good pilots. But I hoped that, if the day ever came when we did have to fight a real war, maybe my experience in the Light Horse might be of some account in applying to be a fighter pilot.

So the years at Roseworthy passed by full of interest, learning and increasing good health and physical fitness. I finally achieved the rank of corporal in the Light Horse troop, and graduated from college with an Honours 2 Diploma in Agriculture. The college proved to me that, provided you are of average intelligence and are properly motivated, there is very little you cannot achieve – you just have to be prepared to make the sacrifices necessary to reach your goal. I had not only been educated in many aspects of mental and physical health and how to get along with people of both sexes, but fortunately had a technical qualification which enabled me to get employment, at a time when Australia was still in a state of economic depression.

In our third year, we began to go on trips to various rural industries, and learnt to drink beer between stopovers

My older brother Bob was not able to get beyond his School Leaving Certificate due to financial constraints on the family. At the end of his schooling at St Peter's he had to become an office boy in Dad's business at Broken Hill which was sharebroking and agencies for mining supplies. Bob was, however, a keen student of economics and decided to do a correspondence course in accountancy, and at the age of twenty-one became a qualified public accountant. This was something of a record and an indication that he was to become a force to be reckoned with in future.

My ambitions were still oriented towards life in the open air but we could not afford anything even faintly resembling a property, so I applied for a job with the Irrigation Branch of the South Australian Lands Department, as a junior inspector of leases. This was granted to me and my place of employment was to be at Berri on the Murray River, where a dried-fruits and citrus-growing complex had been built up since World War I by soldier settlers from that conflict.

My initial duties at Berri were to be the surveying of all the fruit blocks and plotting onto plans all the varieties of vines and trees that had been established over the years. Therefore I was required to spend some weeks in Adelaide, working in the plan-drawing office of the Lands Department.

My introduction to life in the public service was a real shock to the system. The plans office was headed by an energetic and hardworking officer with four employees, who spent nearly all their time chatting to each other and accomplishing no more than an effective four hours work a day. When I questioned him about this he admitted that he was literally powerless to discipline these characters, let alone fire any of them. This was due to the rules and conditions that surrounded their employment, in which the goal of security, not productivity, was the main aim.

This shook me somewhat, and after I had picked up enough knowledge of surveying, I was happy to board the bus for Berri in January 1938, hoping that what I had just witnessed was the exception rather than the rule.

2 WAR BREAKS OUT – JOINING THE RAAF

To all swift things for swiftness did I sue;
Clung to the whistling mane of every wind.
(Francis Thompson, "The Hound of Heaven")

I was not disappointed with my fellow workers at Berri, especially with the district officer in charge, Arthur Gordon, who was a former Light Horse officer from World War I. Arthur and his wife Marge, being childless, treated me like a son, and he worked me like a slave. I slotted cheerfully into a life that was spent mainly in the open, surveying fruit blocks, and then mapping them in the office. I was also giving odd bits of advice to those growers who were more ignorant than I (there were not many of them) in the ways they might improve their efficiency.

One could not help but realise that the world was heading for another armed conflict. Being the right age to be dragged into it, one might at least be prepared for it. It did not take long for me to join an infantry company being formed under the banner of the volunteer Militia. At the same time a friend named Arthur Lee (nicknamed "Mert") who was managing the Berri Hotel for his family business, also joined the Militia and we used to race our cars from Berri to the Glossop drill hall every Friday evening.

I had acquired a J-type MG from my brother Bob, who found it an impossible machine for handling the Broken Hill desert climate and road conditions, apart from being second-hand and clapped out when he bought it. I found that each time I raced Mert in his Ford V8, I not only never beat him, but spent the rest of the week trying to get the MG back in tune. If it did nothing else it taught me a lot about cars and the internal combustion engine.

Although I started out like everyone else in our Militia company as a private soldier, I worked hard at learning the art of infantry warfare and was finally promoted to the rank of second lieutenant. Mert, as well, was given this rank and we were both made platoon commanders. Mert went on to great success in the Australian Imperial Force (AIF) during the war. He was highly decorated, and after the war became the National President of the Returned Sailors', Soldiers', and Airmen's Imperial League of Australia (RSL) and was made a knight of the realm.

As a second lieutenant in the Australian Military Forces, Berri Company

Another notable Berri personality, who became my greatest friend, was a young schoolteacher named Alec Ramsay. Alec was a very merry and witty character who came from a hardworking Methodist background. He had a genuine belief in a socialist society and had read and studied reams of books on the economics and politics of the subject. My basically free-enterprise upbringing allowed us to have some mighty debates on the pros and cons of each system but we never let it interfere with our deep respect for each other's views.

In order to supplement his meagre income and be able to marry his Adelaide girlfriend, Amy, he used to spend some hours every Friday evening tutoring pupils from the local high school who wanted to go on to higher education. At the end of this stint I used to drop in and, over a few beers, talk over the experiences with which we met during the week, the future of the world, the state of society and the way in which its ills might be cured, together with countless other subjects which were not usually discussed by our age group. We were all mainly products of an era in which the job of youth was to listen to its elders and move in the directions laid down by them.

It was Alec who also introduced me to the works of Havelock Ellis and his *Studies in the Psychology of Sex*, which opened windows of knowledge on the subject which Victorian society had kept slammed shut, or darkened. My relationships with girls from then on changed somewhat from the ethic of St Peter's College, whose only pronouncement on the subject of boy-girl relationships had been, "Do unto the other fellow's sister what you would have him do unto yours." The mess that blind ignorance of normal sexual behaviour produced in a lot of our generation, with a society based upon the dominance of males and the role of women being bed and kitchen, was avoided by me as a result of my understanding that, in matters of female relationships, one must not gain one's enjoyment at the expense of the other's. Thereafter I hugely enjoyed the company of girls, as they always felt that I treated them as equals. This led to many wonderful relationships, even if a few finished with some heartbreaks on both sides as the war took its toll of our destinies.

Alec and I also endlessly discussed the coming war. He was against all war in principle but realised that, in the final analysis, it might be the only way to right a basic wrong. As it turned out he was never a soldier, owing to his chronic asthma. After the war he acted as my best man at my marriage. He went on to great success in life as manager of the South Australian Housing Trust, the creator of the town of Elizabeth, a member of the board of the Australian Broadcasting Commission, and commodore of the Glenelg Yacht Club, and was created a Companion of the British Empire for his contributions to his country.

During a dinner with him, my wife Stella and other friends, at the Adelaide Club in 1983, he suffered a massive attack of asthma and, in spite of attempts at resuscitation by some doctors then present, he died in front of me. His whole life was an inspiration to me that eclipsed all others.

In 1938 a gliding club was formed at another settlement down the Murray River, a place called Waikerie. At last I was in a position to satisfy my craving to be an aviator and many weekends were spent helping to rebuild a primary glider which had been crashed by the owner at Murray Bridge and purchased by the Waikerie club for £5. The president of our club, Jock Barrett, was the fountain of information (mainly gathered from books) for the rebuilding program. His dear wife sewed up all the fabric for covering the wings. After all the doping and painting was finished, the wire-and-wood flying machine was towed out of its shed and onto a local pasture with an old Dodge six-cylinder buckboard. Fitted on its back was a drum with 100 yards of manila rope wound onto it.

The drum was also equipped with a handbrake. A ring on the end of the rope fitted onto a hook on the front of the glider. However, nobody knew how to fly the beast, so we organised a Waikerie Gliding Club Inauguration Ball in the town, which netted us a profit of £20. In those days one could get flying tuition in aero clubs for 10 shillings an hour, so we gave Jock the money and asked him to get as much dual and solo flying as the £20 would buy at the Adelaide Aero Club, and also pay for his other expenses. Soon after he returned he was promoted to the rank of chief flying instructor and our flying tuition began. It consisted of being towed along behind the buckboard on about 200 feet of the rope, while Jock stood on the back, near the winch drum, with one hand on the brake and the other holding a megaphone to his mouth, through which he shouted instructions to the pilot.

A primary glider is really only a wooden skid with a metal facing underneath it, a wing and seat on top, together with a rudder worked by the feet, and the ailerons and elevator operated by a joystick – no instruments, no fuselage, and only the noise of the wind to indicate airspeed. When things got really quiet you could anticipate being in real trouble. The glider was towed along until it reached flying speed and then the fun started, with Jock calling out instructions and the pilot trying to obey them. If things got too hairy, Jock simply released the brake, the rope ran free and the glider "clunked" back onto the ground.

A primary glider, the same as the Waikerie machine. It was a German design, and similar to the gliders which were used by them after World War I to train pilots (especially their potential German Air Force ones) in the early fundamentals of aeronautics

One's first lift-off from the ground, however (even if it meant flopping back on again after 100 yards), was a unique feeling. An almost indescribable elation was my reward. A conviction soon took hold of my every wakening moment that herein lay my future – a bit like Toad of Toad Hall.

As training progressed we gradually increased the height above ground level and learned gentle turns to left and right, and started to overcome the first problem that every student has, which is over-controlling. My confidence increased gradually to the stage of overconfidence. On one evening at the end of the day's flying this almost involved me in a disaster. I was scheduled to make this last flight of the day and it was from the opposite side of the field to the shed we called our hangar. I convinced Jock that we would be quite safe if I was able to go up to 200 feet and land straight ahead before reaching the hangar. Having achieved that height the machine drifted off-line to the right. Without thinking, I pushed the rudder bar with my right foot as though it were a motorbike handlebar, anticlockwise in order to turn it to the left.

This was exactly opposite of what I should have done, which was to have pushed the left foot forward to turn left. Thus the machine's nose swung to the right at the same time as I pushed the joystick over to the left, to aid what should have been a left-hand turn. This was the method of making what is known as a sideslip and is normally learned as an advanced manoeuvre. It certainly resulted in a mighty one as far as I was concerned. Fortunately I seem to have been blessed with very fast reactions and immediately corrected the rudder as the machine got near the ground. It straightened out just in time to finish in a nice smooth landing. Jock ticked me off for being too bloody clever by half and for showing off by doing sideslips, but I did not let on that it was a fearful error of judgement. My reputation as a top learner remained unsullied.

Before very long we converted the old buckboard into a power winch with some 2,000 feet of high-tensile steel wire on it, which gave a potential launch height of 500 feet. The more advanced pupils were able to attain this height and do a full 360-degree turn after the wire released from the glider. This gained them their first gliding qualification, called the A certificate.

Later on in 1939, after the war had begun, we had a real mess-up when another friend, Jim Gillespie, who worked in a bank at Berri, bought his attractive girlfriend to the field so that she could see him fly. It was my turn to fly first, so I had pestered Jock to take me up to 500 feet on the winch so that I could do a full turn and get my A certificate. Being a cautious bloke, he said he did not think I was quite ready, so he would throttle the winch back at 300 feet and I could do a 180-degree turn instead.

Jim and I towed the glider across to the start point and he asked me, because his girlfriend had to leave before he was due to fly, could he have my flight and simply land straight ahead, as he was not yet allowed to do any turns. I could see no problem in this and was sure Jock would agree because Jim had done this before. We strapped him in and I stood there chatting to his girlfriend. I waved the flag to the winch to take up slack and then gave the full-speed-ahead signal.

Up went Jim and soon reached 300 feet. Jock, who was feeling sorry for me, decided he would continue the launch to 500 feet and I would obviously take it as read that I could do my 360-degree turn. So poor Jim was pulled up to 500 feet before the winch stopped and the launch wire fell off.

He was then in the classic situation of being up the well-known creek without a paddle. He decided to dive at the ground in the hope that he could land before he reached the edge of the field, which was bordered by mallee trees about 20 feet tall. Alas, Jim ran out of aerodrome before he ran out of speed. He pulled the joystick back in the fond hope that he might have enough lift to get him over the trees, but Newton's law intervened and he landed in the treetops. Jock came racing over yelling, "Monty, why the bloody hell didn't you turn?" and then, with open mouth said, "Good God! Jim! What are you doing up there?" Jim, still strapped into the twanging wires and creaking remains of the glider, explained the problem. It was a good lesson to everyone that proper communication was one of the first requirements for safe flying. Needless to say the glider was almost a complete write-off, but by this time there were many willing hands to repair it and we were soon back in the air again. Jim Gillespie later joined the RAAF and was killed in action in the Middle East in 1941, flying a Martin Marauder bomber. Sadly, by this time he was married to his lovely girlfriend.

After the war began, no doubt every parent of an eligible son must have been in the same state of fear as were my parents – that he would immediately rush off and join the nearest fighting unit. At the very outbreak I put my thoughts down on paper to my parents and this is what I had to say:

BERRI

Sunday. 3rd Sept.

Dear Mum & Dad,

Tonight I have purposely postponed my letter to you because I thought that I may have been able to rejoice with you, should Germany have replied favourably to our last note.

It is now 9.15 and I have just finished hearing the speeches of Mr. Chamberlain and our own Prime Minister and you yourselves will too have heard I guess, that it is to be war again.

It is at times like these that one comes really face to face with oneself and at the present moment I feel no tremor of fear at what I know must come. You too, however much you may have refused to believe it, have known all along that should this horror be imposed upon us that no power on earth would stop me from doing what I think fit and what I have been taught is fit to do. I am old enough now to realise and feel very deeply that what success I have made so far in life has been due to a long fight by your two selves to keep me on the right paths. Subconsciously I have made you my standards and though I naturally have my own secret thoughts, most of the big things I have ever done have been done with the thought behind them, "How will Mum and Dad think of me for this".

Tonight I ask myself the same question and though I can see the tears springing to your eyes I know that what I have to do is exactly what you both would have me do. There can be no shirkers in our nation. Those who are not for us must be against us and anyone who does not discern the sincerity behind Britain's last moves is not only bigoted but self-deceived. It is our duty once again to try to maintain right and freedom in the world and to do this we are about to sacrifice a few million lives in the hope that eventually law and order may prevail.

One cannot help but ask, "Since the last war was fought with the same intention and has failed, then are we making further useless sacrifices". But are we, I wonder? Don't you feel in your innermost hearts, that despite all the arguments, this is our last resort and one which we must all face up to? I would never forgive my country and her leaders if I ever lived to find out that we are being inspired by propaganda and trickery as so many were last time.

There is a song on the wireless coming through now, "Two O'clock in the Morning". Do you remember it?

It may seem a funny sort of song to bring back memories but every time I hear it I think of us as kids in our old home, singing around the piano with Clarrie Howie. If ever kids worshipped a man we did. I guess I am very lucky, taking everything into consideration, since I have good memories of good times and no remorseful ones.

It is quiet here now. Nobody except Jim Gillespie has come in since war was declared and since he has now gone I am alone with my thoughts and find, to my surprise, that they are still intact; nothing has changed except perhaps that my subconscious mind has begun to build up its wall of fatalism.

It seems funny that amidst such a terrible catastrophe human reason is still present and that no strong emotion sways me. I feel much calmer than I did during all the previous tense moments. It brings me to the conclusion that I am not afraid to meet my maker and perhaps I have saved myself up for this. I always knew that some such big demand on my independence and life would come some day. I had hoped it would have been a good wife and family and a career of national good but I guess the powers that fashion our destinies have other aims in store for me. Do comfort yourselves with the thought that you are not the only family that may have to suffer. Please don't take things too hard Mum and Dad. It had to come in the end and no matter how much one may hate a thing, to run away from it does not improve matters at all.

On no account must you let Bob enlist. He has a wife and nipper and he has a big business to attend to which is helping the mines to carry on and that means a national duty unless the authorities decree it otherwise. Please remember this too; that when I go into battle it will be with an environment that has always appealed to me for its cleanliness and high ideals. I think flight is wonderful and no matter to what hideous uses it may be put this time, it will come into the world again in the form of an enthralling relaxation. Our gliding promised to develop into that but I guess that will be postponed indefinitely. The airman who comes out of this war is going to have a lot to answer for and it may take years to ultimately clear the practise of the beastliness which it is going to create, but I feel confident that it will ultimately become to mean more to us than a new manner of destruction.

Of course I am going to see you all again before I do anything; I know that Mums is in Adelaide, but I write this to you all as usual since it may be the "first of the last" and you must keep them all. What my next move is until general mobilization is called I am uncertain but now I am going to bed and sleep and I trust you will all accept the inevitable and do the same. This is a time that we all of us need a courage that will endure anything. I know that we have inherited this from yourselves and hence I have no fear for the future and want you all to be the same way.

I will write you every time anything comes up; at present I am trying to puzzle out a way of getting down to Adelaide to see Mums. I may ring her up if she is on the phone. Be of good cheer all you good lads. I do love you all so very much.

Mont.

In spite of that letter, I still recall to this day the feelings that overcame me at the outbreak of the war. There was a mixture of apprehension and excitement which I did not carry into my letter to Mum and Dad. I knew that one of my ambitions, to command a fighter squadron, might now be within reach. At the same time it was tempered by a vivid imagination as to the price which might have to be paid to reach and hold it – knowing from my studies of World War I that the chances of survival in fighters were extremely slim.

I am now sure that the conditioning I received, by being educated in my schools that service to God and country was paramount over self-survival, was also one of the reasons that I immediately put the wheels in motion to join the Royal Australian Air Force. This was strengthened by the training I was receiving in the infantry, where one was taught to suppress initiative and follow orders without question. The rebellious streak in me decided that lone combat, where one did not have to depend on or be responsible so much for others, was another powerful reason for aiming for the skies.

At the time that I applied for the RAAF I was in camp at Woodside in South Australia with our Militia battalion, and after I got back to Berri I wrote the following letter home:

Irrigation Office
Berri

Thursday

Dear Dad,

Further to the phone conversation which we just had I feel that I should write to you now. In any case I intended writing tonight and am sorry that I have not been able to do so before, owing to the rush and tear which I have been in since the camp and during same.

Naturally the first thing to talk about is my application to join the Air Force, about which I think you are unnecessarily concerned. I offer no excuses for my joining up because I still think that what I have done is not half so disastrous as you all seem to think. I have however many reasons for joining which I consider completely justifies my attitude, the main one being that I have bottled up my desire to join the flying corps for so long and have had to lead such a damned prosaic and unadventurous life that I refuse to be dragged into staying away from the scene of action doing a job which another person, with half my training, could do equally well.

In any case your argument that I would be much more use to the country if I remained behind must apply equally to all the Battalion Commanders, Company Commanders and practically every officer in the present A.I.F. because at least 75 per cent of them must have been holding down jobs which were more vital to the country than my own and, if you still think that these men should not have to go then who in the hell is going to run the military machine?

Also using your argument that the military machine will not be used to any extent by us, but that we will gradually starve the Germans out, then why worry about me joining the Air Force if we aren't going to fight anyway?

However I could go on bringing up arguments against yours and you could do the same with mine, and better perhaps, but this still does not alter the fact that Australia is scheming to train hundreds of pilots and to build up a tremendous Air Force and the only way to help this to happen is for those, who are not at present engaged in a job of national importance, to throw their weight into it.

I wish I could share your confidence that the Germans will not launch a big air or land offensive during the whole war, but will sit down and be quietly starved out. I share the opinion of many others that this is going to be very far from correct and in fact the only way that Germany can gain success is to strike hard and quickly. Should they do this and we still find ourselves in the glorious military muddle in which we are struggling at the moment, then we will realise the necessity of having men ready to do the job in hand rather than say "Let's sit down and see what happens before we do anything".

No doubt, had I already been engaged in running a property in Western Australia then I might have been persuaded to stay behind, but whatever gave you the idea that a person can walk out from Roseworthy and not have anything to do with fat-lamb raising for 3 years and then manage a new property straight off the bounce, I don't know. It requires an apprenticeship of at least one year under some other pastoralist in the district before one could even get used to the seasonal conditions and the methods of management, which are peculiar to each different locality. In plainer words Roseworthy is not W.A. and unless I received special training and advice for a year or more then you would be definitely risking your money.

Finally, so much am I convinced that I would not be doing the right thing, then to pull out and run off to a nice safe job of farm managing would leave me thoroughly disgusted with myself and since I have to live with myself (I say this without any desire to be selfish and exclude the rest of you) then it is up to me to keep this relationship a clean one, where I can examine my conscience without feeling like a worm. In any case I haven't passed the quack yet, but in the condition I am at present any doctor who doesn't let me through would need examining himself.

I meant to tell you all about the camp and may elaborate on what I have to tell you when I get more time. I undoubtedly enjoyed the life when I was well enough to appreciate it (due to the tonsillitis) but seeing things with the eyes of one who is anxious to see the country organized and the war over and done with, I was absolutely and thoroughly disgusted.

Firstly no effort had been made to organize the troops into definite training units, nor effort made to supply the officers necessary to carry out this training work. The men knew as much as most of the officers and when the latter made mistakes then it was patent to all and loss of respect and discipline followed as a result. Take this as an example of the inefficiency of the administration.

Owing to the fact that all other officers in our battalion were engaged in doing duties around the camp, which could have been equally well performed by men of lower rank, I was sent out on my own in charge of a whole Company and told to teach them Advance Guard work.

This meant that besides being Director of Operations I had to be also the Umpire, Critic, Officer Commanding Main Guard and Van guard. Naturally I taught them "a la book" how the whole show was carried out; but what a futile waste of time and money when they should have been trained by somebody at least twice as well trained as I was. If they desire trained men why in the devil not send them to an Officers school for a couple of months at least, so that they can return secure in the knowledge that they can gain the respect of the troops.

I can see now how hundreds of men's lives must have been sacrificed in the last war because of this lack of the right knowledge and proper organization and it looks as though they are walking into the same trap. They can count me out of it if they are. If I can't get into the Air Force then I will consider your proposition because I refuse to be led out to slaughter by a lot of bloody fools whose main object seemed to be moaning at the sentries because they wouldn't salute them and getting drunk in the Officers Mess. The main saving grace of the camp was the companionship of the good fellows in our own Company and amongst the men of our region but perhaps this was because we had worked together at Berri for so long.

Well I have already taken about two hours of the precious Dept's time and if I don't stop now somebody will be sure to write a memorandum about it so to save them the trouble I had better try to reduce the pile of dockets in my basket which frightens me every time I look at it. My love to Mum and all the kids.

Your very loving Mont.

Having made up my mind to join the RAAF, and being somewhat browned off at working for the government, I felt it would serve no useful purpose if I remained at Berri until called up to report for aircrew training. I decided I would be better off to resign and go up to Broken Hill, where there was an aero club in which I could train to be a pilot, and get some experience of power flying at a cost of only 10 shillings an hour. This I managed to do to the tune of almost sixty hours of flying, involving lots of stunting and throwing a Gypsy Moth or the Moth Minor around the skies and often taking movies with Dad's cinecamera while doing it. Those few months in the autumn of 1940 were also enjoyable because most of my contemporaries were waiting to be called up into Army, Navy or Air Force. The girls wanted to make the most of them while they were there, so the barriers were somewhat lowered, to the immense delight of all.

The day dawned in April 1940 when I was directed to report to Adelaide for a physical examination by the RAAF. This held no fears for me because at Roseworthy I had reached a high peak of physical fitness with all the farm work. I had maintained it at Berri as an active member of their rowing club, where I once stroked a maiden eight to victory in a regatta. Then, due to gliding and Army training interfering with the schedules needed for crew rowing, I took up single sculling.

At Adelaide I was duly examined, pronounced fit, sworn in and given a number, 407041, which remained with me for the next five years. The first 40 in the number stood for the year in which one enlisted; that is, 1940. The next number was the state in which one enlisted. Number 7 stood for South Australia. The last number, 041, meant that I was the forty-first person in that state to be enrolled. The organisation which we all joined was known as the Empire Air Training Scheme (EATS) and it finally trained more than 28,000 of our Australian airmen, in Australia, Canada and South Africa, before the war's end.

After our swearing in, the intake of ninety aircrew volunteers were lined up and told that, since not everyone in an aircraft could be a pilot, some of us would be mustered as observers and some as air gunners. To my consternation my name was included among the observers and I was sent off by train, with others, to Cootamundra in New South Wales.

I knew that this was no way to being a survivor (let alone a fighter pilot) so, soon after reaching Cootamundra, I asked for an interview with the Commanding Officer, Flight Lieutenant Murdoch. I pointed out to him that the Allies could possibly lose the war if I was not remustered as a pilot. Instead of throwing me out of his office, he suggested I should finish the first thirty-day initial-training course and he would assess me at the end of it. Motivation took over at full throttle and, while the other guys were pub-crawling and girl-chasing during their hours off, I was squirreling away at improving my studies, deportment, drill and discipline. The joy with which I was able to write the following letter home can be imagined:

No. 1 Air Observers School.
Cootamundra
Sunday

Dear Mum and Dad,

This morning is a perfect one and I am sitting in the sunshine feeling fit and thoroughly pleased at last, for the reasons which I will give you.

You remember my mentioning how the Group Captain came up and interviewed some of us? Well it has so transpired that I have got a recommendation from my Commanding Officer for a pilot's training course at Somers (near Melbourne) and I leave here on Tuesday morning about 2pm with about four others who have also cracked a pilot's job.

I topped the course and am very pleased indeed. I am going to send you a wire so you will know where I will be when next you write, When I came here I realized that with hard work I could get on well and I certainly have!

Here are my exam results:-

First Exam:-
Maths. 83 per cent.
Spelling. 96 per cent.
English Essay. 97 per cent. I topped the whole lot in this. I wrote on Compulsory Military Training, and the Education Officer said to me:
"It was a pleasure to read. I wish I could write as well as that myself".

Second Exam:-
Rifle shooting. At 100 yards with the .303 I scored 75 out of 75 which meant 16 bullseyes out of 16 shots i.e., 1 for a sighter and 5 points for the remaining 15.

This was the top score of the whole school and I won 10 Shillings and sixpence out of pools and £1 on a bet with a chap – who still owes it to me by the way. The marker in the butts said it was so good that all the shots were in a 3" circle which pleases me greatly since we had no rests and open sights. Further to this there was a carnival here at the showgrounds last Wednesday and I joined in the winning Tug O' War and won 4 bottles of beer. Again I came 2nd in a 100 yard championship and won 10 Shillings. Haven't finished yet because I must tell you about my Morse code work, I can now receive at the rate of 7 words per minute and was given an "Excellent" award.

Naturally I have not been backward in endeavouring to impress all this upon the Commanding Officer and I know from what I have been told that he is extremely pleased but I'll bet he's not half as pleased as I am.

The other day I received a pleasant surprise when Mr. Rabbit called in from Young and had a chat. He said he would write and tell you that I looked well and was enjoying myself. I have by no means neglected the social side of life and have made some good friends in a country family here called the Scotts. They have a beautiful home and property about 10 miles out and I played tennis there last Sunday and dined remarkably well. Naturally the main attraction lies in one of the fair daughters, Alice by name, who, being so stricken by my leaving the district has promised to knit me a pair of socks and, in view of the fact that she actually bought the wool, it looks very likely that I will get them!

The life here has been really good after the exams. Every other night we generally troop down to the local pub and chat over a beer or two and we have been practically overwhelmed by dances and balls to which we are always invited and at which we always make terrific enemies of the locals by getting away with their lasses.

In a more serious vein. What do you think of the war news? I only hope that there is some force working behind us that we know nothing about because on present showing we have lost all the way. Today we all attend a church parade and I do hope that our prayers for the British Empire will again be answered by a final victory, but it may take a long time as you say. Well, I must tear off now so with best of love to all I am,

Your loving Mont.

After I arrived at Somers I found out the reason why I was at first mustered as an observer. It was due to the fact that I had failed to hold up a column of mercury for more than sixty seconds by blowing hard into a tube. This surprised me, but a friend, Pat Field, whose dad was a doctor, told me that it was taken as an indication of excessive nervousness – which I believe was true on that occasion. I was informed that I would have to pass another medical, and of course the vivid imagination got to work and I started worrying about it. Pat suggested that I should go home with him and see his dad on the day of my exam to see if he could give me something to calm me down. This we duly did.

His dad was an awfully nice man, and quite sad at seeing Pat and myself so keen to be heading devotedly into what to him must have seemed certain death, which it did turn out to be for Pat. He gave me a bottle of pills called Luminal. He told me to take one of these one hour before the exam. To be certain of it, I took two of them, and on entering the exam felt I was walking on air about 6 inches above ground level. I duly held up the mercury for 108 seconds, creating an Air Force record, and eliciting from the examiner the observation that my previous examiners must have been idiots.

I just made it back to Pat's place and slept for twelve hours straight, and vowed to keep my tablets at the ready for any future exam that might possibly prejudice my overweening need to keep flying. As it happened I still had them at the end of the war because nobody ever asked me again to hold up the mercury. Maybe this was because they did not want to take a chance of grounding someone in whom, by the end of the war, they had a hell of a big investment.

Our commanding officer at Somers Camp was Squadron Leader T.W. "Tommy" White, who had flown with the RAF in the Palestine and Middle East campaigns during World War I. He had been captured by the Turks and wrote a book of his experiences, called *Guests of the Unspeakable*.

He was a member of the House of Representatives in the Australian Government. Small, energetic, serious and a true patriot, he was ideally suited to head up such a school and we all thrived under his administration. We managed to pull his leg at times, notably when a section of ten of us were returning from a rifle shoot and decided to keep in step and thump our feet up and down in unison on a suspension bridge, over a creek, near the administration area. We had the bridge leaping up and down close to the point of collapse when Tommy came bounding out of his office calling "Halt, halt!" in his loudest voice. We were duly lined up and given a lecture by Tommy as to the grave dangers to structures from resonance caused by rhythmical loads taking the structure to the point beyond its designed stress. With straight faces (lying like pigs in clover) we thanked him for dispelling our ignorance and promised always to break step in future.

Rifle shooting at Somers was carried out on an 800-yard range with only four target mounds, and consequently there was a lot of standing, or lying, around done while waiting to shoot. Since this became rather boring, things began to happen. First, somebody who was reclining gracefully in a small bush suddenly sprang into the air with a loud shout, having discovered that some bright spark had crept up behind him and set fire to the bush. All around the range was a thicket of thin tea-trees. As some of the lads were leaning against these, watching the firing, it was but a moment before they were lightly tied to the trees by the brace which ran horizontally across the back of their overalls, much to everyone's amusement when they stepped (or tried to) smartly away from the tree as they were called to the firing line.

Another joke, against myself this time, was perpetrated by the lads with whom I came from Cootamundra. Knowing that I had gained the highest score off the rifle at Cootamundra (and was all set to clean up at Somers), after my grouping practice on the 100-yard range, they altered my sights to 800 yards while I was examining my target. When my next ten rounds all went exactly 9 inches above the target, great was the badinage and my own consternation.

An extract from my diary at that time reads:

8 June 1940

Talking to Bob Hay of Roseworthy today and he told me that the Department of Agriculture in South Australia are not making good the difference between his civil pay and military pay, This means that the government, who, at the beginning of the war asked private firms to make up differences in pay are not doing so themselves and this is, in my opinion, pretty scurvy treatment especially in view of the fact that he is married. Bob is a very fine chap, being Dux of Roseworthy while he was there and has just left a job as lecturer in fruit culture.

There is a young chap from the Australian Broadcasting Commission in our hut who plays the ukelele well and is generally a lively character, one of his jobs in the Commission was to entertain celebrities and he knew Harold Williams the singer very well. We naturally drifted into conversation about singers and songs and he informed me that he learnt the following marching song from H.W. who came out with it at a dinner party in this chaps home. It is sung to the tune of "Colonel Bogey March" and is at present our marching tune at Somers and is often sung at our musical gatherings in the evenings:-

Adolf has only got one ball,
Goering's they say are much too small.
Himmler, is somewhat similar,
While poor old Goebells, has no balls at all.

Bob Hay's experience confirmed the suspicions I had during my last months at Berri, when I was doing my own job plus a large amount of that carried out by the previous inspector of leases, who had been promoted to district officer and not replaced by anyone. I wrote home at the time that I suspected the department were going to try every trick in the book to prevent my getting a higher salary because they knew they might have to make up the difference when I joined the Air Force. It was this mistrust I had of their motives that made me decide to reject their offer at the end of the war to become the district officer at the Loxton Irrigation Settlement. This was then scheduled to expand into another soldier settlement for World War II veterans.

I worked very hard at Somers, and we were all issued with a Pilot's Training Card, which we had to carry throughout our training period up to the time we would be posted to squadrons. Mine read as follows:

1. Maths. 96 per cent.
2. Navigation. 97 per cent.
3. Signals. 100 per cent. (8 words per minute Morse Code)
4. Law & Administration. 93 per cent.
5. Gas & Armaments. 75 & 80 per cent.
6. Drill & Physical Training. 95 per cent.
7. Medical. 95 per cent.

General Remarks:
"Distinction in all subjects. Excellent type. Considerable flying experience. Has all qualities as officer. Third place out of 98 in school for all round excellence".

Signed; T.W.White, Squadron Leader.

Not long after this I was informed that I was to be posted to No. 4 Elementary Flying Training School at the aerodrome at Mascot in Sydney. Much to my delight, I learnt that two pals of mine at Somers, Selwyn Clark and Alex Kerr, both from Western Australia, would be there too.

3 ELEMENTARY FLYING TRAINING

Now God be thanked who has matched us with this hour,
And caught our youth, and wakened us from sleeping.
(Rupert Brooke, 1887-1915)

On 27 June 1940 I was enrolled at No. 4 Elementary Flying Training School, which was based on the main airport for Sydney, originally named Kingsford Smith, but now mainly known as Mascot. It is named after Sir Charles Kingsford Smith, Australia's most famous aviator. To my delight, I was to be taught my elementary flying training at the civilian aero club known as the Kingsford Smith Flying School. This was an organisation started by Sir Charles and, I guess, then belonged to his estate.

The RAAF was in the throes of an enormous expansion program in its role of training aircrew under the newly created Empire Air Training Scheme. It just did not have the aerodromes, instructors or aeroplanes to do it. This training was therefore contracted out in some areas to accredited civilian schools, of which Kingsford Smith was one. I was duly fitted out with a SIDCOT flying suit, wool-lined flying boots, gloves, helmet and goggles, and assigned to B Flight, under the tutelage of my instructor Mr Bayliss (age nineteen), who reported to the Chief Flying Instructor, Allan Clancy. The SIDCOT suit was invented by and named after Sidney Cotton, a World War I Australian pilot with the RAF. He also pioneered photographic reconnaissance in specially modified Spitfires and formed the first Photographic Reconnaissance Unit in World War II.

The aerodrome at that time was overall grass with no paved runways and the only airline traffic was two Douglas DC2s which plied between Sydney and Melbourne, and Sydney and Brisbane, twice a day. Our aeroplanes were a mixture of de Havilland Gipsy Moths and Tiger Moths, all painted a bright red

Training with the Kingsford Smith Flying School, Sydney, in 1940; the aeroplane is a Gipsy Moth

with chequered tailplanes, and looking more like Baron von Richthofen's World War I circus than RAAF trainers. My logbook shows that Mr Bayliss and I did four flights together, consisting of circuits and landings, spins, and so on, for a total of two hours and twenty minutes, and then I was sent off on my first RAAF solo flight on 1 July 1940.

At this time the Battle of Britain was in its initial phase and those of us in training often wondered if the war in the air would be all over before we could get there. It is as well that we are not in any way gifted at foretelling what lies in the future. We all spend plenty of time guessing what is going to happen but there is no foolproof system of actually pinning it down, in spite of the would-be soothsayers. Had there been, then those of us who were concerned about being too late to get into action would have had the willies had we known what really lay ahead for the next five years.

At Mascot, as at my previous training units, I had made up my mind to try to top the course, so I did not overdo the social life and got on with learning as much as I could. Looking back, it is now apparent that I had a natural urge to want to be at the head of any group I was involved with and always felt uncomfortable if I was not. This urge really never left me until I retired from business in 1982 and it is only today that I have achieved a peace of mind that overcomes ambition. My letters to home reflect this desire to do well, and some of them also reflect a fair degree of overconfidence and some egotism, which, as the war progressed, toned down considerably. Extracts from some of these letters rather than all the scribble, will be chosen to illustrate this.

However, we spent from 27 June to 20 August having the fun of our lives being trained in the classic style of Air Force flying. This included flying "under the hood" on instruments only, aerobatics of all description, forced-landing practice, sideslips, cross-country navigation flights and inverted flying. The first time that Mr Bayliss turned the Gipsy Moth upside down in order to familiarise me with inverted flight, I nearly died of fright as I fell into the shoulder harness and noticed odd bits of dirt and other strange objects drop out of the aeroplane in front of my eyes. My initial reaction was to grab hold of the side of the cockpit and hang on like grim death. On landing after this session, Mr Bayliss asked me how I liked inverted flight and I confessed that it scared me. As a result of this a little note appeared in my record that, "He does not feel confident in the inverted position."

Being a civilian flying school, Kingsford Smith did not have parachutes, and I believe that this was the reason I was not enamoured of inverted flight, because as soon as we were equipped with chutes on our next course, and later in our squadrons, I used to love belting around upside down, or any which-way, as long as it was not straight and level for too long. The sequel to this is quite macabre because when I was on the high seas to Canada, Mr Bayliss was instructing another pupil in exactly the same techniques when his own safety harness broke and he fell out of the aircraft to his death over the Sydney suburb of Randwick.

Some of the training was interspersed with amusing incidents, two of which occurred on the same day when a strong south-westerly wind blew up while we were flying. Ken Hicks, a trainee from Western Australia, came in for a landing and was caught by a very strong gust during a turn, to avoid another aircraft, at the end of his landing run. This flipped his machine over onto its back. He was relieved to find that he was quite unhurt and released his safety harness only to fall on his head and hurt a muscle in his neck.

The other thing that happened was when I was flying over the top of the drome in one of the Tiger Moths which are equipped with wing slots – allowing one to fly right up to the point of stall in safety. I found that by flying directly into the wind, 1,000 feet above the drome at just above the stall, the aircraft actually moved backwards over the ground from one side of the drome to the other – to the amusement of all and sundry.

Another episode which caused us all some mirth and brought forth some caustic comment was the making of a film by a Sydney company, which included a night-time scene of a German Luftwaffe transport aircraft disembarking a number of armed German troops and taxiing off into the night. A DC2 aircraft, which was one of the daily Australian National Airlines flights to and from Melbourne, was branded with German Air Force insignia by pasting paper crosses on its fuselage, which of course all blew off as soon as the engine started. So the troops all knocked off while someone replaced them with a washable paint. No one in their right mind would mistake the aircraft for anything but a DC2, but that's entertainment.

After the troops had rushed about and fallen over one another in the dark, or tripped over their (British) rifles, the hilarity was further increased when the DC2 ran one wheel into a pothole in the dark and the whole thing had to be scrubbed. I would hate to have seen the final product and been ushered from the theatre for making rude remarks.

In one of my wanderings around the aerodrome after the flying day had finished, I strolled into a hangar owned by ANA. To my surprise, tucked in the back behind the DC2s and other modern craft was the Fokker tri-motor, the *Southern Cross*, which had created aviation history with its first flight across the Pacific in 1928 from San Francisco to Brisbane. It also created another record in making the longest ever nonstop ocean flight, between Honolulu and Suva, which took them $34\frac{1}{2}$ hours.

I crawled into the cavernous fuselage and clambered up into the pilot's seat. The joystick was equipped with a wooden wheel to work the ailerons – just like the steering wheel of the motor cars of that day. I gripped it and sat there by myself, dreaming of the experiences they had with their flying through tropical storms, a breakdown for three hours in their radio, failure of their compass on the leg to Brisbane, flying blind and being tossed around in one storm so violent that it broke their windscreen and flooded the cockpit. Electrical flames from the storm played around spark plug leads, and the copilot, Ulm, was so exhausted that he could only make one entry in the aircraft logbook between 6.15 in the evening and 3.20 next morning. Reading of the deeds of the great adventurers in history has always been a source of inspiration during my life and few have influenced me so much as the exploits of airmen. This communing with the spirits of Kingsford Smith, Ulm, Harry Lyon the navigator and James

Warner the radio operator, was a unique experience which has stayed with me ever since.

As our training progressed, the instructors begin to weed out those who were obviously not going to make the grade as pilots, and the following extract from one of my letters home tells of the sadness that accompanied some of the decisions the Air Force had to make:

Letter, 8 July 1940

One of our lads today was grounded because of lack of ability, together with one of the seniors who was grounded for the same reason. They have been hanging about for a fortnight and you can understand how rotten they must feel about it. An Italian chap called Ruggerio was given the order to "cease flying" by the Air Board about a week ago, because of the entry of Italy into the war, and has left for civilian life again, Undoubtedly it is the wrong thing to have a potential enemy in our midst, but what a time to find it out when the poor devil was so keen too and actually would have made an excellent pilot and seemed patriotic enough. However war is like that; no respecter of likes or dislikes but just a huge juggernaut that has to be left alone to eventually tire itself out.

One of the great benefits of not being on a formal RAAF station was that we were issued with passes into and out of the aerodrome. This meant that when we had finished with flying or lectures for the day we were free to do what we wanted until 8.30 next morning, when the formal day began again. While our money (10 shillings a day) lasted we would be on the phone to the girlfriend of the moment, or to any chaps who had something lined up in the way of entertainment, and would hightail it into Sydney in quest of fun and frolic. One of our favourite haunts was Princes nightclub in Martin Place, where the very latest and most popular dance band was to be found. This club was always crowded out by Army, Navy and Air Force blokes with their girl-friends, so much so that the small dance floor only allowed a basic step of about 6 inches in each direction. Since the fashion of the day was dancing cheek to cheek and getting as close a body contact as possible, everyone thought this was great.

We made friends of some very nice people in Sydney (particularly the Whitford family), and of all the cities I have been in since, I know of none where people are so natural and outgoing, even if they are obsessed with money. Getting close to the end of the course meant that I could really begin to relax, as the following extract from a letter shows:

Letter, 30 July 1940

On Saturday night I took Margaret Kneebone to see "Charley's Aunt" at the Minerva and she enjoyed herself thoroughly; it was screamingly funny and at one stage I nearly died laughing. She is going back to Melbourne some time this week and is spending her term holidays home. I sent our regards to Dr. and Mrs Kneebone as you doubtless would have wished.

The flying is intensely interesting now and lately I have been doing all sorts of stunts such as slow rolls and flick half rolls etc., where in the first one the machine is slowly rolled about the fore and aft axis for one complete revolution and in the inverted position one hangs in the straps for some appreciable time. The second manoeuvre is a flick half roll onto the back and a dive recovery which brings one facing in the reverse direction, it is done very quickly and looks very effective from the ground.

By the way, I have our last exam results and I obtained the following:

100 per cent for Armaments,
95 per cent for Engines and 97 per cent for Airframes, being top in each subject.

I have finished the whole of the flying syllabus already and in the next two weeks I may be able to relax a bit from study. However we still have another bout of exams to go through and for the last week or so things will be pretty willing. If I can't pass out top then it won't be for the want of trying.

I notice from my logbook that on 14 August I was sent off on a cross-country navigation course which took some one hour and forty-five minutes. It consisted of flying a compass course to Windsor, then to Penrith and return to Mascot. On the way back to our aerodrome from Penrith I started getting interested in the traffic on the Main Western Highway as it rolled by underneath my wings. Then this palled and I noticed a large percentage of the buildings looked like poultry farms, so I dropped down to have a look. In fact I came down so low that I could see chooks scattering themselves all over the place, and I realised that I was committing the cardinal sin of unauthorised low-flying. This did not cause me any great concern because it was most exciting to see the trees and buildings rush past, instead of hardly sensing any movement over the ground at our lowest legal height of 1,500 feet.

Next day I was in a class on armaments when an order came through that, "Leading Aircraftsman Cotton is to report to Flight Lieutenant Hicks immediately." I was suddenly seized with a feeling of dread that someone had read the letters on my aircraft when I was low flying and reported the misdemeanour.

I thought that Flight Lieutenant Hicks (a strict disciplinarian), who was the chief flying instructor for the whole school, was about to give me a rocket. I knocked on the door of the classroom in which he was teaching. He appeared, acknowledged my very military salute and gazed at me in his usual gimlet-eyed style. He then, without a smile on his face, asked: "Cotton, how would you like to go to Canada?" Without breathing an audible sigh of relief, I assured him that this would suit me admirably. Next day I found that four of us from Mascot were selected to be among the first forty Australian pilots to go overseas for training in a more advanced school in Ottawa, Canada. The other three trainees were in A Flight, and I was delighted to find that Alex Kerr and Selwyn Clark were two of them. The third was Ken Hicks, famous for hurting his head while upside down. Later on in our association we called ourselves the Four Mascoteers, for fairly obvious reasons.

In the last week or so at Mascot I had my Exacta camera, mentioned in the preface, and started taking pictures using Kodak Super X film. This, being very fast, allowed a lot of shots taken in bad light to come out quite well and overcame some of the problems of not having a flashlight.

Before being posted off to our embarkation centre at Bradfield Park in Sydney I was notified that I had come top in our course. I was given my Pilot's Training Card with the following information on it:

Ground Training:- Well above average in all subjects. Excellent type. Selected to proceed to Canada prior to holding final exams.

Flying ability:- Above average. Flying very sound in all departments. Very high degree of airmanship.

C.O.'s. Report:- Exceptional trainee. Above average and will do extremely well in any sphere. Definite officer type.

As can be seen I did not let much grass grow under my feet at Mascot and was enormously pleased to be presented with a prize, a book on navigation, from the Commanding Officer, Squadron Leader Ellis, maybe as a hint that this was my weakest subject. I was invited to have a whisky with him in his office and we yarned about his own experiences in World War I as a fighter pilot in France.

During my final leave at Broken Hill I managed to do a couple more flights with the aero club. I also took a trip to Tibooburra with the Flying Doctor, John Woods, and his pilot Hugh Bond, in a de Havilland Dragon Rapide. I took quite a bit of colour movie film of this episode, which I titled after the war and which is still in very good condition. Farewells to all my friends, both male and female, occupied a lot of my time. Finally the day came when some of them and all the family gathered at the railway station to see me off on the *Silver City Comet* to Sydney. My last impression of this was Dad, with tears running down his cheeks, taking movies of me as I waved from the train.

Arrival at Bradfield Park meant the meeting together of the First Forty for the first time. The Station was a specialised camp where all troops were fitted out with kit for their overseas postings. Our group was a selection of airmen from every state in Australia. Most of them had done their elementary flying training at Narromine in NSW and were chosen not necessarily because they were all high achievers, but, no doubt, because the politicians felt that it would be more acceptable to have each state represented. However they were all a pretty merry lot (with the usual exception of at least one real stinker among them) and, at the end of the book, in Appendix A, they are listed, together with their final achievements or fates.

We were all soon jabbed with various needles – which put me into the camp hospital with a raging temperature for twenty-four hours. We then had stacks of kit dumped on us and spent lots of time sewing "Australia" name badges onto our uniforms and had movies taken of us doing so by Cinesound, which was a newsreel outfit. We were told that these would not be shown on our national screens until we arrived in Canada, which naturally had us all asking if they anticipated we might be torpedoed en route.

We are inspected by a high-ranking officer prior to em-barkation on the SS Awatea

We were bashed into some reasonable shape on the parade ground to make us look like a real unit. At our final parade we managed to present a fairly military look, which brought a pat on the back, and a farewell, from a high-ranking officer whose name has unfortunately escaped me. His World War I medals and the gold braid on his cap (known to we philistines as "scrambled egg") were most impressive, as was his news that we were to embark on the morrow, but must not let anyone know, including our relatives.

So, on the next day, we embussed for the wharfs at Pyrmont in Sydney Harbour and duly filed on board the SS *Awatea*. Belonging to the New Zealand Union Line, she was said to be a miniature copy of the *Queen Mary*, and was fast enough to outrun any enemy raider and therefore needed no convoy protection.

An RAAF photo of us about to pull away from the wharf as we leave for Canada

After being photographed again by the newsreel cameramen who, together with RAAF photographers, had latched onto us at Bradfield, we finally steamed out of Sydney Harbour on the way to the adventures that lay ahead.

Nobody was there to wave us farewell.

4 ADVANCED TRAINING IN CANADA

No young man believes he shall ever die.
(William Hazlitt, 1778-1830)

If anyone was homesick or despondent it was not apparent. I must confess that I had no qualms as to whether I might not return, in spite of the fact that we had steamed past a hospital ship as we left our wharf at Pyrmont. The old "it can't happen to me" attitude was enough to make me quite cheerful about the outcome and determined to fill as many moments as possible with interest and enjoyment. The next three days crossing the Tasman Sea were then spent by me hoping that we might be sunk by a German raider so that I could be relieved of the seasickness which laid me low (together with most others) after leaving Sydney Harbour. However, as we were nearing Auckland in New Zealand a steward brought me a cup of beef tea and a Sao biscuit, which started the process of recovery and a desire to research what was going on around me.

The other passengers on the boat were mainly Americans returning to the USA. One couple who were particularly popular had a rather attractive daughter, so the trip began to look a lot better. My first letter home reads as follows:

On board "Awatea"
8th September

Dearest family,

This is being written while we are berthed at Auckland and just after I have finished an excellent meal. Today I only fully recovered from a rotten bout of sea-sickness which started when we left Sydney last Thursday and continued up till yesterday. Although many of the lads were a trifle perturbed about the German raider which is ticking about the place, there was a time when a fleet of them would

Across the Tasman Sea to New Zealand. Left to right: self, Ron Phillips, "Bluey" Lloyd, Ron Damman, McCullough

have left me completely unmoved. However I am glad to say that I have got my sea legs now and tonight, when we walked through Auckland, the ground felt quite unsteady underfoot. The little that we have seen has rather impressed me; most of the architecture being old and exactly what one would imagine England to look like. We travelled past numerous volcanic islands on our way in and the scenery is quite unusual, the land looking very rough and mountainous right to the water's edge and the clouds, rain squalls and oily calm sea makes it very enchanting atmosphere.

Getting back to our stay at Bradfield on Wednesday last; we spent the whole afternoon being speeched at by Air Commodores, photographed by the press, interviewed by same, photographed again by all the newsreel people in the Commonwealth and inveigled into recording a broadcast for the Australian Broadcasting Commission. As soon as we reach Canada a flood of films, words and pictures will burst upon Australia like a monsoon and you will see me in the movies and papers and hear me over the A.B.C. giving ourselves and Broken Hill a bit of publicity. It was a terrible show actually, but will undoubtedly give the Empire Air Training Scheme a boost and I believe the films are to be

A birthday party. Left to right: Allan McSweyn, Alex Kerr, Selwyn Clark, self, Freddie Drummond, Ken Hicks, Ron Damman, Ron Phillips

shown, wherever possible, all over the world to indicate that the boys of the Empire are on the job; good idea I s'pose but we felt dreadful asses while it was all going on.

The voyage from Sydney (or what I have seen of it) has been very uneventful, most of the conversation centering around the German raider and, even though we have the paravanes out all the time, there is always an uneasy feeling of what might happen if we smacked into a mine.

There is a fair amount of distraction at present in the form of a musical in the lounge and it is rather hard to concentrate so maybe I will conclude this; if we do not stop here for long my next letter may come from Suva, where I understand we will be stopping. Lots of love.

Mont.

After the arrival in Auckland we were made welcome by a group of New Zealanders and taken in their motorcars on a day tour of Auckland and its environs. We were most thankful, and very impressed with the beauty of the country. We were also intrigued to find in the hotels we finally visited that a popular drink was beer flavoured with raspberry cordial. I am not sure to this day if they were not having us on.

Next stop was Fiji and, as we steamed through the break in the coral reef into the harbour at Suva, I was fascinated to see the park where Kingsford Smith landed the *Southern Cross* on his epic transpacific flight. It looked too small for even a Tiger Moth to safely set down in. The Fokker wing must have generated enormous lift to have got them airborne again, even with a minimum load of petrol, which they finally topped up at Naseli beach before setting off for Australia.

We approach the wharf at Suva, Fiji

Before we were allowed to disembark, a lot of stevedores came on board and they, being Fijian natives, were interested to hear Selwyn Clark, with his ukelele, accompanying Ken, Alex and me singing some Australian songs in our cabin. We soon all joined together in a jam session, with the Fijians naturally harmonising some of their own songs – something we would have had to rehearse for ages – and teaching us a Polynesian song called "Isa Lei", which we sang many times together afterwards. The stevedores got ticked off by their boss for not working but we all parted the best of friends. We four decided to continue singing in a group in future and learning more songs of the islands as soon as we were allowed on shore.

We went on shore together, with the instruction from our officer in charge to be back on board before sailing time next morning at 8 o'clock. We first went to the Grand Pacific Hotel, where the white sahibs and their ladies acted out their roles as leaders of the Empire. After a few decorous beers, we hied ourselves

Selwyn Clark, Alex Kerr and Sergeant Brown disembark at Suva

off to the city of Suva to look for something more exciting. We were walking along the main street having a look at the sights when a chap in shorts, sitting in a car at the side of the street, asked us if we would like a ride around the island. When one of the lads asked him how much it would cost he said: "Cost be damned; this is a government car." So we piled in and had a wonderful run around. He turned out to be a civil engineer and, when we came back from our drive and were having a few beers with him, we met the chief magistrate. He also took us for a run around in his car, to the places we had not already seen.

In the evening we were shown over the military barracks and were sung to by some of the native troops. The rest of the evening was spent at the Defence Club. It was an all-white club patronised by sugar growers, businessmen and Army personnel, whose main occupation therein seemed to be consuming grog and playing billiards. Thus in the late hours, when the club shut down at 3 a.m., we had no alternative but to wend our way back to the boat, somewhat the worse for wear, and to wake up next morning with varying degrees of hangover. We did not learn a great deal about Fiji but, as the boat pulled out, we at least farewelled those at the wharf with our version of "Isa Lei".

Nothing much of note took place on the way to Honolulu, which was our next stop, except for some shooting with our ship's armament – a 3-inch calibre gun – at a wooden crate tossed over the stern. Needless to say the crew of the boat, whose job it was to handle this weapon, were not as expert as they might have been were they Navy gunners. We volunteered our assistance, which was even more amateur, and I cannot recollect any shell even looking like getting within cooee of the target. We all thanked providence that the *Awatea* was faster than any German U-boat or raider, and spent our time from then on playing deck tennis, quoits, singing to and flirting with the bright young things on board – until one morning we saw the clouds in the distance which indicated the nearness of the romantic Hawaiian Islands.

We docked near the Aloha Tower at the end of a busy street and parkland to be told that, because we were combatants and the USA was neutral, we would not be allowed to disembark. If there is one thing that Americans hate to be thought of in their own country, it is that they are not hospitable, so the irate citizens got together, hired the Royal Hawaiian singing and dancing troupe and sent them on board to entertain us. Alex, Ken, Selwyn and I just lapped it up. The singing and the music were things with which we were enraptured. At the end of the session we made friends with the three stars of the show, to whom we gave the names Hilo Hatti, Smiley and Bright Eyes. They taught us the music and words of such numbers as "Lovely Hula Hands", "When Hilo Hatti Does the Hilo Hop", "Song of the Islands", and others. After entertaining them to a merry lunch on board, we even got them to lend us their grass skirts and leis and to teach us how to do a hula.

At our protracted farewell to these delightful girls they gave us their leis, accompanied by the traditional kiss, and told us that as our ship cleared the harbour we were to toss them overboard so that, in floating back to the shore, they would ensure our eventual return to the islands. None of them accepted the invitation to stow away on board, so when we regretfully cleared the harbour there were very few of us, unless we were totally devoid of romance, who had not sworn they would come back and meet up again with the girls of the Royal Hawaiians.

The trip to Vancouver, Canada, was scheduled to take only a few days, so one of the officers on *Awatea* decided that some farewell functions would be in order. The first of these was a concert, with the First Forty providing all the entertainment for the rest of the passengers.

Ken, Alex, Selwyn and I were billed as Four Boys and a Ukelele – later in our "careers" changing our group name to the Four Mascoteers. We thought we

We gaze longingly at downtown Honolulu after being told we are not allowed ashore

We are entertained by the Royal Hawaiians, and afterwards make friends with (from left), "Hilo Hatti", "Smiley" and "Bright Eyes"

Fraternising with the hula girls. Left to right: self, Bright Eyes, Peter Wilson, Hilo Hatti, Phil Harbottle, Smiley, Eric McLeod, Ron Damman

easily outclassed the rest of the mob on the program because of the applause we received, and if we did, then it was due to the fact that we had rehearsed fairly solidly. The next celebration was in the form of a banquet and a fancy-dress ball, which I duly reported home as follows:

Letter, 25 September 1940

We also had a banquet and a fancy dress ball on the second to last night of the boat journey and again it was a roaring success and produced some very original costumes. I went along as a pirate and since I was wearing a tattered shirt and trousers it was not long before they both were playfully ripped clean off. Being prepared for such an emergency by wearing a pair of bathers underneath (having in mind our party at home when Pat Peoples lost his strides), I was not left in an embarrassing situation!

The next few days passed by uneventfully, until the coastline of British Columbia appeared on the eastern horizon and we steamed through the Strait of Juan de Fuca to the town of Victoria on Vancouver Island. It was said to us that Victoria was more English than England, and the styles of architecture, gardens, parks, trees and lawns were certainly quite different to most parts of Australia and looked a picture-book copy of our ideas of England. The enormous firs and pine trees that lined the shores and blanketed the far mountains belonged to the land of the big hills and forest giants. These timberlands, together with those of the north-west coast of the USA, were the areas that supplied Australia and the world with enormous quantities of Western Red Cedar, Californian Redwood, Douglas Fir (known as Oregon in Australia) and Spruce. They were also the lands of the world's biggest sawmills, fed from huge rafts of logs floated down the rivers to the sea and brought by tugboats to the mills along the foreshores of the Straits of Georgia, between Vancouver and Seattle.

We disembarked for a few hours at Victoria and were registered and fingerprinted by the Canadian immigration authorities, given some Canadian money and let loose on the town to do some sightseeing. On returning to the ship we were greeted by reporters and photographers from the Canadian media for interviews and pictures as we set sail for Vancouver. All the usual clichés about being "keen, tall and bronzed Aussies" were trotted out, there being possibly about half a dozen in the whole forty who would have met this standard.

"The Four Mascoteers" besides being top-whole fliers [how could they know?] are also singers. They started to sing as a quartet over the Canadian Broadcasting

Commission's microphone while news men were moving about getting brief interviews ...

So the blurb went on in a Vancouver newspaper later on. I do not remember what we sang, but no doubt "Waltzing Matilda" took a beating.

Before we landed at Vancouver we were herded into the theatrette on the boat and lectured by a Royal Canadian Air Force officer on some aspects of Canadian ways and customs. We were warned that some of our Australian colloquialisms carried quite different meanings in Canada. For instance, to "keep your pecker up" was not nice in mixed company, as a "pecker" was synonymous with a penis, whereas in Australia the phrase meant keep your spirits up. Also, to complain that one was "knocked up" meant, in Canada, that one was in the family way, as opposed to our use of it to indicate we were exhausted.

Thus armed, we duly marched off the boat when we reached Vancouver, to the newspaper report that:

> A Vancouver crowd cheered wildly as the first contingent of Australian fliers to participate in the Commonwealth Air Training Plan reached this country to complete their training ...

I think they were exaggerating a bit because I have no memory of any wildly cheering crowds. The Cinesound movie people, however, took pictures of us, which were duly shown in theatres in Australia, where my family saw a shot in Broken Hill with number-two son fair in the middle of it. My dad was a great believer in the saying "Ask and ye shall receive", so he wrote to Cinesound and asked for a frame of that particular shot, which was duly posted to him. I recently turned this up among all the other records he had kept of me and my adventures, and converted it to a negative, an enlargement of which came out extremely well.

Vancouver made us feel very welcome, and we chummed up with our counterparts in the Royal Canadian Air Force, visited them at their aerodrome and met some of their Women's Auxiliary Air Force and other girlfriends. Their Tiger Moths had to be modified for flying in the sub-zero winter climate and looked very cosy with sliding canopies and internal heating systems, but I still fancied the helmet and goggles and wind in the face that we were used to in Australia. Later on we learnt why they were so keen on protection from the cold.

There was not a great deal of time given to us to see much of Vancouver before we were installed in Pullman cars on the famous Canadian Pacific Railway and informed that our destination, Ottawa, was nearly three days away,

We pause to say goodbye to the engine that hauled us across the Rockies

and would be our new home for the next twelve weeks or so. The trip took us through some really awe-inspiring scenery in the Canadian Rockies. Names such as Frazer River, Glacier National Park, Kicking Horse Pass, the Great Divide and Banff reminded me of the stories I had read of the opening up of this part of North American continent to European settlers; tales of gold rushes, timber mills and forests, railway work gangs, grizzly bears, salmon fishing, Indians, ice and snow. One could imagine it all as the train steamed its way through the tunnels, past enormous mountains capped with ice and snow, along the banks of the streams and skirting the thick forests.

At Banff the train halted while an engine more suited to the faster journey across the plains was coupled on, and we set off at speeds up to 90 miles an hour across the prairies and the wheat fields. We stopped briefly at towns and cities such as Calgary, Medicine Hat, Regina and Winnipeg, where some of the later contingents in the Empire Air Training Scheme would finish their training as observers and air gunners.

It was an odd feeling to be in a Pullman car where the bunks were a double line of upper and lower ones on each side of the car instead of the small sleeping-car modules that we knew of in our country. We had to dress and undress in the seclusion of our bunks, behind curtains, as pedestrian traffic wandered through. The Pullman was obviously made to accommodate the maximum number of bodies but lacked the privacy of our system; not that this worried us, because any over-rowdy elements were soon shouted down by the majority. Fraternising with all-and-sundry Canadian travellers and spectators at the railway stopovers kept us interested in the journey. One never lacked for conversation, or time to chat to strangers, something which is missing from air travel today.

On arrival at Ottawa, we found that the Canadian Pacific Railway had its own private railway station in the basement of a most beautiful hotel called the Chateau Laurier, and we were ushered into rooms therein for our first night. We also found that this was because we were going to be pestered by the Canadian Broadcasting Commission and other media representatives. We were getting a bit fed up with being publicity fodder by this time and not much came of the tall stories a lot of us invented about our lives in our homeland.

A quick look around Ottawa caused some puzzlement at their strange drinking habits, because there were no hotel bars as we knew them at home. There were sterile-looking beer halls where one drank the most vile, chemical-tasting, headachy brew from bottles. If one wanted anything stronger one had to buy spirits from a drugstore and presumably drink these at home or in one's car. This soon convinced us that this particular part of Canada was a bit odd.

It was exciting, however, to be, at long last, delivered to our training aerodrome at Uplands airport and allocated to our training flights. We met up

We couple up with this big fellow. Those large-diameter wheels will pull us across the prairie at speeds of up to 90 miles an hour

with our new instructors, mine being a Flight Lieutenant Broadbent, who turned out to be quite a character with a hidden sense of humour which manifested itself on occasions when some drink had been consumed. Otherwise he was a careful and knowledgeable aviator and I was indeed fortunate to be assigned to him. The various slang expressions were sorted out, so that we all understood each other, and in no time at all we were told that we sounded like Canadians and our instructors like Aussies.

The first procedure we went through was a line-up for a course photograph and the installing in our caps of a white flash which denoted that we were aircrew, as distinct from ground crew. Not to be upstaged, the Canadian ground crew started a rumour that anyone with such a distinguishing mark was suffering from a venereal disease. We managed to scotch this by countering with another rumour that we were actually marked down to be commissioned officers, accusing our opponents with being jealous.

The first aeroplanes we were introduced to were Yales, possessing a fixed undercarriage but having landing flaps, and made, as were our later Harvards, by the North American Aviation Coy in the USA. It did not take us many flying hours to get to the stage of conversion to the Harvard, which turned out to be quite a machine. It had a 550-horsepower radial engine, retractable undercarriage and a top speed of 205 miles an hour, cruised at 170 miles an hour and was fully aerobatic. Alongside our Tiger Moths, they looked huge, and the instruments inside were a frightening array of switches and knobs.

The noise they made on take-off was incredibly loud. We were told that this was brought about by the tips of the propeller exceeding the speed of sound, causing shock waves. Little was known then about the effect such continued high noise levels could have on one's eardrums. One wonders how many of our instructors finished the war with permanently impaired hearing. None of this worried us as we gleefully went through the new routines of pre take-off checks, the use of variable-pitch propeller and retractable undercarriages. My letter home at this time recorded the experience:

Letter, 3 October 1940

I had two hours and twenty minutes dual instruction and then went solo for 1 hour 50 minutes doing circuits and landings.

My instructor was interested in the way I sneaked in over the perimeter of the drome at the same height and landed on the same spot each time without wasting a yard of aerodrome, even though it is a beautiful big one with long bitumen runways and plenty of space. He asked me where I learnt to fly . When I told him about the size of the Broken Hill drome he could understand why I was so economical of runway.

I learnt later on that this helped me considerably in the final assessment of my flying ability, so luck was with me. Later on in the war, the Harvards were also fitted with a machine-gun in each wing and bomb racks under the wings to carry light practice bombs. Trainees could then be given some early tutoring in air-to-air and air-to-ground gunnery and bombing, but (like a lot of the rest of the facilities at Uplands) these modifications had to be postponed because of the more urgent need for basic training of pilots to replace the Battle of Britain casualties.

Nevertheless, we were very busy polishing up our instrument flying and general airmanship, including our first taste of formation flying which was to be so important to those of us who were to become fighter pilots. I enjoyed formation flying and I believe now that this was one way in which the Service Flying Training Schools sorted out the bomber and fighter pilots.

A natural fighter pilot, while in formation, would react very quickly to slight changes in position, and could often stay glued in one spot (which was designated as being one wingspan away from and one wingspan behind the formation leader's wingtip) no matter what manoeuvres were carried out. A natural bomber bloke, on the other hand, might take a millisecond longer to react, and was often more heavy-handed and slower, but was perhaps more thoughtful and less excitable than the fighter jockeys. Not always would an individual make the grade for which he thought (or hoped) he would be best suited. Only practice and observation, both in the air and on the ground, by properly qualified instructors could detect the strengths and weaknesses. Our course did well, however, in that only three out of the forty were taken off the course altogether and sent back to observer or air-gunner duties, and did not get their pilot's wings.

Not long after we started our course, we were informed that the Australian High Commissioner for Canada was inviting us to a party at his residence. Shoes were polished and buttons shined, and we waited to be taken by bus to the gathering, eager to meet some of the bright young things of Ottawa. As I remember it, the bus either got lost getting us there, or broke down before picking us up, and we arrived about one hour late to find that the gathering was reasonably high on cocktails. A bevy of socialite mothers and daughters had been recruited to welcome us, and we joined in the downing of the free grog and answered the usual questions about ourselves.

It did not take long for the decorum to be somewhat shattered by some of our members innocently (?) referring to how knocked up they were at the work they had to do but, in spite of being so far from home, they were all keeping their pecker up. I believe that after this there were very few gatherings of that nature without a careful screening of the invitees.

Nevertheless, we did make some very nice and jolly friends with some of the daughters and I, with my usual luck, became the escort of one damsel who owned a Ford coupé and used to call at the camp guardroom for me when I had leave to attend the odd party. The looks I got from some of the Canadian airmen, waiting patiently for buses into town, were shafted with daggers. We Australians became looked upon in Canada as were, later in the war, the Yanks when they invaded Australia and caught up with lots of friendly Aussie girls; so it was not all one-sided, as our countrymen at home thought at that time. An extract from the next letter after this says:

Letter, 4 November 1940

I must finish this off soon since I am dining out this evening with a Mr. and Mrs Sherwood whose fair daughter, Miss Penelope, I have been escorting to various functions. I met her at Sir William Glasgow's party and she is a very bright lass. Dresses simply and well and is most entertaining, having a charming personality. Her Papa is an estate agent and I am told owns half Ottawa. They have a lovely

Miss Penelope Sherwood sells buttons for charity

home and 3 sons in the Navy. I must send you a picture of her which I took one day in Ottawa when she was selling buttons for Armistice Day. P.S. (I have no views towards matrimony, so relax).

Although the reader of this might think that we were living a lotus-eating existence we were in fact being pushed to our limits. The normal course of eight weeks had been compressed into seven weeks, and we were required to attend lectures and fly on weekends.

I read in one of my letters (and remember it clearly) that we had a visit from Air Vice Marshal Billy Bishop, who was the highest-scoring ace in World War I on the Allied side. He had just come back from England, where he had (being a Canadian) paid a special visit to the all-Canadian squadron then operating there. He said that when he called on them, the fifteen minutes during which they had leave to see him was so appreciated by them that it seemed like a holiday. Some of them were married men, too, and all older than us, being prewar members of the RCAF, so it showed that this was not at that time a young man's game, as it is so glamorously depicted by Hollywood. This made us all feel a lot better about the pressure we were under, and we appreciated even more the odd chance we had to enjoy some leave.

Towards the end of five weeks, we were introduced to night flying, and this was something with which I became quite taken, even though it required an enormous concentration on pure instrument flying which, at the end of an hour, left one completely wrung out. It was fortunate that I was able to do a full course of night flying, in spite of the fact that fighter pilots traditionally battled in broad daylight, because later on in England it stood me in very good stead.

As we neared the end of the course the examinations in ground subjects took place and the results were reported home in this letter:

Letter, 17 November 1940

We have all been through six weeks of some of the most strenuous training up to date and for the last fortnight I have had only two evenings off and all the rest of the nights have been spent in studying, but it has been worth it because I came second in ground subjects with an average of 86 per cent.

The bloke who topped it is a real wizard, a nice steady lad called Ron Phillips. He was I believe the youngest qualified accountant in South Australia when he took his degree, or something, and he socks into it properly.

I have also passed my "Wings" test fairly high I think (no results of this yet), the wings test being about the hardest flying test that one does in the Air Force.

By passing this I am now entitled to wear my wings and we are to have them presented to us at a huge parade next Friday and the celebrations afterwards will be loud and continuous.

The Canadian Broadcasting Commission have been recording a series of sketches about us Aussies and I was commissioned to write the script for the different scenes and also to talk in the whole ruddy lot. Up to date I have figured in the following:

1) A Canadian National program entitled "Carry on Canada", wherein I had to say a set piece which is recorded and in which I laid on the colloquial Aussie accent thick and heavy, for that was what they wanted. This recording is being sent out to you by the Commission because of the favours I have done them and I hope it arrives safely.

2) A night-flying sequence (actually recorded on the ground) wherein the instructor runs through all the patter and, while he does this, I have to speak out my thoughts of the different incidents in the flight, This is all cooked up but sounds very effective and is to be sent back to Australia for public consumption.

3) A discussion between three officer instructors. One an Englishman, one Canadian and one Texan, with myself as an Aussie airman, This was funny because my instructor was in the show and he and the others proceeded to get tight and they all got horribly merry. Since this was the night before my wings test, my instructor and I proceeded to get the Chief Flying Instructor as stinko as we could so that he, too, would not be feeling up to the mark next day, We, however, made the mistake of getting him so blithered that next morning he rang up the flight and said he was too ill to fly and sent the other CFI along who was quite sober the night before, so I had to clear the old head and really concentrate on the flying and luckily enough flew quite well. It was as funny as hell though because my instructor, Flight Lieutenant Broadbent (who is a real character), kept belching into the microphone while the recording was on, besides telling rude stories while we were doing the actual flying.

However they will doubtless censor these tit-bits and you will hear our conversation with all the noise in the background. So now you can see that I have developed into quite a public figure (or should I say spectacle) but it leaves me dead cold and, except that I was told to do it, I would normally rather see less time wasted in talk and publicity and more effort given to prosecuting the war.

Our total exam results were finally published and confirmed the fact that I had come second on the course to Ron Phillips. Although I had beaten him in the flying, his lead in the ground subjects gave him the top position, which was richly deserved. The list of pilots in Appendix A shows that Ron was killed very early as a pilot officer, but I do not know the cause.

With some amusement today, I read on my Pilot's Training Card:

Above average. His confidence in himself appears to be justified.
Very popular. Good personality.

On the flying side it says:

An above average pupil who shows very good judgement.

And finally, in "General Remarks":

This pupil is extremely hard-working. Very suitable for a Commission.

The time for our Wings parade duly arrived and we were lined up on the tarmac, together with all the station personnel and aircraft, and ceremoniously had our wings pinned on our chests – real Hollywood stuff, tempered only slightly by some Canadian reserve. We were also advised of our new ranks and I was very disappointed that Selwyn was not given a commission. It did not take long for the war to redress that problem, once he got into action on his squadron.

Sergeant Pilot Selwyn Clark, maestro of the Four Mascoteers, and my firmest friend of the First Forty

In spite of our different ranks, we were all given a party in the officers' mess and joined in some games new to us. One was to stand with one's back to the edge of an open door, clasp the hands together over one's head on the top edge of the door and pull oneself up and over backwards, in one swift movement, to finish up sitting straddled on the door. This, together with games of Rugby, high cockalorum (a pyramid-building melee) and numerous other merrymakings were among those which only the worse for wear with drink could survive.

I could begin to see what life ahead was going to be like. Billy Bishop had said to me before that being a fighter pilot was (compared to soldiering) "a life of extreme ease, punctuated with moments of intense fear". Although I only half-believed it at the time, in retrospect that tended to sum it up fairly well.

We still kept on with our flying after the Wings parade, and one day woke up to find the aerodrome covered in the first snow of the season. To us Aussies this was excitement indeed, and the Canadians highly amused at the lengthy and exhausting snow fight we turned on. Life took on a new aspect, with wearing heavy clothing and overshoes being the order of the day. Centrally heated barracks kept us reasonably warm at nights, but when one night the outside temperature dropped to 20° below zero (Fahrenheit) – that is, 50° of frost – we were less than happy.

Our relationships with girlfriends, however, took on a new dimension when a few of us were invited out by one lass to her family ski-lodge near Ottawa. Dressed in what warm gear we could muster, we set off on a cross-country trek of a few miles, which sorely tested untried muscles. We finally hurled ourselves off a ledge onto a nursery slope near the lodge. Nobody hurt themselves seriously

Jock McKechnie decides that it is safer to ski with his undercarriage retracted

but I managed to plough to a stop after falling, and pranged, nose first, into a stook which had landed ahead of me after I had "spun in" (a type of aircraft crash) – nothing broken. Here we were also introduced to the rituals of *après-ski*, with its mulled wine and snuggling up near a roaring fire.

Another result of the decrease in temperature manifested itself on one flight with my instructor, in the back seat of the Harvard, suffering from a hangover from a beery party the night before. We were about ten minutes away from our home base, on a ninety-minute cross-country flight, when my headphones were nearly blasted out of my helmet by a string of Canadian invective issuing from the back seat. After enquiring what I might have done wrong I was met by the curt reply: "Nothing. Just apply full throttle, return to base and land as soon as possible."

When this was duly accomplished, I was puzzled by the departure of my instructor, without any goodbyes, before the aircraft had stopped rolling. I was also puzzled to see him waddle like a duck towards the flight office and, after some discreet enquiry found out that, soon after take-off, he had decided to empty his bladder into the "pee" tube with which the Harvards were equipped. After starting the operation, the urine, which exited through a small external suction venturi, had frozen on contact with the extremely cold air and backfilled the tube until it overflowed into his flying boots before he could turn off the "tap" – no doubt made more difficult because of the excesses of the night before. Before we could reach the drome his boots had also frozen. No wonder that his normal cheerfulness was somewhat subdued!

Now that we had our wings, we had some more time to spare for our social lives and spent as much of it as our money would allow at a dance hall over the border in Quebec at a place called Hull, entertaining our girlfriends. Here we were able to imbibe our drinks at leisure at our tables, because Quebec State (being virtually French-Canadian controlled) made sure that its citizens might behave as they were used to doing in their homeland. This was a good fun place where we generally relaxed and were taught some strange dance of the day called the "Hokey Pokey". I believe that one of our course actually returned to Ottawa after the war and married one of his then Canadian girlfriends.

My firm resolve was that I would never get married during the war, because I felt it would restrict me in my flying to have such a responsibility. Also, it would be difficult to make the correct judgements of one's future mate in such an uncertain world, where it would not be easy to be in the long and close contact necessary for the early sorting out of the different traits of character that often lie hidden in each partner.

5 ENGLAND AT LAST

Let us therefore brace ourselves to our duties,
and so bear ourselves that, if the British Empire
and its Commonwealth last for a thousand years,
men will say, "This was their finest hour".
(Winston Churchill)

In early December we finished our course, and the final hours flown, since I began training in the Air Force in Australia in June were as follows:

	DUAL		SOLO	
	Night	*Day*	*Night*	*Day*
EFTS		23.05		25.25
SFTS	1.20	33.55	4.10	46.20
Totals	**1.20**	**57.00**	**4.10**	**71.45**

I did not realise until well into the war that this total of just over 100 hours was often a danger period in a pilot's life because he had by now reached a stage when he had begun to really know what flying was about and began to explore the boundaries of his capacity. After his first solo, and at about ten hours flying, he was in another danger period, because he really knew very little and also had no experience to cope with any emergency. The 100-hour mark, however, made us all feel that we were now able to take on the whole Luftwaffe single-handed, and we were delighted to be entrained from Ottawa on about 8 December and off-loaded onto a ship at the port of Halifax in Nova Scotia, bound for England.

The vessel was a Dutch ship named the *Penland* and, unlike the *Awatea*, had nobody on board but airmen and soldiers, and was under convoy protection by the Royal Navy. She also smelled like a doghouse, no doubt due to the overcrowding and closed portholes in all cabins to ensure a full blackout. Each cabin had also been fitted with extra bunks, and we could see that the next week or two was not going to be at all comfortable. Fortunately by this time I had acquired a better set of sea legs and for the initial day or so I kept seasickness at bay by eating nothing, and in the daytime walking up and down the limited deck space.

The Atlantic turned on its usual frightful weather, and this, combined with the fact that the convoy sailed northward close to Greenland to escape German submarines, meant that we not only had snowfalls covering the decks, but any spray froze where it landed. Lifeboat drill was practised until we were all proficient at finding our places but to a lot of us it seemed a waste of time because we doubted if anyone would survive for more than a few minutes in one of those open boats, let alone the time it might take to be rescued. In spite of this, we also had to remain fully clothed at all times except for a quick body wash which became known as an APC, standing for " Armpits and Crutch".

The time passed very uneventfully, in my case reinforcing the decision I had taken long ago that the air was the place to be in this man's war. Towards the end of the journey, we ran into a 60-mile-an-hour gale lasting for thirty-six hours and finishing up as a thick fog, in which we lost our escort for the last two days of the voyage. Before we rounded the northern end of Ireland on Christmas Eve, a ship in another convoy was bombed and sunk by a German aircraft about 15 or 17 miles ahead of us. In one of my letters I noted that I was asleep at the time and did not know that he also flew over the top of us but was obviously out of bombs, because we escaped any attack. We eventually sailed into calmer seas in the North Channel and a fly-past by an RAF Stranraer flying boat gave our spirits a lift. If our convoy had met any submarines or suffered any damage we certainly did not know of it, because most of the time we could hardly sight each other through the murky weather or hear anything over the howling of the gale.

Pitch and toss in a howling gale across the Atlantic

Thus, thankfully, we finally berthed at Glasgow and set off by train for the Royal Air Force Station at Uxbridge, near London, to be transferred to the keeping of the RAF and kitted out with uniforms and flying gear. The first night there introduced us to a bombing raid. At this time such raids were being conducted by the Germans against English cities in an effort to disrupt the civilian war effort. A letter extract tells of the result:

Letter, 28 December 1940

We saw ample evidence of the damage caused by air-raids and when one first sees the ruins of the beautiful old buildings it really burns one up. On our way out of London to Uxbridge we passed through, or by, places with such famous names as Baker Street, Harley Street, Regent Street, Piccadilly Circus, Hyde Park, Regents Park and countless other names that one continually comes across when reading English books.

Naturally, when one sees these buildings in complete ruins and shops in a whole street with absolutely no windows left, then the first question that hits one is, "How are the people standing up to it?" Believe me their courage and bravery is something to be wondered at and deeply admired. Suburban London has suffered also but actually when everything is added up the Germans have not accomplished one useful thing and have only made the people here more determined than ever to win the war.

Fortunately nothing fell on our camp, but the noise of the anti-aircraft guns and that of exploding bombs was enough to bring our thoughts to the realisation that we were now heading into some real danger, and had best learn to cope with it without dying of fright. The day after our arrival was spent in our usual fronting up to the media and the end result made interesting reading because, as reported in one paper, nobody ever recalled anyone being rendered temporarily helpless by having his limbs frozen while flying in Canada, apart from my aforementioned instructor (as recounted in Chapter 4), and he was a Canadian and only temporarily discomforted.

I am sure, however, the English were immensely cheered by our arrival and by the Germans thinking about suing for an armistice. We did not let this go to our heads, because we were too busy getting fitted out with our new gear and dashing off to London and back to see the sights and get measured for uniforms. We were told that every Sunday night the Grosvenor Hotel put on a tea-dance for officers, so a few of us duly turned up in our new uniforms – courtesy of Simpsons – and introduced ourselves to some English lasses so that we could study the behaviour of the natives.

The London press report our arrival on 27 December 1940. This is also recounted to the people of Australia in a newspaper which my dad saved

AUSTRALIAN AIRMEN ARRIVE

First Contingent From Canada

WARM WELCOME IN BRITAIN

Australian Associated Press

LONDON, December 27.

The first R.A.A.F. contingent under the Empire training scheme has arrived at a British port.

These Australian pilots set a new high standard in Canada, where their instructors declared that succeeding recruits would have great difficulty in living up to their performance.

Batches of Australian airmen will now arrive in Britain at regular intervals. Only three of this training batch failed to obtain their wings. One withdrew, owing to illness, one because he received poor marks in ground subjects, and the third because his instrument flying was defective.

The trainees used machines originally intended for the French air force and taken over by Canada after the

NEW CHAPTER OPENED IN OUR HISTORY

First Empire Trainees To Reach Battle Zone

MELBOURNE, December 27

The Minister for Air (Mr. McEwen) said tonight that Australia would receive with elation and pride, the news of the arrival in England of the first batch of Australian Empire air trainees. They were the first Empire trainees to reach the battle zone, and Britain's enemies would soon know their quality. The men had received their primary instruction in Australia and had graduated after the completion of immediate and advanced courses in Canada

"The strength of the movement which has now begun must be viewed in the light of the knowledge that only a small percentage of Australia's pilots, observers and air gunners will be trained in Canada," Mr. McEwen said. "The first batch from schools in that Dominion has reached British soil, but approximately four-fifths of the total to be provided will graduate from R.A.A.F. establishments in Australia.

"The young men have been drawn from the finest types in the Commonwealth, Mr. McEwen added. Choosing its aircrew trainees, the R.A.A.F. had set high standards of physical fitness and mental capacity, and the policy of the Government had been to insist upon the most thorough training methods which experts could devise.

"I am confident that time will prove

Needless to say we were most impressed by the roses-and-cream complexions, and even more so by the fact that when the hotel began to shudder from nearby bomb hits the girls turned not a hair, but consumed their gin and limes at no faster pace – as we felt like doing. One of the lasses suggested that we were all unwise to be staying in the crowded room in case the hotel took a direct hit, and that we might be better off at a nightclub called the Hungarian, in Piccadilly. So two girls, with us as escorts, came out of the front door to be greeted with the awful din of ack-ack guns just across the way in Hyde Park and great flashes of light and noise as the German bombs hit their targets nearby.

Little did we realise that this was the night when Hitler decided to burn London and then bomb it to bits. It was the night of 27 December, if my memory serves me correctly. Fortunately, London became obscured by 10/10ths cloud during the night and the bombers could only drop their loads indiscriminately on the glow of the fires which they could see while flying above the clouds. This meant nothing to me at the time except that I was petrified, and I asked one of the girls what the funny slapping noises were on the pavement. To be told that they were ack-ack shell fragments made me feel my brain was exposed, and I longed to don my tin hat, which we, as servicemen, were compelled to carry but felt I should offer it to her.

This was refused, so we all decided to catch a tramcar up to Piccadilly Circus to have some shelter on the way. The conductor somewhat rudely accused us of being responsible for the raid, because the RAF had bombed Berlin the night before, but was mollified when assured we had just arrived from Australia – which won us a free ride. The Hungarian turned out to be an underground nightclub near Piccadilly Circus, where the music was supplied by a Hungarian (at least he was dressed like one) playing a zither and accompanying a very nice orchestra of violins and piano. We drank, listened to the lovely music, nattered and danced our way through the night until the late hours of the morning.

I saw the aftermath of the inferno later next day when I went to the City area to call upon a businessman who was associated with the North Mine at Broken Hill, and whose name and address had been given to me by the manager, Mr Oliver Woodward, before I left Broken Hill. Over a cup of tea, we looked from his office window across acres of smouldering rubble with the dome of St Paul's still standing in the background, untouched. I remember him saying that the Germans would be made to pay for this because there was no way that England was going to give up, and that she would fight her way to victory, no matter what the cost. I recalled at that time another saying of Billy Bishop's while in Canada: "Remember lads, it's not the amount of dogs in the fight that counts, it's the amount of fight in the dogs."

On another night in London a friend and I had finished dining on curry at Ventachellums near the Strand and decided to visit a nearby club called the Liaison Club, which we had been told, although it was private, might make us welcome without any formal introduction. After being quizzed by the doorkeeper as to the nationality represented by our uniforms, the door was flung open with a hearty, "Welcome, Down-Unders."

It was a nice cheerful place and we were introduced all round, and especially to a civilian sitting, hands on a walking stick, near a warm coal-fire. I was delighted to meet none other than one of my boyhood heroes, Negley Farson, whose book *The Way of a Transgressor* had, in my youth, held me spellbound and full of envy for one who had, in his own youth, cast aside convention and given life a good shake. We sat and chatted about his books, and I mentioned his leg war-wound that he had inherited from World War I when fighting on the side of the Italians, and found that it still troubled him, hence the stick. I delighted in his company and would have been happy to have sat there all night grogging on and talking about our likes and dislikes of the authors whose works we had read, when he said there was a girl he would like me to meet.

I then found myself looking into the most beautiful cornflower-blue eyes I have ever seen, in an equally beautiful English rose-petal complexioned face, crowned with long raven-black hair. Nor did her lovely figure do anything to calm my rapidly beating heart. I was absolutely stunned by the astonishing combination, and even more stunned to find myself dancing with her and trying to think out ways by which I might prise her away from her RAF flying officer escort. It was all to no avail and just remains an indelible memory of sheer, unusual beauty.

At one stage of the evening, and amid the noise of the usual air raid outside, someone called out "Here comes a stick!", meaning a stick of bombs, which, they could recognise from past experience, was going to straddle us. Sure enough, a series of awful bangs grew closer and we were duly straddled by the explosions, and watched the wall above the bar crack from floor to ceiling. All that happened to the club members was a temporary cessation in lifting of glasses and a continuation of normal imbibing and conversation as the bomb bursts retreated away from us. One could only try to emulate the lack of any abnormal reaction or panic and begin to marvel at the sang-froid of the English under their enormous stress. It was certainly a lesson in how we had best learn to behave in their company.

As much as we were enjoying the lures of wartime life in London (in spite of being bombed every night), some of us, to be trained as fighter pilots, including Selwyn, were soon posted to No. 56 Operational Training Unit at Sutton Bridge in Norfolk, East Anglia, where we arrived on 7 January 1941. This was hardly recognisable as an aerodrome because it was grassed farmland which had obviously been resumed for the duration, had Nissen huts plonked around half the perimeter and (as we later found) former Battle of Britain Hurricane fighters dispersed around the other half.

Nevertheless, excitement on my part built up as, next day, I examined them after reporting to A Flight, commanded by a Flight Lieutenant Hellier, DFC. I learnt later on that Hellier was the sole survivor of the original pilots on his fighter squadron after Dunkirk and the Battle of Britain. All the rest were killed. Hellier could not have been much taller than 5 feet 4 inches (162 centimetres), sported an RAF moustache, jacket with the top button undone, identifying him as a fighter pilot, and an air of cynicism and insouciance. All of this was carried off with no indication that he was entitled to be a complete nervous wreck.

He ushered me into the front seat of a Harvard trainer and said: "Cotton, do me some circuits and bumps and try not to kill me." Having carried this out successfully, I was then told to spend the day studying the pilot's notes of the Hurricane Mark 1 which was equipped with a two-bladed, fixed-pitch, wooden propeller. The Mark 1 was one of the original eight-gun Hurries which started operating at the beginning of World War II, and I avidly devoured all the

"A" Flight at Sutton Bridge Operational Training Unit, with Flight Lieutenant Hellier on the far left, and instructors in dark uniforms or flying suits. Trainees are wearing Sidcot suits

information and enquired of the other instructor on our flight as to those elements I could not understand. Flight Lieutenant Greaves checked me out for fifteen minutes in the Harvard, saying at the end of this: "Cotton, that was a frightening experience. However, go over and fly Hurricane Number 320 and don't bend it."

Number 320 had patches on wings and fuselage which looked suspiciously like war wounds from previous dogfights and one could only hope, on being strapped in, that they had healed properly. "Best of luck, sir," was the parting greeting from the flight sergeant, who then jumped off the wing to switch on the mobile battery trolley which assisted the aircraft starter motor to swing over the twelve-cylinder Rolls Royce Merlin engine. At my thumbs-up sign we both pressed the required buttons and the engine coughed into life, and I knew that it was my first time to face my destiny in an aircraft designed to carry only one pilot and with no aid from any instructor in any back seat.

Taking off was in fact easier than in the Harvard trainer and, once airborne and with the wheels retracted, the acceleration was breathtaking compared to that machine. It did not take long for me to realise that I was handling something entirely different. The controls firmed as the speed built up to

My instructor, Flight Lieutenant Greaves, welcomes me back from my first solo in the Hurricane

180 miles an hour and only hardened slightly more at 240 miles an hour. Theoretically it would fly straight and level at more than 300 miles an hour, but I had been told not to exceed 240, and in any event that was thrilling enough. I took the plane through a series of steep turns, climbing turns, stalls, stall turns and a quickly corrected spin, realising as time went on that this was a real thoroughbred which flew in a most forgiving manner and felt firm and steady under my hand. An hour went by very quickly and the approach to land and touchdown were smooth and uneventful, with the feeling on my part that I had now begun to climb the ladder towards my ultimate goal and nothing could stop me, unless fate intervened.

Very quickly we began the exercises which were supposed to turn us into qualified fighter pilots able to take our places in front-line squadrons. Letters to home began to wax eloquent:

Letter, 15 January 1941

The weather caused a washout as regards flying yesterday and today was my next flip in the little darlings. We are able to receive and transmit by radio telephony to one another and to a central ground station and life has become most complicated and vastly more interesting than formerly when we flew out of touch with both ground and other aircraft. It is now possible to fly back to one's station by radio when lost and I had practice in that today when I set out to do some map-reading and pin-pointing in particularly foul visibility and, after flying about at 300 feet for an hour and locating and losing myself regularly every 15 minutes or so, I eventually came home by wireless right on the button.

All around the aerodrome are trenches and anti aircraft guns with soldiers on duty day and night and it makes one realize that the war is coming a lot nearer although Jerry has left this place alone so far.

Today I also had somewhat of a thrill when I was doing some aerobatics. I had just come out of some weird and wonderful manoeuvre and I saw a ruddy great bomber pooping along about a mile off. I yelled out a "Tally Ho" on the radio and proceeded to tighten my straps, switch on the reflector sight, turn the gun button onto the "Fire" position and give chase; practically drooling with excitement at what was going to be an easy victory. However, when I came up within firing range of 250 yards I saw it was one of our own bombers so I buzzed off in "fine pitch" before the rear gunner mistook me for an enemy and got nervous on his triggers.

Selwyn, who is on "B" Flight, today rather demoralized the station personnel by accidentally leaving his gun-button switched on and, in an attempt to straight-en the aircraft while making a landing run, touched it. His eight guns gave a bloody roar and everybody fell flat just in case he kept it up, but he rightly desisted and peace was restored because, due to the attitude of the Hurrie when the tail is on the ground, all the bullets went winging over Norfolk some miles away.

I have been made the senior student pilot of our flight now and lead the formations in practising attacks etc. I was raised to this position after my effort this afternoon when we were taken up in formation by our instructor and he really put us through our paces.

His first effort was to go into a howling engine-on dive. I managed to stick right by him but the other lad got horribly left behind to the extent of a mile or so. We tried again for his benefit and this time we really went to town and he got left very badly. The instructor had pushed his nose down so that we were diving at about 70 degrees and as I glanced at the Air Speed Indicator it was registering 350 miles per hour! We peeled off about 5,000 feet and in a few seconds came screeching out at about 100 feet above the deck, whence we howled into a tight turn and generally tore holes in the atmosphere. My leader was as pleased as punch about my show, so now I will be taking up the other blokes and giving them the same treatment.

I spent Saturday afternoon, night and Sunday morning in Spalding which is a town about 12 or 15 miles from here. The attraction there is a very pretty lass whom I met at a dance there about two weeks ago. Her Dad is a big shot in the Home Guard and a fine chap too. He has a few farms about the place and this is an extremely rich district where they grow lots of potatoes and sugar beet. His first greeting to me was a question as to whether or not I was always in the habit of low-flying over the home of the young ladies I had met – which was exactly true in this case and I had to admit it – to be told that it frightened the daylights out of the whole village and, please don't do it again! We were lucky to get the time off but it began snowing heavily about Saturday mid-day and it has been coming down solidly ever since.

Cheers Dears, Mont.

As our training time at Sutton Bridge was going to be all too short, I bought myself a second-hand, rather clapped-out Hillman 10-horsepower sedan, at the cost of £10, to do some sightseeing, and also to take me to wherever my future squadron might be. This was given the name Ermintrude, and served me faithfully for the next six months before being sold for £5. It kept me in touch with life outside my RAF stations, as can be seen from the above visit to Spalding.

I flew Hurricanes for a total of twenty-two hours and twenty minutes at Sutton Bridge. I fired my guns once at a ground target, did about forty-five minutes practice dogfighting with Flight Lieutenant Hellier, carried out various cross-country flights, practised lots of formation flying and had very few lectures on anything. In retrospect the training was laughable. One was, at the end of it, not much better equipped to fight than the World War I pilots who arrived on their squadrons in France with a total flying time of only twenty hours. Although we thought we were ready, the reason behind the paucity of training was that we were being used to fill the gaps, caused by the Battle of Britain, in the ranks of pilots. These gaps were large and had to be filled quickly.

In the last week at Sutton Bridge a new instructor was posted to A Flight and was also bunking in my room. I noted very quickly that he was wearing the DFM (Distinguished Flying Medal) and bar, which is only awarded to noncommissioned officers. He was now a pilot officer, and introduced himself as Bert Hallowes. On questioning, he revealed that he was newly commissioned and had just returned from fighting in the Libyan desert after completing his operational tour on fighters. This was twelve months on a squadron, or 300 hours of operational flying, whichever came first.

He was a neat, quietly spoken man, whom one would have taken for a bank clerk in civil life, but the story of his Air Force career was fascinating. He was a permanent prewar RAF pilot on one of England's most famous fighter squadrons, No. 43, which he insisted was actually the most famous. They were known as the "Fighting Cocks" because of their emblem (see Appendix B), and he was with them at the outbreak of war and fought with them in France and through the Battle of Britain at Tangmere in Sussex. At the end of this conflict, they had shot down ninety-seven enemy aircraft for the loss of eleven pilots. Hallowes was awarded the DFM during this time, and finally was posted to Libya. His full wartime story is told in Appendix C.

After yarning with me off and on for a few days, he obviously had my measure as being one highly enthusiastic pilot, but who was totally incapable of surviving in any real brawl. So when I asked him one day how could one get to join 43 Squadron, he replied: "Forget it, old chap. They're out of your class until you have a hell of a lot more experience." I felt that this was not the answer I wanted and, in my usual brash Australian way, asked the adjutant if I could have an interview with the station commanding officer about my posting to a squadron after my training.

The interview was granted, and the commanding officer (a nice, polite wing commander) enquired of me what he might do for me. I asked him if he would be able to get me a posting to 43 Squadron and he looked at me in disbelief as though I was asking for the crown jewels. After getting his breath back he asked for my logbook and Pilot's Training Card. On studying these, he looked at the ceiling, paused thoughtfully, and sang out to the adjutant: "Adjutant, find out where 43 Squadron are and get Tommy Morgan on the line."

A few minutes later the adjutant called out: "Squadron Leader Morgan on the line, sir."

"Hullo Tommy, Wingco McGuire here."

"Well, thanks Tommy. She's fine. How's Margaret and Tony?"

"That's great Tommy, how are things up there at Drem?"

"Tommy, how are you off for replacement pilots?"

"Yes, I know, it's a bugger isn't it."

"Tommy, we have a young Australian bloke here, keen but no operational experience."

"Yes, I think I can recommend him, but he's a hell of a long way to go yet."

"OK, Tommy. Love to Margaret."

He looked at me. "Well, Cotton, I don't know if you're lucky or not, but 43 are at the bottom of the barrel for pilots. They are at Drem in Scotland and may be able to get time to knock you into shape before they come south again. Squadron Leader Dalton-Morgan will accept you. The adjutant will give you your movement order. Best of luck."

When I got back to my billet and told Bert Hallowes what had happened he was dumbfounded. He said: "Cotton, if you can fight as well as you can talk you'll be a squadron commander in no time. Congratulations anyway; you are about to join the best fighter squadron in the RAF."

Naturally I was delighted at what lay ahead in the way of opportunities to achieve my ambition, which was still as strong as ever. I was reminded of the words that my dad had often said to me: "If you want something badly enough in this world you can't be stopped if you are prepared to make the efforts and sacrifices necessary to achieve it."

Within days my movement order came through. I was entitled to get petrol for Ermintrude because this would save the RAF the rail fare. Trusting that no policeman would notice that it was not registered, I said goodbye to the last few members of the First Forty who were training with me at Sutton Bridge (and who I would not see again for forty-five years), and set off for Drem in Scotland.

6 JOINING THE "FIGHTING COCKS"

Fierce, fiery warriors fight upon the clouds,
In ranks and squadrons, and right form of war.
(William Shakespeare, *Julius Caesar*)

It took me all day on 24 February to get from Sutton Bridge to Drem (a distance of about 500 kilometres) and it was nightfall before I arrived at the tiny village consisting of about twenty small stone cottages. A knock on the door of one of these to ask the way to the aerodrome resulted in it being opened by a large tough-looking Scot who, when asked, replied, "Och awa ludddy, herr be doon the noo un awa oer tharr aboot the larrn a wee bitty," pointing to the lane going off the road I was on. I hardly understood a single word he said, and felt that I was in a totally foreign country instead of a bit of the British Isles, this being my first encounter with a really broad Scottish accent.

I set off in the direction indicated. Finally, in the cold and darkness of a Scottish winter night, I arrived at the entrance to the airfield, was checked in by the guards, and one of them rode with me, as a guide, to the officers' mess. I gingerly entered the anteroom and asked someone if the adjutant of 43 Squadron was available. In a moment a very likeable fifty-year-old flight lieutenant came out, introduced himself as Stewart Carey, and invited me to hang up my cap and come and meet the commanding officer and pilots.

The scene that greeted me was one that will always live in my memory. A crowd of young fellows, all obviously about my own age or younger, in RAF blue, were gathered around a log fire. In a preferred position in the middle, with a pewter tankard of beer in hand like all the others, stood a pink-cheeked, young-looking squadron leader with fairly long hair – as was that of most of the others. The top button of his tunic was undone, and he had a DFC under his pilots wings and a small enamelled fighting-cock emblem on his left pocket. This was the

Squadron Leader Tommy Morgan, DFC and bar, the commanding officer of No. 43 Squadron – "the Fighting Cocks"

Commanding Officer, Thomas Frederick Dalton-Morgan. If I remember correctly, he was also born in March 1917.

He took one look at me in my dark-blue Australian uniform and called out, "Look chaps, a Bastard from the Bush," whereupon I was given an all-round handshake, had a full tankard of beer shoved into my hand and was made to feel instantly at home. Later on, Tommy Morgan shortened his name for me, firstly to "the Bush Bastard" and finally "Bush", by which name I became known throughout the whole of my time with the RAF. I am still addressed as such by most of the ex-members of it by word and by letter.

I have set out, in Appendix B, a short history of 43 Squadron which had served with great distinction in World War I. In World War II, up to the time I finally left them, they had shot down more than 110 enemy aircraft for the loss of eleven pilots killed in action, and were one of the most forward-placed units in the Battle of Britain, at Tangmere, on the south coast in Sussex.

They were among the Hurricane squadrons which, because they were outclassed by the German Me 109 fighters, were required to intercept the bombers. Among those in our mess, there were a few from that time who had come north to rest after the Battle of Britain, to train new pilots and to defend the Edinburgh-Glasgow sector of 13 Group. Along with Tommy Morgan was Flight Lieutenant Frank Carey, DFC and bar, DFM, Flight Lieutenant "Killy" Kilmartin, DFC (also sometimes known as "Iggy" because of his first name, Ignatius), and Flying Officer Danny duVivier, a Belgian whose family had been decimated in the German blitz on his country in 1940 and who had escaped to join the RAF.

A book called *Aces High*, written by Christopher Shores, contains many of the names and the experiences of the lads I met during my time in the RAF and I have included them in Appendix C. This includes the abovementioned, and also some later pilots with whom I trained or served in No. 43 and 17 squadrons during the years I spent under service with the RAF.

My admiration for these veterans knew no bounds, and I was delighted to be posted to Killy's flight after recovering from the very beery welcome on my first night. I was posted after an interview the next day with the commanding officer, who said (after taking a look at my logbook and Pilot's Training Card, with the comment that I was literally "cannon fodder") that he was sending me over to Killy because there was not much he did not know and, if I listened to him, I might have a chance to survive. My first letter home from Drem had its opening as follows:

RAF Officers Mess
No. 43 Squadron
DREM
East Lothian
SCOTLAND

19/2/41

Dearest family,

Things have certainly happened since I last wrote the main item of news, being my posting to the above squadron. You may not know it but this squadron ranks among the very best in England and while I am only posted temporarily at present it will depend on how I shape with them as to whether I remain as a member or get posted at the end of my 50 hours training when I become fully operational. They don't know it yet but I will be a full member just as soon as I get cracking on the flying. These lads have over 90 Huns to their credit and they were the squadron that bagged about 25 Junkers 87's last September in one day and the mess is simply thick with DFC's and DFM's.

Their headquarters are in the South of England and they are up here resting, more or less, and have been given the job of training pupils from Operational Training Units up to the 50 hour mark on Hurricanes. If the pupils are only average they send them on to other squadrons but, if they show plenty of promise, then they keep them back as members of their squadron. As soon as one has been in action with the squadron against the enemy he is presented with a small badge of a fighting cock to be worn on the left pocket. The mascot is a beautiful metal model of an English gamecock and is quite the best one I have seen. It is the habit of the good squadrons here to have such mascots and badges and some are very good indeed, but this is really the tops.

As an aside, I would point out here how this example, such as giving a visible reward to enhance motivation, is often used today in industry and government when management are trying to discover ways and means of reaching top-line efficiency. It is truly surprising, even in today's materialistic society, how much can be achieved by recognition of excellence with something other than money. In our case it was a little badge or a piece of coloured ribbon.

Number 43 prided itself on being the squadron which used to do loops, with their wingtips tied together, in their Hawker Fury's at prewar air shows. Consequently they were really keen about formation flying. Their idea of keeping station was that the wingmen should fly with their wingtip 3 feet away from the leader and 3 feet back, and you had to concentrate mightily to keep to their requirement. It transpired later on in the war that the pattern we flew, in four "vics" ("vees") of three aircraft each, was superseded as not being flexible

Learning formation flying, a few feet off the leader's wingtip. The letters FT designate all 43 Squadron aircraft, while V is the serial letter of this machine

enough, or tactically sound. At the time however, it drilled into us the need to be able to join up as a squadron of twelve aircraft into formation quickly, and also to maintain station under all circumstances, until the leader decreed otherwise, or the squadron was "jumped" by an unseen enemy.

The next most important thing that was drilled into us was air-to-air gunnery. This was practised in two ways. One was by using a 16-millimetre cinecamera mounted in the wing and activated by a button next to the true gun button. The other was to have 100 rounds loaded in only two of the eight wing-guns, with the bullets painted red, blue, yellow or green so that at least four aircraft could fire at a towed aerial target and their hits could be identified by colour and counted.

Cinecamera attacks were good for ensuring that the aircraft were actually firing inside the maximum range of 250 yards, at which distance the eight machine guns were harmonised. This meant that all the guns, which were in the outer section of the wings, were pointed at a spot 250 yards ahead, at which all the bullets would arrive in harmony. Hurricanes equipped with a camera-gun, also in the outer wing, could act as a target for another one, and camera-gun work could be easily carried out by squadron pairs, and dogfighting could be done so that all angles could be practised for shooting. One had to be careful to press the correct gun button.

It used to be interesting, when viewing the films and listening to the comments on our techniques by the squadron commander, to sometimes see a second or two of film of one of the practising pair, taken by an unknown "attacker". Without knowing it he had been "shot down" by the commanding officer who jumped him while he was concentrating on his exercise. It was not only embarrassing, but a very good way of learning that, no matter where you were or what you were doing, you had to keep an ultra-high standard of vigilance or you were dead.

For practice-shooting with live ammunition, a towed target in the form of a long, white, cloth sleeve (like a windsock) was generally towed at 200 yards behind a Fairy Battle – an outmoded, single-engine, two-seat bomber. One had to meet the target at a special firing range out to sea and make a head-on approach to one side so that the attack was initiated by turning into the target and firing the two guns (see above) when between 90 degrees and 45 degrees on a converging course from behind. Known as deflection shooting, it was an excellent way of proving that the target was actually being hit. It had been practised by the RAF for many years and prizes been given for marksmanship to both pilots and squadrons.

Frank Carey, in his prewar days, once scored 185 hits out of 200. The best I ever did was thirty-six but, if one was allowed, one could get a good score by doing about five attacks and squirting only twenty bullets at a time out of each of the guns. The rate of fire of one of our Browning guns was 1,200 rounds a minute; that is, twenty a second. If one was truly on target and laying off the proper deflection, or lead, on the target, and one was at the correct range, then it did not take long to make a reasonable score. It was hardly likely that the enemy would be as obliging as a towed drogue, but the object of the exercise was to make deflection shooting become second nature to us.

As the weather improved later in the year and we wanted to do more air-to-air gunnery, we devised a method of towing a target off our grass aerodrome with one of our own Hurricanes. We did not have to wait for a separate unit to tow targets for us, thus increasing our time on the range and the teaching of the pilots whom we were training.

The weather in Scotland was awful in the long winter that kept up until well into May of that year. On one occasion we had a very heavy snowfall that had to be rolled down so that we could operate. The next day it froze solid and we could take off, but not land, so we were sent across the Firth of Forth to operate from an aerodrome, belonging to the Fleet Air Arm of the Royal Navy, at a place called Crail. Because it was right on the seacoast it did not freeze over. It was amusing when we landed to be given directions to report to the "Bridge" for further instructions. The Bridge turned out to be the control tower. We also learned that our billets in Nissen huts were given "deck" letters, such as A, B and C deck. The hut that was the officers' mess was "the Wardroom".

The "ship" – HMS *Jackdaw* – which was actually the aerodrome, resounded now and then to weird commands over the loudspeaker system. The advice that, "A liberty boat will leave for the shore at eight bells," meant that a bus would depart from the guardroom for the local township at a given time, and so on, in accordance with Royal Navy tradition.

One thing that did impress us mightily, however, was the duty-free liquor and tobacco that could be purchased. A tot of whiskey or gin was only threepence, and cigarettes sixpence a packet, so we pooled our money resources and bought up scads of grog and fags. The Navy were a great bunch of fellows and made us very welcome for the three days that we were there, but when we had to go back to Drem we did not have enough room in our kites to store all the contraband we had amassed.

One of the Navy aviators had the bright idea of suggesting that, if we removed our radios, we could pack our loot in the space thus provided, and they would send our radio sets back to Drem for us by lorry. We therefore flew back home and puzzled the ground controller while in the air by not replying to any messages, explaining to him, when on home ground again, that the sets must have been made unserviceable due to our close proximity to the cold ocean. In the meantime, our cooperative ground crew retrieved the radios for us from the Navy, and it was no time before we were operational again and our fitters rewarded with a share of the goodies.

As the days went by, and the weather gradually improved, we began night flying in earnest. This was something I enjoyed when the weather and visibility was good but it was a hell of a strain in bad weather, of which Drem had more than its fair share. England and Scotland were totally blacked out. In a time of no moon it was pitch-black and, with no horizon, one had to be extremely careful to watch the height above the ground and ensure that one knew where he was in the sector, and could "blind-fly" navigate out of trouble if necessary.

Navigation was assisted by the ground control having us always pinpointed by our own automatic radio signals, which were broadcast by our aircraft for fifteen seconds in every minute, and which were picked up by three receivers, plotted into a "cocked hat" on their sector map. This could assist them in getting us back over, or near, the aerodrome, unless our radios failed. The concentration required to do this in a single-seater was a severe drain on the nerves and very tiring, but we were training to be ready for night fighting in the summer, when it was considered the Germans would begin night bombing of Edinburgh and Glasgow.

The method we used for landing and taking off at night was known throughout the RAF as the Drem night-operating system. It had been developed at Drem in the prewar years. The first requirement was to enable our own machines to find the aerodrome without the field being also detected by any enemy aircraft. This was done by the ground controller directing us towards our drome and giving us a course to steer which would take us over a single, fairly dim, ground light some miles downwind of the runway in use.

Once over this we turned onto a set course and flew an exact pattern at a set speed and height and let-down on set right-angle turns until we could, at about 300 feet above ground and a mile away from the runway, see another dim vertical light. On looking to the left, one then expected to see a row of six small lights on the left-hand side of the runway, and a left-hand turn then set one up for a landing approach. These lights were only visible for a few degrees to each side and upwards, due to their shielding, and one had to be spot-on to maintain them in view.

As the aircraft turned onto this approach, one also picked up, at the beginning of the runway, a slope-path indicator light. This had red, green and amber beams directed towards the machine. These coloured beams, plus the angle of the runway lights, helped the pilot to maintain a let-down that was neither too high nor too low, by staying in the green. Red was too low and amber was too high. There was only a single line of lights on the left-hand side of the runway for its whole length, with a red one at the far end. It required very neat judgement to assess how high one was above the ground, so that one would not fly into the deck and bounce or, if too high, stall and drop a wing in.

Pupils were aided by the temporary switching on of a small searchlight, which illuminated the landing area momentarily, known as a chance light. One soon got used to judging the landing without it, especially if it was known that there were Germans about. There was also a landing light set into the leading edge of the left-hand wing, but most of us considered it too much of a distraction rather than an assistance, because it tended to dazzle one rather than light up much runway.

Another of the training routines that we went through, time and time again, was learning how to "scramble". This was the codeword for immediate take-off

I am at readiness, with all the necessary gear at hand

because of enemy aircraft, or probables (known as "bogies" when first sighted and then "bandits" when confirmed as enemy), within the sector. The proper execution of this required the aircraft to be fuelled and armed, with its engines warmed for emergency start-up. The pilots were at a state called readiness, which meant being in full flying kit with the Mae West life jacket done up and the parachute draped over the left-hand wing of the machine.

The first time that one scrambled, it was very exciting, but as the war went on and one seemed to spend one's whole existence on readiness and scrambling at the least threat of the approach of enemy aircraft, it became quite a drain on the nerves, and the best thing to do was to try to sleep. This often meant a rude awakening when either the telephone rang or the loudspeaker came forth with, say, the order for "Clearing Red Section, Scramble", a section being two aircraft. Number 43's radio call-sign while in the air was "Clearing Squadron".

On receiving the above order, there would be a mad rush from the flight hut (or chair if outside in the sun) and a dash for the parachute, previously laid on the wingtip. This was then buckled up as one ran around and was helped to

Hurricanes at readiness outside A Flight at Drem. The authorities would have had a fit had they known I took pictures such as this

climb up the wing by one's crew, who had already started the engine. As the engine fitter hopped out of the right-hand side of the cockpit, the pilot climbed into the left, was smartly strapped in, connected up his radio and oxygen leads and slammed the throttle wide open to take off straight ahead with minimum regard for runways or other aircraft.

Unless the machine was actually airborne inside two minutes from the time of the order, one got no marks for the effort. This letter extract tells of an actual "flap" soon after I joined the squadron:

Letter, 15 March 1941

The other day I saw the fastest piece of work at getting off the ground that I have seen, or will ever see. I was not on readiness at the time but was sitting in the flight hut when the order came over the Tannoy (as we call the loud speaker system) for the whole of B flight (6 aircraft) to scramble and patrol a certain point. In less than two minutes the lads were out of the hut, dashing to their kites which were immediately started by the "erks" (mechanics), were strapped in, chutes and helmets buckled and off the ground.

That's pretty fair in my opinion and I believe our squadron actually holds the RAF record for refuelling and re-arming. One day in the last blitz the whole squadron landed, refuelled, re-armed and were off the ground in twelve minutes!

It is only when the ground crews take a pride in the squadron and everybody co-operates together that this sort of thing can be done and believe me, the spirit that permeates this unit has to be seen to be believed. This same squadron was famous in the First World War and was actually led by Sholto Douglas [see Appendix B] who is now the Commander in Chief, Fighter Command.

Our squadron leader (Tommy Morgan) gave us a talk on the squadron and its history one wet afternoon and I think the most outstanding item was, when during August last year 43 Squadron (then comprising only ten machines through losses) intercepted 500 German bombers on a daylight raid, went in and attacked. They brought down 17 machines for certain and something like ten or twelve probables. How's that for sheer guts, ten against 500. A chap certainly has something to live up to in order to be able to remain with them.

While the weather is bad we often dash into Edinburgh and go to the flicks or a pub. Our meeting place on most of our times off is generally the Royal Hotel at North Berwick and one can always find about half of No. 43 squadron pilots in the private bar in room number 8. We have lots of fun and quite often finish up by getting behind the bar and serving drinks for everybody. Being 43 Squadron we don't seem to be able to do wrong anywhere and consequently have some grand times together. One of our chaps, "Mae" West, plays the piano beautifully but never properly when sober as he is too shy, so every time we want him to play we have to get him merry and then the singing and general fun begins. Miss Lorimer, who is the owner of the Royal is awfully good to us as she lost her fiancee in the RFC in the last war. Peggy the barmaid is a true Scot and hard to understand unless one has had a few beers and then everything seems to become clear.

About six of us had been stood down from the squadron one evening so we went to the pictures after a small session at the Royal. Feeling rather full of "joie de vivre" we took our seats in the circle and settled down to watch the news. Then came a documentary film on the Indian Army. We had seen it at the station about two nights before so waited disinterestedly for it to finish. Not so did one of our number. He remembered a scene showing some very smart marching and a very snappy about-turn on the march by some sepoys. Timing it to a nicety he watched the same scene and, at the crucial moment, roared out at the top of his lungs, "About turrrn"! As the soldiers on the screen obeyed him instantly the whole audience was hushed into amazement for a brief second and then roared with laughter.

By the time we had been well trained in scramble techniques the weather began to gradually improve. As the days lengthened, night readiness became as important as daytime, and every moon period saw us on constant stand-by both night and day. We had to implicitly trust the ground controllers at 13 Group Headquarters at Turnhouse to assess the conditions for night flying because we had no way of doing this ourselves until we were airborne. One night, one of the very best friends I had made on the squadron was killed by flying into a hillside in bad weather in which nobody should have ever been sent up. His name was David Bourne. He was about nineteen years old and by nature a sensitive, poetic idealist who reminded us all of Rupert Brooke, who died in World War I. He had written some beautiful poems, which his Dad finally had printed by Jonathon Cape.

His parents were terribly affected by his death because it was obvious to everyone that David would have become one of England's great writers but, like so many, they believed in their cause and would only say that David died doing what he loved, so they must not falter in their own duty. At first I had found it difficult to understand the English and their reserved ways, but as time went on I discovered that, beneath the apparent aloofness, there lay an awe-inspiring determination and a great sense of service and dedication to the winning of the war.

It was also a revelation to one such as me, who had been brought up in the free-and-easy style of Australia, where there were few social boundaries, to see how the English people accepted the stratum of society into which they happened to be born and got on with the job of working within those constraints, with a minimum of rebellion against them. Later on I discovered under my command some who, once let loose from not being so confined, became superb leaders, but this was a rarity. I believe the reason so many Australians did so well in the RAF was because they were never taught from childhood that "there was a place for everyone and everyone in his place".

I concluded that over a couple of thousand years, on such a small island, the people would have had to learn who were to be the leaders and who the led, otherwise there would have been continuous chaos. The RAF was perhaps more free of "dyed-in-the-wool Englishness" because of the mixture of races they accepted into their aircrew. A photograph of a group of pilots on 43 Squadron in May 1941 contained the following nationalities: American (joined the RCAF by hopping over the Canadian border); Australian; Canadian; Indian; Belgian; Scotsman; Englishman; and Czechoslovakian.

This picture was taken by the RAF and publicised around the world as the members of the "International Squadron" and appeared in *Pix* in Australia, along with a lot of close-ups of the individuals. There never was a true International Squadron, but the media at the time had to hang the label on somebody, so we were chosen and a motion picture was made around the idea. If I remember correctly, the movie was called *International Squadron*, and starred Anton Walbrook. The musical theme which ran throughout it was Tchaikovsky's Piano Concerto in B Flat Minor, Opus 23. Although this was written in the 1870s, a more fitting piece could not have been chosen (or written today), with its soaring passages and the feeling it gives of victory and spiritual uplift.

It certainly made an interesting time, for all of us from different backgrounds, to have to work together in the closest harmony. The adjutant handed me a form one day, which was sent to all Aussies serving on RAF units in the UK, asking them if they would like to apply to join all-Australian squadrons. There was an Australian sergeant pilot, Allan Sands, on the squadron at this time, and he and I had a talk about it and both decided we did not come overseas to join a "Little Australia". We felt that we would benefit more by staying where we were and learning how the other half lived so that, if we survived, we would be able to use better judgement in our assessments of overseas people.

By the end of April my fifty hours in Hurricanes were well past and my place in the squadron as a full-time member was confirmed. The only problem was that, in his search for perfection in his pilots, Tommy Morgan was quite ruthless, and we kept receiving, and getting rid of, people at an even greater rate. This threw a big load on the remainder. I began to feel the strain of constant day-and-night readiness during the moon periods, and started to realise that the maintenance of a constant flow of adrenaline had to be paid for. I had, as a result, my first aircraft accident, described in a letter thus:

Letter, 28 April 1941

Altogether, in the squadron, we have had only twelve operational pilots for two weeks. We should have twenty four but the Commanding Officer will not tolerate mediocre pilots so we pick the pearls out and fling the shells away. This will pay in the long run when we go South again but in the meantime we work and are on duty exactly twice as hard and long as normally, for our full strength should be twelve machines on the top line all the time and twenty four pilots. In the last month we had only two whole nights off and were released at times for a few hours for a stretch. We not only flew hard but could not get away from the job and this, together with a piece of poor work by an equally over-the-counter mechanic, led to my first aircraft accident.

A week ago nearly, I took off with Freddie Lister alongside me to do some practise dog-fighting and, after climbing to about 8,000 feet, levelled out, gaining speed rapidly and noticed a hell of a draught about my legs; looked down into the cockpit and saw a corner of a panel beginning to peel out. The locking screw had been left undone. Slowed down, called up Freddie who came alongside to have a look and told him to buzz off and do some aerobatics, put my wheels down and came down in a long slow glide using no motor, because of the panel, to get a decent rate of descent. Came in too slow, ground coming up fast, pulled the stick back smoothly enough but too quickly, stalled a wing (the starboard one), hit pretty hard and bounced up, throttled on and let the kite down nice and gently not realizing I had lost my right wheel in the first bounce. Left wheel and tail wheel touched gently, waited for the nice rumble that tells of a good three pointer and in a split second, crrrrrump!

I sat in the middle of the strip facing back the way I had come, feeling a hell of a fool. Switched my radio on, told control what had happened and to warn other machines coming in to land. Switched everything off, climbed out absolutely unhurt except for a large dent on the ego. Our harness prevents us being flung forward against the reflector sight even though the kite did stop from 80 mph to 0 in about ten yards. Surveyed the wreckage. Machine on its nose, propeller in small splintered pieces spread back along my skid track, tail in the air about ten feet, wing tip in the deck, flaps, radiator, oil cooler intake written off and me nearly crying with shame, having damaged my first aeroplane in nearly two hundred and fifty hours flying.

Of course I took some photos but it was late in the evening and they may not come out. The Commanding Officer was as wild as hell (being fully entitled to be) but his report was not too bad, making allowance for the panel etc., but it means a black mark in my log book and though we laugh at it now, for a few days I felt pretty depressed believe me, I had been told that every pilot must crash before he really can say his education is completed but I, who thought differently, must now agree. It is over and done with now and I am physically and nervously untouched, but it does mean that I must shoot down at least two Huns to be in front.

The mention of Sergeant Freddie Lister serves to remind me that I had been transferred to A Flight at that time and Freddie had been allocated to me as my wingman, as the Yanks would say, but number two in the RAF. Freddie had represented England in prewar Olympic speed skating, and was also a Wembley

My number two, Flight Sergeant Freddie Lister, poses in front of my Hurricane

soccer star, and one could not have wished for a nicer offsider. He flew well with plenty of dash and was altogether a great personality – not at all egotistic about his prewar fame, but just as young and crazy as the rest of us. We got to know each other really well because we were always on readiness together, both night and day, and I was really sorry to lose touch with him when I left the squadron, and never did learn if he survived the war.

At about this time, I was detailed by the RAF to appear on a BBC radio program called "In Town Tonight", and was given a rail pass to London. I wrote the following letter to home after getting back to Drem from the broadcast:

Letter, 28 April 1941

I hope you got my cable in time and heard my broadcast on the "In Town Tonight" programme of the British Broadcasting Commission. It came about suddenly and I left here on Friday evening at 10.40pm. Had a grand sleep in the best train I have ever travelled in; namely the "Flying Scotsman". Arrived in London at 10am Saturday morning after lying in my bunk for an hour or two, watching the countryside flash past and thinking how peaceful it looked and how well-worth fighting for it is to keep it thus. Spent the rest of the morning getting shaved and doing some shopping and reported at the studio at 3pm. We rehearsed until 6pm and I was not too pleased because they had altered the original script and turned it into a hell of a "line". However it was beyond my power to make any alterations then and I just had to imagine the lads back in the mess thinking up rude remarks for my return.

I met the rest of the cast and became quite pally with them all. The most fascinating bloke was an old cove of 70 years whose staple diet is ordinary grass and who runs a mile or two every morning just to make life interesting. He was not at all eccentric but a very decent, well-mannered, natural and likeable character. The announcer, or interviewer in my case, was Ray Rich and he gave me great comfort when he said to me "I know what you think of it and you know what I think of it, but it's good publicity so lets get it over with".

A Canadian comedian and a Cockney chap of the same calling, were also good lads and the four of us popped out to the local at six, when the rehearsal finished, and got outside a few stiff whiskeys. At a few minutes to seven we were sitting at our tables swapping rude stories and then the yellow light came on and my piece went out to the listening millions. I do hope you were able to receive the show alright because I was thinking of you at the time and wishing very much that I could have been allowed to add a few words of greeting to you all.

At about eight o'clock I went around to the Liaison Club and met some of my old pals, all of whom knew the broadcast was coming off and, so many and varied were the drinks, that I was duly poured into my sleeping car at 10.45pm and arrived in Edinburgh at 9.45 next morning a little the worse for wear, but richer by two guineas and plenty of experience. Back again and we are now supplemented by four new pilots, untrained as yet and thus unable to relieve us of our fairly heavy-duty periods. They are all officers, one English boy and three Americans. The USA lads are the absolute opposite to one's picture of the typical Yank. They are from the Middle West and Texas, short and fat and fairly quiet. Nice lads all but too old and slow; still it's too early to tell now and they may surprise us yet.

I cannot think of much else to tell you except that Ermintrude is on her last legs and may soon become completely decrepit and useless. She was fairly cheap and has taken me (and many others) a few thousand miles and gave good service while she breathed, but now old age has caught up with her and her ancestors prepare to receive her withered and misshapen form.

My fondest love

The same letter enthused about a remarkable flying display at Drem, which was put on for the media by a Wing Commander Stainforth, who was in charge of a Beaufighter night-fighter squadron doing experimental development work on airborne radar. He had been a member of the high-speed flight which won the Schneider Trophy for England in 1931 at a speed of 340 miles an hour in a machine built by Supermarine and designed by R.J. Mitchell, the father of the wartime Spitfire. The display he turned on was done with one of the other Drem squadron's Spitfires, and he did things with it that one sees today only performed by very special aerobatic machines like the Pitts Special.

His final *pièce de résistance* for the display was an inverted pass over the aerodrome at 10 feet above the ground and half-rolling out over the far boundary. This was especially dangerous because, soon after they become inverted, the Merlin engines cut out because they were normally fed by a carburettor which relies on gravity. The German aircraft were fuel injected and did not suffer from this problem. One can imagine the nice timing needed to come back to upright flight before this cut-out, especially when flying about 10 feet above the ground. Staniforth was a really odd character who rarely mixed with any of us, hated our modern music (or music of any kind so far as we could tell), and was respected for his incredible expertise at flying, but was avoided as a social being. His whole attitude was perhaps typical of those whose minds are so concentrated on one single issue that their achievement in that particular field causes them to lose touch with the rest of humanity.

That letter was dated 28 April, and after it was written we were brought to night readiness at the beginning of the full-moon period in May. The RAF had been warned by secret agents in Norway that it was a certainty that the Germans would begin night raids on the north of England, and very likely Scotland, at this time, and the commanding officer briefed us on the technique we would be using if Edinburgh or Glasgow were raided.

Four machines would patrol the Firth of Forth at heights to be determined at the time by the controller, and the remaining eight would be stacked up at 1,000-feet intervals over the area being raided, beginning at 1,000 feet above the ack-ack height, which was to be up to 12,000 feet. This meant that the top bloke would be at 20,000 feet, and he turned out to be me. I suspected that this was because it was my first operational night flight and I needed to be kept well out of the road of the more experienced chaps on the squadron; that is, out of harm's way. We were also told to not fly through the "GDA" and, because I did not understand what this meant, I intended to find out after the briefing, but forgot, with later interesting results, as described in this letter to home on 7 May:

> For the past three nights we have been up all night till 3 or 4am chasing German night bombers and the Commanding Officer has bagged three in the past two nights. The first night, low cloud prevented us from doing much more than just stooge around but on the second night things cracked wide open.
>
> At eleven o'clock we were given the "Fighter Night" order over the loud speaker and at four minute intervals we took off and climbed up to our designated heights over the blitz area, which was about fifty miles away at Glasgow. I was over the target at around twelve o'clock. From then on things fairly began to happen for we could see huge areas of incendiaries lighting up acres of the city and now and then ugly flashes told of high explosives bursting indiscriminately among the houses.
>
> I had been over the area for about half an hour when suddenly a black shape came at me from the port quarter ahead and I only just had time to recognize a Ju 88 before he whistled underneath going like stink. I howled into a steep turn after him, hit his slip-stream and spun. By the time I had recovered I had lost sight of him and positively yelled with rage. I only saw another one that night and he shot into the clouds four thousand feet below me before I could do anything about it.

Coming back was just no joke either because like a dope I flew fair through a large gun defended area [the aforementioned "GDA"] which also bristled with searchlights which kept sweeping around towards me. I first got a surprise when it felt as though somebody had given my machine a kick under the tail plane and when this kept happening I looked in the rear vision mirror and saw flashes of bursting shells trailing me up from behind. I split-arsed around and got out of it as quickly as possible and then, as the cloud had thickened and covered the ground, got lost on the way home. However four of us were eventually brought home on the radio, two with about six gallons of petrol left (out of 90) and myself with 15 because I had nursed it to the fullest extent.

Our Squadron Commander shot down his two near the drome, which was a good effort because it is almost impossible to see anything, but he was crafty and flew so that the moon path reflected across the Firth of Forth towards him, and anything that crossed it he could pick up the silhouette, fly carefully in behind, and cut loose without being seen. The next night was the same and the Commanding Officer got another one and this being the fourth night we have been on "fighter night" and getting to bed about 4am, we are all as tired as hell.

The next afternoon I was on day readiness with Freddie Lister in the flight (as "Yellow section") and we were scrambled to chase a "bogey" (unidentified, but suspected enemy) that was coming in off the sea. We took off in 57 seconds and climbed up to 15,000 feet on a given course, The controller then gave us differing courses and we eventually saw a small black machine silhouetted against the clouds, coming in like a bat out of hell. I yelled at Freddie to get into line astern and we turned and began to chase him.

I managed to keep in the sun so that he would have trouble picking us up, but we had everything wide open and had to come down in a long dive from 15,000 feet to his level at about 11,000 in order to catch him. I sneaked right up on his beam about 300 yards away and above. He was a Junkers 88 painted all black and a nastier looking specimen I have never seen. I sang out "Attack, attack, go" and peeled off, came in on the port quarter and opened up at about 250 yards closing to 150 yards dead astern and giving a long five second burst of fire. I saw my bullets smacking into his wings and engine cowlings, making lovely white flashes and tearing pieces off.

I had to break away otherwise I would have run into him and, as Freddie came in, a large piece of the Hun broke off and floated back as Freddie opened up. Of course as soon as I opened fire he began to dive for the clouds about 1000 feet below and disappeared in a matter of seconds before we could have another go at him. We howled into the cloud after him doing about 350 mph but he must have turned inside the cloud for we lost him. Freddie saw lots of return fire coming at me from the rear gunner but curiously enough I did not see a darned thing, too intent on hitting the cow I think.

We came back excited as hell about it then heard that Red section had just shot another one down, which had been circling some wreckage in the sea. This really lifted the lid off and although Freddie and I can only claim one damaged we are waiting on a verdict from Group Headquarters because the wreckage was a Hun rubber dinghy with a dead Jerry in it, and must have been ours, for nowhere else for miles around had any other squadron encountered a thing.

I think the funniest thing about our Hun was told afterwards. The lads in the flight knew we were after a Jerry and were waiting anxiously to hear what was happening when the phone rang and operations said, "Pilot Officer Cotton has just informed us over the radio that he has clouted a bastard". This really broke them up and although, in the excitement of the moment, I cannot remember saying this I would not doubt it. That brought our total up to five in 3 days and the whole mob at Group were simply wild with joy. There was no relaxation though for we were on the line again last night up till two in the morning. I am really stinking tired, so tired I can hardly sleep and by the end of another week of this will be getting some well-earned rest.

The Commanding Officer is certainly a slave driver and spares nobody, including himself, but this may be a bit short sighted in my opinion because the squadron is supposed to be resting now and if we go on at this rate we will be thoroughly teased out before we are sent back into action!

Even though we sometimes are too tired to think about flying and just lie back in our chairs hoping to hell we won't be sent off, as soon as we are airborne the thrill gets to us and, once up there, we wonder how we ever thought that we wanted to stay on the ground.

The night before last, one of our Aussie Sergeants (we have two, Sands and Haley) got lost and ran out of fuel and had to bale out. He came down safely in the Lammermuir hills, spent the night in a crofters cottage and is now back with us. I'm afraid this thought is always at the back of our minds, especially when we are flying above cloud. If one's wireless goes bung or one runs out of petrol above cloud at night, then it is a matter of baleing out or crashing into the ground.

We have a very funny chap in the mess at the moment who is doing radar calibration flights in a Cierva Autogyro. He says that the only way he can land it safely is that when he nears the ground he locks the control column, puts his arm over his head to protect the face of the one he loves, shuts off the engine and trusts that God will pull his finger out!

I did not tell them at home that the reason he was flying these missions in this awful looking thing was because he was discovered in bed with a WAAF at his last station and this was his punishment.

The photograph of the gadget with German instructions on it is a parachute harness device into which the canopy supporting straps are locked, and is also a quick-release mechanism to get rid of the chute after one lands. This one was taken from the body of the rear gunner of the Ju 88 which Freddie and I shot down. The words on it translate into: "Harness Release. Turn, then Strike." The most interesting thing about it is that the locking and release mechanism on our own parachutes was exactly the same, and the words (in English) were also the same. Obviously, since our harness releases (and parachutes) were made by the Irvin Parachute Company in the USA, they had at some stage sold a stack of them to the Luftwaffe as well.

A parachute harness-release mechanism from the rear gunner of Freddie's and my Ju88

I am sure this trade would have ceased when war began, because the company presented a small insignia to all Allied fliers who had to bale out (wearing one of their chutes), consisting of a small golden caterpillar with ruby or emerald eyes – the caterpillar being the spinner of the silken canopy. The ones with ruby eyes were given to those airmen who were shot down in flames and the emerald-eyed ones were for those who landed in the ocean. I hardly think our side would have allowed our chaps to wear these if the enemy were doing so as well.

About 33,000 lives were saved by the use of Irvin parachutes alone during World War II.

7 MEMORIES OF SPECIAL FRIENDS

The friends thou hast, and their adoption tried,
Grapple them to thy soul with hoops of steel.
(William Shakespeare, *Hamlet*)

At about this time, the Allies were given a surprise by the sudden arrival in Scotland of one of the Nazi German hierarchy, Rudolf Hess. What they were not told was that he was very lucky to be in one piece, because Danny duVivier and his number two were chasing him as a bogey (unidentified aircraft), and were only minutes behind him when he baled out of his Me 110 near Turnhouse. We did not learn about this ourselves until we read about his arrival in the papers and, putting two and two together, realized he was nearly another statistic on our list of "confirmed destroyed".

After July, we found that the Germans scaled down their night raids over 13 Group, no doubt because, after their invasion of Russia on 22 June, they were busy over there, rather than because we frightened them away. We went back to our main task of the training of fighter pilots from the Operational Training Units and thus the strain of constant readiness decreased.

I had some time off on one occasion and went with the other pilots into Edinburgh, where we had booked out the four stage boxes at the Edinburgh theatre to see a show called *Up and Doing*. The cast included Leslie Henson, Binnie Hale, Cyril Richard and Stanley Holloway, and for about three hours I ached with laughter. The highlight of the show was the last scene where Leslie Henson and Cyril Richard came into our box to carry out a bit of backchat with Stanley Holloway, on stage, who was trying to recite "The Green Eye of the Little Yellow God", and we had a close-up view of the whole episode.

After this show, we went on to a popular nighspot near our operations room at Turnhouse, called (if I remember correctly) the Roadhouse, where there was dancing and drinking to be enjoyed. When ordering some drinks for the lads, I was standing next to a very attractive WAAF corporal who suddenly turned to me and said, "Good evening, Pilot Officer Cotton." I was a bit startled and asked her how she knew my name, to be told she recognised my voice from the radio in the Turnhouse operations room, where she worked in the intelligence section.

Dancing with her was the beginning of what turned out to be a real romance on our part and, had it not been for wartime disruptions, might have led to something more permanent. As it was, I used to call for Corporal Pearl Highett on any occasion I could get leave, and once had to go to the rifle range at Turnhouse. I found her there on the firing mound with other WAAFs, banging away at the targets with .303 rifles under instruction from the armaments warrant officer. He soon dispelled my doubts that they would be of much use in an invasion by showing me some of their targets and inviting me to do better. I must confess that I did not create any better records than they did, and finished up with an even greater respect for English girls and the job they were doing for their country.

Pearl and I had some great times together, and fortunately Ermintrude lasted long enough for me to be mobile enough to be able to join her in Edinburgh, now and again, for dancing or films. Her companionship certainly lightened the serious and sometimes risky business of training, in which we were heavily involved. With a female companion, one could escape from the eternal pilot's

Corporal Pearl Highett of the WAAF – just as bright and smart as she looked

talk of flying, even in the mess where one was enjoined to never talk flying, politics, religion, or to involve in gambling for money, which, in fact, were the main topics of entertainment anyway.

Not far from North Berwick was a hill about 1,050 feet tall, which looked like a pimple rising out of the surrounding flat country and was known locally as the Berwick Law. It made a splendid landmark and also provided a few of us with some fun at climbing it and fooling around at the top, as shown in some of my photographs. At one time I was flying around in a Miles Magister (a small two-seater) and saw a mist, only about a hundred feet deep, creeping in from the sea. It covered North Berwick, then crept up over the Law, which stood out like a lump under a blanket. The same mist is a phenomenon known as a Scots "haw", or "har", and comes from the North Sea under certain meteorological conditions. On the day we were flying, it covered the countryside so quickly that we just got back to our aerodrome and landed before it totally blanketed the field and we lost our way in it. We had to shut down the motor, abandon the aircraft and grope around the aerodrome to find the flight hut, leaving the aircraft on the field until next day when the mist lifted.

There is no doubt in my mind that there could not be, anywhere, much worse weather than Scotland, and it cost us dearly in men and machines in that winter of 1941. My sister Betty lost her fiancé, Phil Hart, who crashed while flying in fog at a bomber training field not far from Drem. The English seemed to accept it as inevitable, but those of us used to the sunny skies of Australia hated it. In spite of this, we had a lot of very funny times together, and it calls to mind some of the characters in our unit.

Chris Doll (also in Appendix C) was singing and drinking around the piano in the mess one night and a steward brought in some sandwiches. Chris, torn between carousing and a desire to eat, took out a false front tooth, opened a sandwich, placed the tooth inside it, closed the sandwich and slapped it on the piano with the admonition, "Eat that you bastard," and kept on merrymaking. Odd snippets from letters tell of other events that coloured our lives:

Letter, 16 May 1941

The pilots in the squadron were all issued with revolvers the other day and any stray ammunition has been fired off at a great rate and we are now anxiously searching for more to blaze away with; although nobody can hit a damned thing with them so it is really quite wasted but good fun. There are a number of hares on the drome and when we are taxying around, they run along just in front or to one side and now the lads have the bright idea of using their revolvers on them.

Ronnie West about to drown at the seaside

Hare-hunting in Hurricanes is going to make this drome a very unhealthy place to live in until the boys find some new and less hazardous occupation.

The three American lads who were posted to us have been transferred to the Eagle Squadron and are as mad as hell about it, for they all very much wanted to stay and we also wanted them. They were all decent chaps, full of fun and not at all like the chest-beating Yankee types one often runs across. When told of their posting, Bob Reid rang up the Adjutant of the Eagle Squadron and told him they will apply to go back to America if they have to leave 43 squadron, but even that was of no avail and they left us a few days ago; but we had a pretty wild party to farewell them and they won't forget us for some time to come. In any case they all intend to apply for a posting back again as soon as they get to their new station.

Four days later:

"Tex" Mize is back from his Eagle squadron today and has been telling me how, as soon as they had arrived at the Eagle's lair (?) and had been suitably welcomed, they all with one accord said. "Thanks very much, here is our application for transfer back to 43 squadron". Since then their Commanding Officer has been a most outraged person but they just live for the day when they can come back again. Tex tells me that Bob and Fred have been tight as ticks for about a week straight, in fact having drinks between drinks. They all aim to be here for tomorrow night's squadron party and with them here, a good time should be had by all.

In June we celebrated our early victories of May, and Tommy Morgan's bar to his DFC, with a lovely "do" at No. 8 at the Royal at North Berwick:

We celebrate our victories at room No. 8 at the Royal North Berwick in our usual style. Miss Lorimer is behind me, to the left

Letter, 2 June 1941

Did I tell you about our squadron party to celebrate our 6 victories? I do not seem to remember, but perhaps none of us do remember quite distinctly exactly what happened. I do remember taking a photograph of all the gang packed in behind the bar of the Royal in North Berwick but very much doubt if it will be a howling success because they none of them could be kept still for a second; Tommy would persist in waving a lily over everybody's head or thumbing his nose at the camera. The party finished up as usual in our own mess at about 3 am and, after raiding the kitchen for food, spilling soup everywhere and making a hell of a noise we all gathered around the piano and sang rude songs and generally cut loose.

I was told afterwards that I had considered the general tone of the piano was much below standard and poured my beer inside to improve it. In any event next morning the keys and things refused to function as well as usual and it has since been given an overhaul and general clean-up, which it has needed actually for quite a time, so perhaps it was a good thing after all.

Letter, 9 June 1941

Starting off with our squadron "do". We all arrived back at the drome from the extremely wild night to find next morning that the whole squadron (pilots and machines only) was to proceed to the RAF aerodrome at Valley, on the Isle of Anglesea, to stand-by for Killys's squadron (Kilmartin, ex 43 Sdn. Now Commanding Officer of 602) which was going to Ireland for 2 days on special convoy work. The Flights took off about 11 am with numerous headaches and, in foul weather with clouds down to 300 feet, flew in close formation all the way and landed at Valley. Killy took his boys off and headed for Ireland.

Exactly half an hour after he left, Danny DuVivier was scrambled after a "bogey". He took Frank Czaykowski (Polish) with him and they sighted a JU 88 somewhere over the middle of England. Frank's engine overheated and he was forced to land before he even got his sights on the blighter but Danny waded in – in his inimitable manner – and pooped off everything he had. This all happened at about 23,000 feet and Danny himself copped a packet in the oil cooler and had to land at a strange drome.

The Hun made a crash landing not far away from here and only two of them were alive, the rest being somewhat punctured. The funniest part about the whole show was Killy, when he came back from Ireland and found that we had bagged a Hun in his sector. He was livid for a while but took it like the good sport he is and stood us many drinks. The poor cow has been where he is for nearly two months and not chased one damned Hun which is bad luck indeed.

The Commanding Officer received a signal from Bob Reid who was posted to the Eagle Squadron about 250 miles South, saying that he had been granted 5 days leave and could somebody come and get him in the "Maggie" (Miles Magister). I thought I was lucky to get nominated for the trip so set off from here about 2 pm, took 2 and 1/4 hours to get there but it turned out to be awful weather all the way. I had to fly at about 500 to 700 feet and go through a lot of industrial haze which was exceedingly foul but arrived safely.

I saw at the same station a lot of Aussie lads (four from my course in Canada) in No.1 Australian Squadron and we swapped experiences, whence it turned out that I have been the first and, so far, the only fighter pilot in the Empire Air Training Scheme to have bagged a Hun, but offsetting this by far I heard that one of the bomber lads has been decorated with the D.F.C. and they are carving a good name for themselves and Australia.

Bob and I left the drome at about 6.30 pm and came back the whole way at ground level with a visibility of never more than 1 mile and sometimes less than 200 yards. There was one range of hills that had us both worried and we nearly "had it" because we flew at one stage for about 30 seconds above one hilltop covered in cloud and only 10 minutes gas left. However we arrived safely at 9.15, taking 2 and 3/4 hours and absolutely frozen stiff, for these open jobs are hell to fly in compared with a nice warm Hurricane.

Back at Drem:

Letter, 16 June 1941

Today we had some damned bad luck when news came through that Frank Czaykowski had crashed about ten miles away through a cause unknown. The poor lad is now in Edinburgh suffering from a broken leg and arm, dislocated knee, concussion, severe abrasions and heavy shock. Although none of these are likely to be fatal his condition is critical and he has a bad night in front of him.

He has a splendid record of service against the Hun. He fought them in the Air Force in Poland, escaped to France leaving his family and everything he had in the world behind, had to escape from France after serving in the French Air Force, came to England in August 1940, went through the Battle of Britain, shot down four Huns and was himself wounded by an exploding cannon shell in the cockpit. He spent six months in hospital convalescing and has only been with us for about one month. He is a grand pilot and one of the nicest lads I know. It makes one wild to see fellows like him stopping it when there are so many other useless swabs about the place who will never be able to fly or fight as well as he could. I guess that's the luck of the game.

For some unknown reason, all the letters to home after the above one (up to the last one written while on 43 Squadron in late October) are missing. I believe that they must have been lost at sea on the way to Australia, via the Atlantic, where the submarine war was really hotting up. The last one I wrote while still with 43 Squadron had this to say:

Letter, 14 October 41

No. 43 left Drem about two or three weeks ago and proceeded to a drome just north of Newcastle (Acklington) after a fairly successful nine months; when I sometimes averaged about 50 flying hours per month under some of the most appalling weather conditions during both night and day that I have ever experienced. During this period we shot down eleven Huns, all bombers and mostly JU88's, which brought our total of enemy aircraft confirmed destroyed during this war up to 119. While at Drem we did not lose a single pilot "Killed in Action" but quite a number "Killed on Active Service" through flying accidents, mainly due to weather, and a hell of a lot of near misses, yours truly included.

Our job at Drem eventually evolved into day and night fighting and training of pilots to fit them for operations against the enemy. I have now something like 480 hours RAF flying, of this some 270 hours in Hurricanes, and 30 hours of this last total is operational work at night. However I was never really satisfied with myself in this capacity, no matter how much I told myself that it was for the ultimate benefit of the Air Force. When about one week ago Tom Morgan came to me and asked me if I would like to take over a Flight in a squadron similar to 43 but scheduled for action out East, I gave it some careful thought and decided to accept.

Up to the time I left the squadron we had trained about 170 pilots, the first numbers of whom have brought us lots of reflected glory and fame by their deeds in other squadrons in the battle front down South.

Although I hated the idea of leaving 43 and the wonderful friends and the memories I had acquired, I was really fed up with the weather in the British Isles. I also felt, however, that the promotion was another rung on the ladder towards my ultimate ambition to become a squadron commander, which was just as strong as ever.

The unit I was posted to was No. 17 Squadron (whose history is recounted in Appendix B), who were also flying Hurricanes and were in many respects similar to 43, with an equally distinguished record, and were currently at an aerodrome in northern Scotland, at Tain, near Inverness.

As Ermintrude had finally given up the ghost by breaking a back axle at Drem I would have to go from Acklington to Tain by rail, which went via Edinburgh. Naturally Tom Morgan was always agreeable to the promotion of the love life of his pilots, and arranged for me to take five days to get to Tain, which meant I could meet up with Pearl at Edinburgh on the way through.

We duly got together and managed to spend a weekend at the Royal at North Berwick, where dear Miss Lorimer and Peggy took us under their wings and made our stay a most delightful one. Pearl changed into civilian clothes, as she was fed up with always being in an airwoman's gear, and, for a while, it seemed as though we were back in peacetime. We promised to write to each other and I took some photos of us, and was delighted to be given one of her, which graced my quarters during my time in the East. Although we talked in a desultory way about the future we never raised the subject of marriage or betrothal. I still believed very strongly that any commitment such as this was to become a hostage to fortune and that one must not have any ties to hold one back from full attention to the job in hand.

On my way to join up with No. 17 Squadron, Pearl and I say our farewells at North Berwick

I had seen and heard of too many examples of single pilots, let alone married ones, who were not wholly married to their job, cost their own and often someone else's life by holding back from giving all to the team they were with. It took a rare character indeed to be married, as Tommy Morgan and many other prewar RAF pilots were, and yet be totally unafraid to risk everything. Maybe being professionals, instead of amateurs as we were, had a lot to do with it.

So it was my fault that none of my wartime affairs of the heart had any lasting quality about them and, as it turned out after the war, I bless the fact that they did not.

Before I left 43 Squadron, Tom Morgan wrote in my logbook: "Assessment as a Fighter Pilot. Above the Average." That statement, from that leader, meant more to me than any other awards I had achieved. It is my firm conviction that all the training and flying experiences I gained in 43 were the reason I survived the war, and I believe that, in effect, I owe my life to them.

Part 2
SEVENTEEN IN BURMA

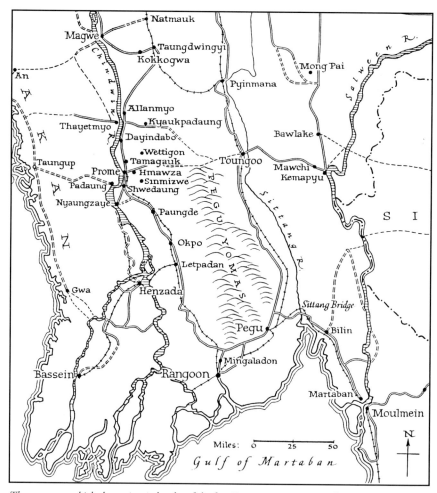

The area over which the main air battles of the first Burma campaign were fought

1 NEW FACES – NEW PLACES

Not Fare Well, But Fare Forward, Voyagers.
(T.S. Eliot)

Arrival at Tain in the far north of Scotland to take over A Flight in 17 Squadron was something of a shock. At first contact the commanding officer, Squadron Leader "Bunny" Stone, DFC, looked and behaved so differently to my previous commanding officer that I wondered if the unit could ever be inspired by him, as was 43 Squadron under Tommy Morgan.

Bunny behaved like a lot of upper-class Englishmen, with a seeming lack of any serious thought and a playboy attitude to everything. Fortunately, I had by this time come to realise that many of the English loved to disguise their true feelings by playing down their achievements and appearing outwardly to be irresponsible fatheads. It did not take long for we colonials to realise that this was a deliberate front calculated to get others to misunderstand them. In fact if one looks back through their history one cannot help but conclude that the path to world domination was strewn with the corpses of the nations who underestimated the English. Bunny turned out to be a true exponent of this tactic, and in fact had a deep core of determination and was a better judge of character than ever given credit for. I came to admire and respect him greatly.

Of all the pilots on the unit, only he and I had fired our guns in action, and I was somewhat appalled at the prospect of facing the enemy with such an untried group. I immediately set about teaching my flight to act as a team, because this way they could at least provide each other with some mutual protection. The first practice at formation flying allowed me to discover that two Americans, "Tex" Barrick and Jack Gibson, were outstanding pilots. Although Tex was a flight sergeant pilot, I made him a section leader, and Jack was given the job of being my wingman. They both exhibited the "damn the torpedoes, full speed ahead" attitude expressed by their famous Civil War naval officer, Admiral Farragut, and I felt that they would be a real inspiration to the others in the flight when we finally got into action.

Before I could get a true assessment of the qualities and airmanship of the rest of the flight, we were directed to fly down to Catterick in Yorkshire, to be fitted out for overseas. We said goodbye to the mud and cold of Scotland and landed in the mists and cold of Yorkshire. We were there for four weeks and did not see the sun, or even its faint orb, through the cloud cover for the whole time. To add to our misery, all of our aeroplanes were whipped away from us and we were not told either where we were going, or what sort of aeroplanes we were going to be flying.

We could understand that security was the reason behind this, and I must say that the English were fanatical about this aspect of the war and rightly so. But when we began to be issued with tropical clothing, some wag said that, if the service ran true to form, we were obviously destined for the snows of Russia. As there was little to do until our new aircraft arrived, Bunny approved some leave, for a few pilots at a time, and I took the opportunity to dash off to London. My letter to home at this time recounted the result:

Letter 23 November 1941

The last two days of my leave in London I called on David's father and we had a very long chat about life in general. He is such a nice chap and I can well imagine how tragic the loss of his only boy must have been for himself and Mrs Bourne. However he is just carrying on with his job and smiling through it all. It makes one realize that we are definitely fighting for something more than vested interests when a man of his calibre can sacrifice his only son and be able to say to me. "I have no regrets that Davy joined the Air Force and am simply glad to know he died on duty" One could not say of David anything more fitting, than the way Rupert Brooke wrote of such as he:-

These laid the world away: poured out the red
Sweet wine of youth; gave up the years to be
Of work and joy, and that unhoped serene,
That men call age; and those who would have been,
Their sons, they gave, their immortality.

There is something rather wonderful in the calm of the English, and their ability to stand adversity and punishment, that would be hard for anyone to better. I take my hat off to each and everyone of them in this regard. Mr. Bourne gave me an abridged version of Doughty's "Arabia Deserta" which work, you may remember, was claimed by Lawrence of Arabia to be one of the noblest works of literature in the English language, and it most certainly is wonderful stuff. He wanted to give me two huge complete copies, each about as big as Lawrence's "Seven Pillars of Wisdom" but I had to refuse them, because of lack of space, which is a shame indeed.

These books were later, after the war, posted by him to me in Australia, where they grace my library shelves as a constant reminder of David and his family.

Lawrence, as you know, had all his work printed by Jonathon Cape, of which firm Mr. Bourne was a senior executive and thus he knew Lawrence quite well and can talk most interestingly about him.

The rest of my time in the grand old city was spent with a couple of Aussie Sergeant pilots whom I know and we did all the shows and had some really slap-up parties farewelling old friends from the Liaison Club. I was given a chrysanthemum by Miss Francis Day, who is the toast of London, in a show called "Black Vanities" at the Palladium and, with others, was compelled (not quite) to dance up and down the aisle of the theatre with a very sweet chorus girl. All this happened to us because we had practically booked out the very front row of the stalls and were naturally right on tap when the prizes were handed out. It was a wizard show; marvellous humour and some beautiful dancing and singing. Flannagan and Allen, Francis Day and Naunton Wayne were the main attractions and they were really screamingly funny. Together with a visit to the famous Windmill theatre (however do those undressed young ladies keep warm?); it was a marvellous send-off and makes up for some of the boredom of the life we are currently leading.

Finally we began to receive our brand new Hurricane fighters, which turned out to be Mark 2cs, armed with four Hispano Suiza 20-millimetre calibre cannons. By comparison, our previous armament of .303 Browning machine-guns had a calibre of 7.5 millimetres. Bunny believed that we were destined for the Caucasus, based on the idea that the cannon armament was specifically designed for ground-strafing of armoured vehicles, as the Germans were overrunning the Russians with their tanks and personnel carriers at the time.

Bunny was so caught up with office work that he detailed me to take charge of all flying and the conversion of pilots to the new models. This did not take long, in spite of the horrible weather, and on one occasion, when I had cancelled all flying due to the lack of visibility, Bunny and I were alarmed to hear the noise of a Merlin-engine aircraft coming into the circuit area for a landing. We eventually breathed a sigh of relief as one of Catterick's Spitfire squadron's machines, on delivery to them by ATA (Air Transport Auxiliary) pilots from the factories, landed safely out of the murk.

We all considered the delivery in such weather to be either the work of an extraordinarily clever pilot or someone too stupid to know the risk – particularly as the Spit squadron had lost a pilot killed a short time beforehand in similar conditions. We watched the pilot climb out – a slim figure in the traditional ATA black slacks and jacket, helmet unbuckled, and long blonde hair shaken out; a young lady hopped down off the wing and started repairing her make-up.

Our welcome was tinged with some awe, but she made light of the conditions and that night in the mess also proved she could hold her own in a game of snooker and swig down many a pint with the best of them. The ATA, and particularly the women pilots therein, did a wonderful job during the war, and delivered everything to the squadrons from the factories, including four-engine bombers. They saved the RAF from a considerable waste of operational personnel by allowing trained pilots to remain in action.

The last letter I wrote home from England says:

Royal Air Force
Catterick
Yorkshire

27/11/41

Darlings,

This will be my last letter to you from this country but by the time this reaches you I may have cabled a new address and preceded this by air mail. We have been here one month now and in that time have flown exceedingly little and rested ourselves an exceeding lot.

Thus we are all mad keen to get cracking again, but the binding part of the whole show is that the Eastern Blitz has already started and we may miss some fun. Of course it is stupid to think that the war is going to be finished off in the next few weeks, so perhaps we will yet have time to really prove ourselves as a squadron.

I have come to know the lads fairly well but reserve all my judgement until I can get them in the air with me and see how they fly; they are all very pleasant blokes and amongst them I can see the makings of a first class fighter unit, as befits the history of this great squadron. During the (almost) year that I have been in

England there have been times when it was everything that any fighter pilot could have wished for, but latterly it has been frustrating due to the lack of the sort of activity for which we are trained. Because of this, and because I cannot see anything else but this same state of affairs continuing in the foreseeable future in the U.K., then I am glad to be getting away from it. In any case we all consider that the training of "sprog" (pilots from OTU's) to be about the most dangerous occupation of the war, and I am damned glad to see that most of my future flying will be operational stuff wherein one has a better chance for a few more victories.

I flew up to Acklington to say cheerio to the boys of 43 Squadron and found them all in good form but still awfully browned off at the lack of Huns, however this is a common complaint these days.

I hear on the radio at the moment a recording of "Begin the Beguine" by Artie Shaw and, as you may remember, this used to be one of my favourite swing pieces at home.

Pearl is at present training at a place called Loughborough and slightly sick of the red tape and "bumf" but expects to get shot of it and down to a real job of work as an assistant adjutant before long. I cannot help but admire her keenness and efficiency, but then she is typical of the young girls who are doing such jobs over here. Only tonight a bright young thing has popped into the mess in a snappy ATA uniform, she having just flown a Spitfire from some far away spot North of here. I must admit that the weather was such that would keep most of us on our backsides in the mess but she, blithe spirit, seemed to take it in her stride.

Naturally she has been invited to our farewell party tonight and, if all goes well, she may become one of the chosen few who have already inscribed their footprints (in bare feet blackened with boot polish) on the ceiling of the mess by mounting a pyramid of tables and chairs. When I inform you that the aforementioned ceiling is about 15 or 16 feet high you will understand that this is an exceedingly tricky operation, especially when the one trying to do it is generally rather "droolers", as we call it.

I must away to dinner chums so cheerio for the present.

Lots of love, Mont.

Those four weeks we spent at Catterick were great from the point of view of a wonderful farewell from the homeland. It was a beautifully equipped peacetime station with all the amenities that one could wish for – central heating, crystal and silver in the mess, plenty of beer, snooker tables, a dance hall and a large contingent of WAAFs to help us while away the boring times when weather prevented flying.

The flying that we did manage to do was not much good to us, because we had no facilities for gunnery practice or night flying, and we were all thankful when we finally entrained for our journey to Gourock, at the mouth of the Clyde, on about 5 December 1941 for overseas embarkation. As it was just less than twelve months since I had sailed past Gourock on the way into Glasgow from Canada, it was with a feeling of satisfaction that I reviewed the time and the experiences I had been through. I felt a lot older than the twelve calendar months should have made me feel, and realised that life was going to get a whole lot more complicated and my responsibilities a lot more wearing before the task ahead was completed.

We sailed on the largest convoy ever to proceed to the Middle and Far East, and believed we were scheduled to sail around the Cape of Good Hope, then up the Persian Gulf to Basra to pick up our Hurricanes and go to the aid of the Russians. With us, along with hundreds of Army people, were two other fighter squadrons. Frank Carey was the Commanding Officer of No. 135 and Jimmy Elsdon Commanding Officer of No. 136 (Frank's and Jimmy's histories are recounted in Appendix C). The pilots of all squadrons were on the *Durban Castle*, and the ground crews and aeroplanes on different ships. After a few days at sea the Japanese bombed Pearl Harbour on 7 December and the whole scene changed with the entry of the USA into the war.

In retrospect, one can imagine the difficulties involved in the reassessment of priorities of the whole field of battle that the Allied war planners now had to make. It says a lot for the speed with which they acted, for, within a few days of the US involvement, the *Durban Castle* was diverted to berth at Freetown in Sierra Leone. Half of the pilots of the three squadrons were off-loaded, and the remainder rejoined the convoy to proceed to Singapore as reinforcements for the squadrons there and, as it turned out, virtual oblivion. One of these pilots was John Gorton of 135 Squadron, who survived Singapore to become a prime minister of Australia.

Being the senior flight commander of 17 Squadron, I was one of the fortunate ones to be off-loaded and, on landing at Freetown, found to my delight that an old friend from 43 Squadron, Killy Kilmartin, was there in command of a small fighter unit at Hastings aerodrome, protecting the allied interests. Through the grapevine, Killy had come to know that we were coming in to port, and our anchor chains had barely rattled out when we saw a Hurricane appear, low among the shipping. He then turned on a hair-raising display of low-level aerobatics, culminating in a fly-past 10 feet beneath us as we stood on the bridge and gazed into his grinning face.

The ship's captain had by now become very agitated, so Frank Carey signalled Killy with an Aldis lamp: "For God's sake piss off." Half an hour later an RAF launch arrived alongside with Killy on board and our commanding officers and flight commanders were invited to join him for an hilarious Christmas lunch, which was interrupted by his being scrambled to intercept a Vichy French aircraft which had strayed into our territory. This he shot down, and then he rejoined us at the table to indulge in an even merrier celebration.

Here we were taken in RAF DC2s over the African continent to Khartoum, staging via Kano and Fort Lamy. The boredom of droning away over the limitless wastes got to be too much for Frank Carey, who wheedled his way into the cockpit to try his hand at flying the DC2. I am not sure who thought up the skulduggery that followed, but somebody (I think it was Bunny) organised us to all leave our seats and creep to the back of the aircraft, thus upsetting the centre of gravity so that Frank had to level the aeroplane with the elevator trim control. After Frank had got things back into nice equilibrium, we all moved forward, making the machine nose-heavy, thus requiring more work on Frank's behalf to trim it again. After this happened several times he got suspicious, opened the cockpit door, and saw the horde of grinning faces at the back of the machine. This brought forth an admirable string of Air Force invective.

Khartoum was a one-night stopover and a dawn take-off from the Nile in a four-engine Short Canopus flying boat – the civil version of the RAF Sunderland which did such a magnificent job with Coastal Command. We were amazed at the room in this monster and quite fascinated at the cane chairs which the pilot and copilot occupied way up above the other decks. It seemed to us that by all accounts it should not be able to fly at all, but it surely and safely deposited us on the Nile again, at Cairo, where we were billeted at the Hotel National in Rue Suliman Pasha.

It was here that I met and formed a lasting friendship with Barry Sutton, who was my opposite number as a flight commander in 135 Squadron, and set out with him and others to enjoy the sights of the pyramids, Sphinx, markets and night-life of this crossroads of civilisation. The latter seemed to consist of pimps trying to sell the favours of their sisters, or if this met with a blank stare, the similar favours of their young brothers. I also have a memory of being woken up one morning by the sound of empty beer cans clattering in the street below as one of our number pelted them at an organ grinder, who retreated up the street while churning out the strains of "Kiss Me Good Night Sergeant Major" on his machine.

Barry Sutton and I at the Cairo zoo on the way to Burma

Another memory, of a New Year's Eve party at Sheppards Hotel, amid the high-ranking officers of all the services, and their wives or girlfriends, stayed with me because it was in such contrast to the battles raging out west in the desert. It was apparent that not everyone in the services was an active contributor to the war effort, and it tended to spoil one's appreciation at being invited to join in the revelry.

On our arrival in Cairo we had been greeted by RAF Headquarters with the observation: "Who the hell are you and what are you doing here?" After a short space of time, during which we had become thoroughly bored with the fleshpots of Cairo, Headquarters finally agreed to let the commanding officers and some of the flight commanders be loaded once more into a Canopus flying boat and flown out to Karachi in India, via Tiberias on the Sea of Galilee and Basra in the Persian Gulf. Soon after their arrival, Bunny Stone, Frank Carey and Jimmy Elsdon flew out to Rangoon in the Canopus, while I was left at Karachi to try and knock our untrained pilots into shape, using some Harvard trainers, and also to keep nagging at anyone in authority who might be able to make some Hurricanes available.

At this time the RAF had only a few Hurricanes in the Far East, and these were equipped with twelve machine-guns instead of the usual eight. We could

Hank Forde tries his hand in Cairo as a rickshaw wallah. Al McDonald is the passenger

not work out why this was the case, because the extra weight reduced the air-craft performance so much that it lost its manoeuvrability and therefore cancelled out its superior firepower, as it could only be brought to bear on the target with great difficulty. Such was the result of some of the backroom thinking of the time, but we were sure that no real fighter pilot ever thought that one up. They were also equipped, however, with a non-jettisonable long-range petrol tank under each wing, each tank holding 90 gallons of fuel. As soon as some became available, and still equipped with this awe-inspiring load, I sent some out to Rangoon, flying in formation with Blenheim bombers, who did all the navigation.

We were all staggered by the peacetime attitudes of the military services in India, particularly at Karachi, with life being lived as though nothing had happened since September 1939. Servants waited on the officers and their wives, and the built-in routines of social life continued unchanged. One was even expected to have visiting cards available to leave at various clubs and the homes of senior officers, so we tried to break down some of this wasteful and tiresome rubbish by being as anti-establishment as we could get away with.

At a dance which we attended on one occasion, where the formal part of the evening was spent in waltzing, foxtrots and polite conversation, we waited until the orchestra and stuffed shirts had gone and then reorganised the gathering into a jam session. With one of our pilots on drums and another on the piano, we instructed the remaining young ladies in swing and jitterbugging, and general conviviality ruled until the small hours of the morning. The night finished with some of us decorating the solemn heads of the animals (shot by past members) which graced the walls of the officers mess at Karachi aerodrome.

Next morning we felt that the place looked a lot more relaxed and cheerful, with each animal's head having in its mouth either a cigarette, cigar, or old pipe. The senior station officer did not share our enthusiasm and complained bitterly about our larrikin-like and irresponsible behaviour.

On one occasion, I had the job of flying the Army's General Officer Commanding the Sind area over the North-West Frontier terrain. He was most appreciative, but did not respond positively to my suggestion that we beat hell out of some of the unruly tribesmen with our Harvards, just to keep our hands in. These machines were actually fitted with bomb racks under the wings and we did some dive-bombing on the practice range to relieve the monotony.

I was mightily pleased, however, when a signal finally came through that I was to fly back to Shuaiba (near Basra) with five other pilots, to ferry some eight-gun long-range Hurries to Rangoon, where they were so badly needed. I flew as second pilot in an RAF DC2, arriving at Shuaiba on 10 February. We collected our six Hurricanes and flew in formation on three Blenheim bombers, which were to lead us to Rangoon. It would have been a considerable problem for fighter pilots to carry out their own navigation over such a long distance, with nothing more than a compass, and it was sensible to have them led by the Blenheims, which were also badly needed in Burma.

We staged via Bahrain (three hours), Fort Shajah (two hours), Jiwani (two hours and fifteen minutes), Karachi (two hours), Jodhpur (two hours and thirty minutes), Allahabad (three hours and thirty minutes), Calcutta (two hours and thirty minutes), Magwe, Burma (three hours), and Rangoon (two hours). These long flights, sitting in a cockpit where one could not move more than 3 inches in any direction and with one's bottom getting more numb through sitting on a collapsible rubber dinghy on top of the parachute, together with having to concentrate on formation flying, were agonising in the extreme.

It was a wonderful relief to finally stagger out of our aircraft on 14 February and be greeted by the crew at Mingaladon aerodrome, near Rangoon, with a cup of tea and a recital of all their past experiences.

2 AIR BATTLES OVER SOUTHERN BURMA

The time will come when thou shalt lift thine eyes
To watch a long-drawn battle in the skies
While aged peasants, too amazed for words,
Stare at the flying fleet of wondrous birds.
(T. Gray, 1737)

Before recounting the experiences of 17 Squadron after the arrival of their Hurricanes in Burma on 23 January 1942, I feel that it will be best if I give the background of the war in the air as it had developed in the Far East since the Japanese bombed Pearl Harbour on 7 December 1941.

The pilots of 17, 135 and 136 squadrons who had left us at Freetown in December 1941 finally arrived in Singapore with some Hurricanes on 13 January 1942. They, together with their ground crews, were then formed into No. 232 Squadron. They shot down eight bombers from a Japanese formation of twenty-seven on 20 January, but their success was very short-lived, because on the next day the Japanese bombers came over again, this time escorted by Mitsubishi Zeros which shot down five of the Hurricanes. The Hurries were Middle East models fitted with tropical air filters, which reduced their top speed performance and rate of climb and could never hope to compete on level terms with the Zeros, even had they not been so modified. They did better later on when they adopted the tactics of not trying to dogfight at all, but the Japanese had plenty of machines in reserve, and by the end of January No. 232 Squadron had only eight machines left with which to defend Singapore, out of their normal establishment of sixteen.

They continued in the defence of Singapore until the garrison surrendered on 15 February, and after this the remaining Hurricanes of 232 and 605 squadrons went to Sumatra and, together with some remaining bombers, achieved some success in annihilating a Japanese invasion force. But the odds against them were overwhelming; the end was inevitable, and the Dutch Army commander surrendered on 8 March. During the Malayan and Singapore campaigns, the RAF lost a total of 435 aircraft and destroyed 192 Japanese. They did quite well over Singapore, when the Hurricanes achieved 100 victories, but this was at a cost of forty-five of their own number, and it was a case of too little, too late. There is no record of what happened to the original 17 Squadron pilots, but it is presumed they mostly escaped back to Australia. Their story is yet to be told.

The fall of Singapore allowed the Japanese to turn their thoughts towards the conquest of Burma, which was of great strategic value to them because it could potentially lead to the opening of the vast riches of India, as well as shutting the Chinese off from their main source of supply, namely the Burma Road via Rangoon. The Japanese experience in carrying out warfare in the jungles of Malaya would stand them in good stead, and similar tactics were then set in motion in a northern drive into the Mergui Archipelago, which runs along the western shore of the Malay Peninsula.

There have been very few stories written about the RAF involvement in Burma and only one, that I know of, published by a pilot who actually flew in the first Burma campaign. This was *Wings over Burma* by Flying Officer Ken Hemingway, who was a journalist in civilian life and was on my flight in 17 Squadron. It was published in 1944, and although it is a fascinating account of his personal experiences, it is hard to learn from it a broad picture of the whole aerial campaign.

Field Marshal Sir William Slim, in his book *Defeat into Victory* (published in 1956), was very generous in his appreciation of the effort of the RAF in the air, although, in places, critical of their administration. He gave very high praise to the efforts of the pilots of the RAF and AVG (American Volunteer Group, also known as "Chennaults Flying Tigers") by saying on page 7 of his book: "Rarely can so small an Air Force have battled so gallantly and so effectively against a comparable foe."

Louis Allen, the author of the remarkable book *Burma: The Longest Retreat*, has totally disregarded the Allied effort in the air, other than to recount an incident where our own aircraft bombed and machine-gunned our own troops due to being given the wrong bomb line by the Army. Therefore I intend to try to set the record straight by not only recounting my own experiences in this campaign, but also by briefly setting out those of others who were directly involved.

From my own knowledge, the whole of the three RAF Hurricane squadrons together (17, 135 and 136) never succeeded in maintaining more than ten

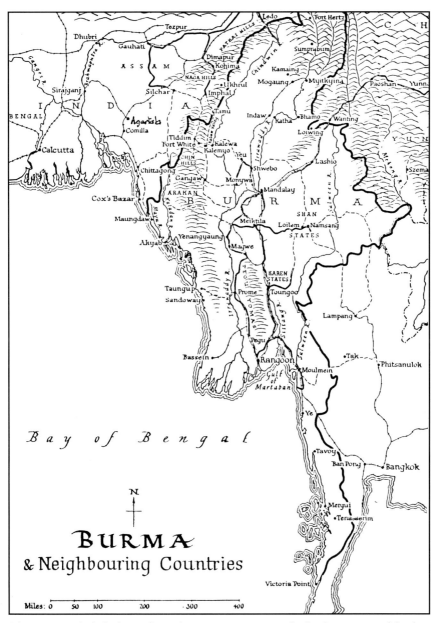

The area over which the first and second Burma campaigns were fought, showing most of the places mentioned in the book

machines between them in the air at one time. Ten aircraft was also the average of the American Volunteer Group's No. 3 Squadron. Number 67 Squadron RAF never fielded more than six Brewster Buffaloes after the Hurricanes arrived and, taken altogether, the maximum number of fighters which could theoretically be scrambled during the whole campaign was twenty-six. There was, however, more often than not at least 50 per cent of the force doing other duties, such as bomber escort, strafing, or reconnaissance, leaving only 10 to 15 aircraft for interception of the Japanese raids.

The Brewster Buffalo

The Japanese, however, have been credited with having (according to Slim) "400 [aeroplanes] available to them for the thrust into Burma". Other sources quote 260 Japanese planes available on a daily basis after the capture of Rangoon on 6 March. Winston Churchill favourably compared the effort of the air forces with that of the Battle of Britain. As Bunny Stone points out in his memoirs (Book Two), the main difference was that in the Battle of Britain the problem was lack of pilots, whereas in our campaign it was lack of aeroplanes.

Bearing the imbalance in numbers in mind, let us have a look at the start of the Burma campaign which began in December 1941. The air defence of Burma at the beginning of the campaign in late December 1941 was wholly in the hands of No. 67 Squadron RAF, equipped with Brewster Buffaloes, and No. 3 Squadron of the American Volunteer Group, flying Curtiss Tomahawks. At

A line-up of the American Volunteer Group's Curtiss Tomahawks

this time, both squadrons had sixteen aircraft each and were normally able to have twelve each on readiness.

The American Volunteer Group had been in action against the Japanese in China and the pilots were mercenaries, recruited from the US forces, and their considerable experience became very valuable to the RAF units associated with them. The only way in which the highly manoeuvrable Japanese Army 97 fighter could be outclassed was to attack from a superior height, snap-shoot, and dive away to gain height again. The Japanese could out-climb our machines but could not out-dive them, or fly as fast in straight and level flight.

Rangoon began to suffer from heavy Japanese bombing attacks from 23 December 1941 onwards, including Christmas Day. On their first raid they lost ten aircraft and the American Volunteer Group and RAF lost nine. Our losses were higher than they should have been because the advice from the American Volunteer Group had not been properly learned. At this time our group, which had been left at Freetown, was diverted for the defence of Rangoon. Rangoon was bombed continually and literally devastated, with a subsequent total breakdown in civil administration and enormous destruction of lend-lease material destined for China via the Burma Road.

When the first Hurricanes from Shuaiba arrived on 23 January, there were only four operational Buffaloes left, but their original sixteen had given a good account of themselves by destroying thirty-seven Japanese aircraft. It is not known how many the American Volunteer Group destroyed but they were masters of the air up until this time and there is no doubt that the majority of the aircraft destroyed fell to them. Their pilots earned US$500 (in gold) for every Japanese confirmed destroyed and those of them who survived the Burma campaign must have been very rich at the end, but we did not begrudge them a cent of it.

On 23 January, however, No. 17 Squadron's frustrations came to an end when the first three Hurricanes arrived from the Middle East. As already mentioned, these were armed with twelve machine-guns, four of which were removed very smartly by Bunny Stone at Mingaladon, but the Air Officer Commanding in Rangoon insisted that the long-range tanks remain fixed to the aircraft. Soon after the Hurricanes had landed, the extra guns had been whipped out and the aircraft had been refuelled, the air-raid warning sounded.

Bunny Stone, together with another pilot and Squadron Leader Jimmy Elsdon, scrambled. The long-range tanks caused them to take ages to get up to 10,000 feet, where Bunny saw a fight going on between some Japanese bombers and the American Volunteer Group. While he was getting his group into position to join the fight, they were bounced by ten Army 97 Japanese fighters.

Squadron Leader "Bunny" Stone, DFC, at the officers' mess at Insein, Rangoon [photo by Ken Hemingway]

In spite of all the stories we had been fed about myopic Japanese pilots who could not even see straight, let alone fly properly, Bunny and his group soon found out how wrong all these tales were. Jimmy and the other pilot quickly realised they were totally outclassed and dived away to land, but Bunny unwisely tried to out-climb the Japanese to stay in the fight. His own description, in his memoirs, records the one-sided combat that followed. Needless to say, his machine was shot-up very badly and the Air Officer Commanding regretfully allowed the long-range tanks to be removed.

After the long-range tank fiasco, Bunny's Hurricane was so badly damaged that it never flew again and was scrapped for spare parts. On the following day he regained his confidence as the early-warning radar (the only one available for the whole of the campaign) detected a large formation of hostiles approaching. Number 67 Squadron's four remaining Buffaloes, plus eight of the AVG and No. 17's two remaining Hurricanes, took off to intercept. With the burden of long-range tanks having been shed, and flying with Jimmy Elsdon as his wingman, Bunny climbed up to 15,000 feet. Coming from the south-east were seven Japanese bombers escorted by Army 97s, which were being kept busy by the AVG.

Once again Bunny's account of what happened is fully recorded in his memoirs. On that occasion none of the Japanese bombers reached Rangoon, but Bunny's aircraft had its propeller damaged by bullets and there were no proper tools to change it. The maintenance crews had an almost impossible task in trying to keep the machines airborne, and it was only with the cooperation of the British Rangoon Railway engineers, who actually made the specialised aircraft tools for them, that the Hurries were kept flying.

The whole of the RAF ground organisation was in a complete mess. Spares and tools from the support depots never seemed to arrive when they were needed. Motor transport was almost nonexistent and 17 had to scrounge some from local car dealers and the American Volunteer Group, whom we helped by lending some ground crew to them.

The saga of the long-range tanks was not yet over, because the Air Officer Commanding issued an order to the squadron to refit them and strafe the airfield at Bangkok – 350 miles away! Bunny pointed out that, by his calculations, they would only have some three minutes over the airfield and they would in any event be sitting ducks for any Japanese fighters because of their inability to jettison the tanks. Even if they did survive any combat, the chances of getting back to their base would be nil because of the time taken and the fuel used.

Headquarters persisted in their request but agreed to let Bunny nominate the pilots. His choice, apart from himself, was Squadron Leader Frank Carey, DFC and bar, DFM, and one of the flight commanders. As soon as someone in Headquarters realised that there was every chance of losing the three most experienced RAF pilots then in Burma, no more was heard of the request. By this time Bunny and the other commanding officers had had a bellyful of the Air Officer Commanding and his disregard for their welfare, beginning from the time they arrived at Rangoon to be told by a sergeant from Group Headquarters, who picked them up, that they were to sleep in the Rangoon gaol. This reception was not appreciated when it was later learned that some 300 Group personnel were, at the time, comfortably installed in the upper middle-class business quarters in Rangoon.

On 27 January, No. 17 Squadron, which had pilots trained in night flying, agreed to try intercepting the bombers then raiding Rangoon at night. The American Volunteer Group had tried this, using the headlights of motorcars to illuminate the runway, but had lost two aircraft in doing so. The Hurricane pilots had been trained in England and the reader will know by now that their night-flying training was excellent.

The night-time weather in Burma is beautiful in the winter and the Japanese normally took advantage of the full moon to mount their raids, so, on the night in question, the AVG took all their aircraft to a nearby satellite strip and left Mingaladon to 17 Squadron. Bunny Stone and Jimmy Elsdon placed themselves on readiness and took off when the warning of a raid came through. They decided that Bunny would patrol above 20,000 feet and Jimmy below. Anti-aircraft fire was noticed, but they could not spot anything at first until Bunny saw what looked like a moving star and realised he was looking at the exhausts of two Japanese bombers flying in formation.

As he moved in for the kill, one of them opened fire, but this stopped as soon as Bunny also opened fire. He lined up on the other bomber and gave it a burst which sent it into a vertical dive, which he followed, firing at it until it burst into flames and crashed into the Irrawaddy.

On landing, he discovered that Jimmy had also located the two bombers and was about to open fire on one, when the tracer bullets from Bunny's guns passed over him and ripped into the bomber. The following day, both machines were confirmed destroyed, and the pilots became the toast of Rangoon for a period.

Frank Carey was still waiting to receive some aircraft and, after persuading No. 17 to lend him one, flew with them, and on 28 January joined in an interception and shot down an Army 97 fighter. But by mid-February both squadrons had received enough machines (delivered by me and others) to allow them to put a combined total of nearly twelve in the air and began to take heavy toll of the Japanese, whose troops were advancing quickly on Moulmein and threatening the Sittang river area. We carried out a lot of Army-support work, knocking out a lot of Japanese transport and personnel by ground-strafing, and sinking boats and barges which they were using to bypass the land forces.

Before I begin to describe my own involvement with the squadron, let us also see what Field Marshal Sir William Slim had to say about the campaign up to this time:

> Speaking generally, all the Japanese fighters were inferior to the Hurricane and the P 40, with the exception of the Navy 0, which was approximately equal to them. The Japanese, however, had a considerable advantage in range, which was of great service to them in a country where distances were vast. The Navy 0, for example, had a radius of two hundred and fifty miles, or five hundred with jettisonable tanks, compared with the one hundred and thirty five miles of the Hurricane. We were thus denied the power of retaliating with fighters against the enemy on their own airfields.
>
> Nor were the superior numbers and range of the Japanese aircraft the only handicaps from which we suffered. With the odds against us, an efficient warning system, which would enable us to defend our own airfields, was essential if our machines were to escape destruction on the ground. Add to the unfortunate location of our main airfields the facts that we possessed only one radio direction-finding set, a meagre complement of anti-aircraft artillery, and the newly raised and hurriedly trained Burma Observer Corps had no wireless, and was thus tied to the scanty civil telephone and telegraph system, and it is easy to picture the disadvantage at which our tiny air force operated.
>
> Rangoon had suffered heavily from bombing, but the two British squadrons and one American squadron defending the city, in meeting thirty one day and night attacks in the first two months, destroyed one hundred and thirty enemy aircraft with sixty probables, and compelled the Japanese to abandon the attacks after the end of February. The majority of the enemy fell to the AVG, who not only had in the P40 the better fighter, but were more experienced than the British pilots. It was thus possible for the last convoys of reinforcements to enter Rangoon and for the demolitions and final evacuation to be completed without serious air interference.

At the same time, P40's and Buffaloes – the range was too great for the Hurricanes – attacked any enemy airfields within reach, and our few bombers ranged far into Siam.

Rarely can so small an air force have battled so gallantly and so effectively against comparable odds. Such an effort could not be maintained. On the 31st January 1942, our operational strength was thirty five aircraft, against one hundred and fifty Japanese.

Appeals for reinforcements were refused; Malaya and the Dutch East Indies still had first call. Singapore fell on the 15th February, and at once the Japanese air forces began to receive heavy additions. By mid-March, there were fourteen regiments of the Japanese Air Force deployed against Burma, a total of some four hundred aircraft with a daily effort of two hundred and sixty. Against this we could produce a daily operation average of under forty-five. The odds were growing too heavy, even for British and American airmen.

In fact the Navy 0 (or Zero, as it became known) did not enter the campaign until towards the end, in April. The Japanese fighter force was composed of the Mitsubishi Army 97 (or Nate), which had a fixed undercarriage and was as manoeuvrable as a Tiger Moth but very vulnerable because of its lack of armour plate and self-sealing fuel tanks. The only way to tackle it successfully was to have an advantage in height and to dive, shoot, and climb away. If one was bounced then the only thing to do was dive away, because the 97 had no chance of catching up. To try to dogfight was a certain way of meeting one's maker.

The reader may remember from chapter one that it was on 14 February that I staggered from my long-range Hurricane and was greeted by Bunny and pilots of the squadron. On the very next day I set off on a fighter sweep over Moulmein. From then on, one seldom flew less than three operations per day. Most of them were low-level strafing of Japanese Army targets, escorting Blenheims on their bombing raids, or interceptions of incoming Japanese raids and fighter sweeps.

Bunny seemed somewhat distraught by the experiences he had been through and, one day at the flight hut on the aerodrome, pulled out a silver whisky flask from a pocket and took a nip from it. He was showing me how it had lost its original curved shape because the high-altitude flying had acted to distort it outwards and, when I asked him why he carried it with him in the air he replied: "Well, Bush old chap, when I have a hangover and I am flying the next day I carry it; then if I see any spots before my eyes I take a quick nip. If the spots go away I know they were liver spots but if they don't, I know the buggers are Japs!"

At Mingaladon aerodrome's 17 Squadron dispersal. Left to right: Ken Wheatley, self, Allen Carvell, Bunny Stone, "Brownie", Jack Gibson, Tommy Thomas, Ken Wisrodt, Tex Barrick, Fuggy Ferguson [photo by Ken Hemingway]

One never could tell with Bunny if he was serious or not, so I never finally determined if he really did have a nip while flying, or saved it to calm himself afterwards when on the ground, because he treated everything outwardly as one big joke. His memoirs confirm that he had to appear good-humoured during the day for the sake of morale, but at night it was a constant worry and strain. This was just one of the prices one paid for leadership – as I later found out.

Later on in the war I was interviewed by an RAF historian (after I had taken command of the squadron), and I was given a record of that interview. I believe that it is more authentic than anything I can today glean from my logbook, or my memory, and I print bits of it hereunder as the best record that I have of the major events of that time:

> We started flying Hurricanes from Shuaiba out to Rangoon on the 9th February, 1942, and flew them with fixed long-range tanks across the Persian Gulf to India and arrived at Mingaladon aerodrome, Burma, on the morning of 14th February. On the 15th February, I did my first high-level sweep which was over MOULMEIN.

Some 17 Squadron pilots outside the flight hut at Mingaladon. Left to right: Al McDonald, Doug Cropper (an Australian), James, Ferguson, "Brownie", Allan Carvell, Ken Wheatley

On the 16th and twice on the 17th we escorted our bombers over the Gulf of Martaban to the front-line area. It was on 16th February we beat up the village of KAMAMAUNG, dropping incendiaries on the village and machine-gunning the woods. Then I lead six Hurricanes, one of which was flown by Sergeant Cropper, on an escort of six Blenheims which made an attack on shipping in the SALWEEN ESTUARY.

We carried out a beat-up of shipping around MOULMEIN in the Gulf of Martaban on the 17th, and on the 18th February we escorted some Blenheims and then beat-up KAMAMAUNG. We escorted Blenheims again on the 20th February. On the 21st February we carried out a front-line patrol, and later in the day there was a scramble but we made no interception. Later we carried out a sweep over KYAIKTO, and we strafed a Japanese Command car which was being concealed in a wood.

We had a scramble on the 22nd with no result, and later provided high cover for 135 Squadron which was engaged in strafing. We escorted Blenheims which did strategic bombing on the 23rd February and then carried out a sweep over the

BILIN ROAD, shooting up transport and personnel and putting one anti-aircraft gun out of action. We also had two scrambles that day, but each was false.

I had mentioned to Bob Neale, one of the AVG pilots, that we were badly in need of transport to and from our pilot's mess at Insein, and he gave me a note to the American Volunteer Group transport pool officer in Rangoon. I grabbed two of our off-duty pilots and fronted up to the American in charge. It was from this pool that trucks had, for some years previously, carried supplies up the Burma Road into China, and there were stacks of four-wheel drive trucks and jeeps sitting there, whose obvious destiny was to be destroyed before the Japanese captured Rangoon. I was wearing a bullet belt and a tied-down Colt .45 automatic pistol at the time, and he looked at me and said that if I gave him six bullets I could have three jeeps. That was the best motorcar trade-in deal I have ever been able to strike. It meant a lot to us to be properly mobile.

It may have even saved our lives one day later when two of us were in the jeeps, Ken Hemingway driving one and myself the other, and were fired on by unknown snipers between our mess at Insein and Mingaladon. We were going so fast that they missed, but the crack of the bullets as they went close to us was more than unnerving, and when we arrived at the drome we pressed Bunny to allow us to return with some extra people and have a man-hunt. Rightly so, he vetoed this because we were needed in the air.

Bunny notes on the back of a further drawing:

> There were nearly 200 Japs in the boat. This was obviously an estimate but I believe that few of them would have survived our strafing and it certainly looked as though it was fully loaded and the return fire from the boat was pretty solid. They were using it to outflank our army and we were able to deter them somewhat, at least by day.

Naturally the Japanese sought to use water transport, via the Gulf of Martaban, to outflank our army, and it was important for us to do as much damage as possible to their shipping because the bridge over the Sittang river was blown up, leaving a large force of our 17 Indian Division on the wrong side.

Because of the tragedy caused by their premature blowing up of the Sittang river bridge on 23 February, the British forces lost an enormous number of men (trying to swim the river) and all their equipment, which was left on the other side. I remember saying to Bunny after this that it looked as though we were in for another Thermopylae – this was a narrow pass in Greece from Thessalonika to Locris, famous for its heroic defence against the Persians in 480 BC by Leonidas, King of Sparta, and his 1,000 men, who fought until all died.

He agreed with me, saying: "Bush, if anything happens to me I want you to know that I have asked the AOC to put you in charge of the squadron." What transpired after this is again taken from my copy of the record of the above interview with the RAF historian:

Most of the ground crews left for Magwe on the 24th February because it was evident that we were going to need that base to be prepared for us very soon, because the Japs were now over the Sittang River and our army simply could not cope with them. We had another false alarm and then provided escort for the AVG which carried out a fighter sweep over Moulmein. An enemy fighter was shot down in flames.

On 25th February we carried out a dawn reconnaissance over the Salween. Someone had told us about some barges being there so we shot up one which was filled with troops. They were then raked with machine gun fire, and after the second attack it went up in flames.

On the morning of the 26th February, Squadron Leader Carey and another pilot from No. 135 Squadron, plus Pilot Officer Warburton and myself from No. 17 Squadron, were on readiness at one of our satellite aerodromes called John Haig. We were scheduled to do a dawn sweep over Moulmein but were delayed by a ground mist. We had very little communication with Mingaladon and we finally took off after the Japs had made a sweep over Mingaladon with twelve Army 97 fighters. They did not see us take off from John Haig because of the mist, and we did not know that they had made a sweep. In actual fact we followed them back to their aerodrome at Moulmein at a 15 minute interval and were over the top of them as they were making their landing circuits. Four had already touched down and eight were in the circuit.

We followed them down from 7,000 feet and then it was a free-for-all. I saw Frank Carey (whom I regard as the finest fighter pilot I have ever seen) coming in behind one as the enemy aircraft was touching down. He gave him a burst and the Jap hit the ground, skidded to one side, and then went through a hangar in flames. Frank zoomed up after that, but I lost him.

I went down on two of them and got one chap after he turned around and started to climb in the opposite direction. He was about 2000 feet above the ground and someone must have warned him because he turned right around. I got a full beam shot into him and gave him about a one second burst. He flipped right over and went straight into the ground just by the edge of the aerodrome. After that I pulled up to about 5000 feet and started getting mixed up with two of them and after getting a few bullets through my rudder did a spiral dive, got away from them, pulled out between a couple of low hills near the aerodrome and, as I zipped across the drome, shot one up as he was touching down.

The Jap swung around, stopped, and as his aircraft was starting to burn it was enveloped in a cloud of dust. As I left the scene I counted five columns of smoke rising on and around the aerodrome.

I had to stay right on the deck and get back home at full throttle because I could see two of the Japs chasing me in the rear vision mirror and we were out to the limit of our range and could not afford to stick around. I caught up with Frank Carey, who said afterwards that he thought he was going as fast as any Hurricane could but was intrigued to see me go past him like a rocket before slowing down. We crossed the Salween and formated together and pointed out each other's bullet holes. I had about six and he had some big ones in his machine just behind the cockpit, obviously from ground fire while he was in the circuit area.

The rest of the squadron went on a sweep in the afternoon and I remained at base as we had insufficient aircraft available for me to make the trip. While they were away another Hurricane became serviceable, except for its radio and, as I was

This photo was taken (photographer unknown) on the day I was wounded. Left to right: Tommy Thomas, Tex Barrick, Jack Gibson, Allan Carvell, with me propping up the Hurricane

the senior officer there at the time, I ordered that it be placed on readiness. Before I could put my parachute in it the air raid phone rang and I grabbed my flying helmet. As Tex Barrick made for the aircraft I told him to stand aside, snatched someone else's parachute and took off. I saw some AVG also take off and head out west but could not hope to catch them so decided to head south towards Rangoon, where there was a huge column of smoke rising from the warehouses on the wharfs, which were being destroyed to prevent the contents being used by the Japs.

I got to 20,000 feet and coming out from behind the smoke saw bomb bursts all over our aerodrome, about five minutes after I had taken off; and then picked up some bursts of ack-ack. I sighted a large bomber formation as they turned around and started back towards Thailand and their fighters stayed over the drome, which gave me a chance to get at the bombers. I was on their starboard side and the fighters were on their port side and well behind, doing lots of aerobatics and generally showing off, as was their custom.

I let the fighters stay there and sneaked onto the bombers and, before the fighters saw me, did two quick attacks. The first was no result, except a lot of return fire and a few bits falling off, but on the next attack I carefully selected the outside one and as I broke away he peeled off and went straight into a vertical dive with smoke streaming from one engine. By this time some of the AVG were attacking the tail-end fighters and one saw the bomber crash and confirmed it as destroyed.

Just as I was about to peel off for the third attack the bombers must have called for help because about ten of the fighters were only about 300 to 400 yards away. I pulled away sharply to starboard and started climbing; I had climbed away from the nearest two and was above them with sufficient height to have at least one shot at one of them before I dived through them for home. As I winged over the nearest one stood on his tail and fired a burst at me which, because of my attitude, went through the side of the cockpit. Had it been from behind it would have been stopped by the armour plate but one bullet hit me just below the left knee and broke both bones in my leg, the Tibia very badly, so I simply went straight on down through them at full throttle, still being shot at but with no more hits being registered, thank goodness. Because the Hurricane could easily outdive the Army 97's they did not attempt to follow me down from the 18,000 feet altitude to which I had climbed after hitting the bombers.

I started trying to pull out at about 10,000 feet but the aircraft would not respond and the harder I tried the more I had to press on the right rudder pedal which simply produced a spiral dive. At the last moment I thought of trying to assist the pull-out by using the elevator trim tab and wound this back, as fast as I felt the elevator would stand the strain, and it worked. The aeroplane came out of the dive at just under 1,000 feet doing about 450 miles per hour. I blacked out momentarily and thankfully only took about ten minutes to get back to base.

At Mingaladon I tried the hydraulics, which still worked and allowed me to land with my wheels down. By jamming my right foot under the toe strap and thus being able to fully operate the rudder bar in both directions this allowed me to maintain a reasonably straight line on touchdown. I managed to taxi the machine back to the flight hut where Jack Alexander (as he told me afterwards) unknowingly parked me over the top of a Japanese delayed action bomb.

The crafty English had learned in the First World War that pilots were often wounded in the legs so they put a loop of leather over the top of each end of the rudder bar. This allowed the pilot to jam the unwounded leg into the loop and thus push and pull the rudder. After the war they carried on this tradition and gave the pilot a brake lever on the joystick to allow him to apply the brakes at the same time. The U.S. made the error of designing toe plates on the rudder bar ends to be used as foot-operated brake levers thus the pilot, if wounded in the leg or foot, could use only one side; which of course invariably produced a ground loop.

There is one drawing with me in the process of being extracted from my Hurricane after tussling with the Army 97s. Bunny notes on it as follows:

I had just landed from a Blenheim escort to Moulmein when I heard you had taken off in the remaining Hurrie left at stand-by. The American Volunteer Group had scrambled and yours was the only RAF machine available. When the American Volunteer Group had returned and the time mounted I started to get anxious and was arriving at the conclusion that you had "bought it" when suddenly a Hurrie appeared. Could only have been you. It carried out a rather corny landing – not up to usual "Bush" standards. After parking you did not get out so I concluded you were wounded and collected the Medical Officer and two Erks (ground crew) and rushed over.

Immediately, I saw that the aircraft was drilled from vertically underneath, but thankfully, no cannon shells. Anyway poor you was still in the cockpit clutching your knee with blood spurting out between your fingers and issuing THE most colourful language.

We got you off to hospital in Rangoon after managing to extract you. I went down to the hospital next morning; there you were, still cussing like mad, with your knee above your head in a large plaster! I said on my return to Ming, to dear old Crowthers (Adjutant), that we must get you back to Calcutta immediately because of the situation. He was bloody marvellous and managed to get a Hudson from somewhere to fly you back to India.

I was taken by our ambulance (which had been ready to set off for Magwe) into the military hospital at Rangoon, where they were just about to shut up shop before the Japanese arrived. I was immediately put under anaesthetic and woke up later to find that the leg had been set and the wound packed with sulphanilamide and vaseline gauze and the whole lot encased in a plaster.

This had been done by an Australian Army doctor, who had volunteered to stay behind, from the Aussie troops who had touched there on the way from the Middle East to Australia. I then had a bad bout of vomiting which was not only from the anaesthetic, but also caused by shock, and it became so bad that I must have strained a muscle in my diaphragm, because it was painful for days afterwards. The thing that stopped the vomiting was an ice-cold drink of South Australian beer, of which the Doc had a few bottles left. We both decided that if anything could stay down, that would.

After a sleepless night, during which Rangoon was plastered by Japanese bombers, I was taken to one of the satellite strips, where a Hudson bomber was parked under some trees. The strip was named Highland Queen and followed the naming pattern of all the satellites, which were called after Scotch whiskies. I always claimed that this was because we had nothing to drink in the mess but sweet sherry, but apparently they were named thus in honour of the Scottish engineer who established them.

The ambulance and my evacuation flight had been organized by Sam Crowthers (a tower of strength during the whole campaign) and I was bundled into it on an army blanket and, accompanied by a medical orderly, took off very smartly, because operations told us there was a raid coming in from the east. We were soon crossing the 10,000-feet tall Chindwin Hills, after staging through Magwe, and landed in Calcutta, where I was transferred to the British Military Hospital.

That incident kept me off flying for eight months.

In the first edition of *Hurricanes over Burma*, I had written into chapter three – using extracts from various books, drawings and stories as told to me by Bunny Stone and Jack Alexander (plus quotes from Slim's *Defeat into Victory*) – all the adventures that then befell the squadron until the time they evacuated Burma in late April 1942. Jack was an airframe fitter on my flight and one of those wonderful erks who kept us flying and who patched up all the bullet holes.

Two readers (for whom I have great regard – plus the publisher) told me that in this second edition I should omit my recounting of the remainder of the first Burma campaign because they are not relevant to my own adventures and tend to interrupt the flow of my story. I am now very happy that my account of my experiences in the first Burma campaign are to be added to by the full recounting of it by Bunny Stone in Book Two, which is the book of his memoirs.

3 CONVALESCING IN INDIA

Rest is sweet after strife.
(Edward Lytton, 1803-1873)

Soon after my arrival at the British Military Hospital at Calcutta, two doctors, one an Indian and the other an Austrian, felt my big toe, which protruded from the plaster cast encasing my whole leg from toes to thigh, and concluded that the plaster would have to be removed. I had been told by the Australian doctor in Rangoon, who put the plaster on, that it should not be removed, because the technique discovered during this war, of letting wounds heal themselves under plaster without the daily routine of dressings, had apparently been proven most successful. However, the leg certainly seemed to have swollen inside the plaster cast and the two doctors at Calcutta were apparently concerned that the blood supply to the foot was being cut off by the trauma associated with the wound higher up, and could cause gangrene if allowed to persist.

It will, of course, never be known if they were right or wrong, but all I knew was that next day there was more agony to go through while the plaster was cut off and the leg finally left resting and strapped with bandages to a slightly raised metal framework called a Braun splint, with me lying on my back. On the night after this episode I had a nightmare which recurred for the next seven nights, and which, at the time, I thought I might be subjected to for the rest of my life; it was so vivid and real. After dropping off to sleep, I would dream that Calcutta was on the point of being invaded and taken over by the Japanese armies. I could hear the rattle of small-arms fire and the stutter of machine-guns, intermingled with the bursting of aerial bombs and artillery, as they neared the centre of the city. This became steadily louder until suddenly there was a long silence, which I knew meant that they had reached the hospital and the staff had surrendered.

Me in the British Military Hospital at Calcutta

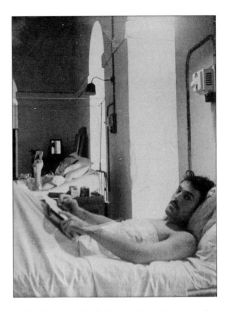

Following the silence came the sound of rubber-soled shoes slapping up the stone-floored corridor, and I knew that it could only be a Japanese soldier running up towards my ward. There were no doors into our wards, only open archways from the corridor to allow free air movement for cooling, and my gaze was fixed on the left-hand side of the first archway, directly opposite my bed. The footsteps stopped. A head, capped in the usual Japanese felt baseball-type headgear, peered around the corner. The face was exactly as the cartoonists had been depicting the "typical" Japanese visage – buckteeth, myopic spectacled eyes, monkey-like ears and a bloodthirsty-looking grimace, supposed to be a smile. The face stared around the ward until its gaze finally came to rest on me in my bed. The eyes flashed, the figure moved from behind the archway holding a long knife in its right hand, rushed over to my bed and plunged the knife into my stomach.

The resulting yell from me not only woke up the rest of the ward, but fortunately drove away the awful image and brought the night nurse dashing in to find out what was wrong. I had the severe pain, from the original internal muscle strain of vomiting, still with me and of course this, possibly combined with sleeping on my back, was the trigger for the dream and the dagger thrust; but it was all dreadfully real and I could only then get some sleep with a dose of pain-relieving drug. It was a great relief at the end of the first week to find that the pain eased off and the nightmare ceased, never to return.

My peace of mind, however, did not increase; quite the reverse. I knew from my days at Roseworthy that broken bones had to be set and firmly splinted in order to knit properly. Here I was with no splints and a break that was not a clean right-angled one but sloping, where there was nothing to stop the bones from sliding over one another. I also knew that the powerful muscles attached to each side of the break would contract and pull the broken parts across each other to result in a grossly shortened and misshapen leg unless something was done to stop this from happening.

Any remonstrating about this with the Indian doctor met with upraised palms and a shrug of shoulders, with an assurance that everything would be "very good finally, sahib". All the Austrian character could contribute was the theory that the bones would knit more rapidly, and therefore stop the shortening, if I was given injections of a calcium supplement, which was duly administered every day, in the alternating sides of my bottom, with a syringe and a needle that looked large enough to dose a bloody horse with.

After a fortnight of this I started really worrying, because I had been measuring the length of my lower leg with a flyswat, by putting it against the inner point of the knee and the inner point of the ankle – that is, the normal top and bottom joints of the tibia – and found that in two weeks it had shortened by three-quarters of an inch, as compared with the same measurement method on the right leg. Providence finally intervened in the form of two British Army surgeons, Major Leon and Captain Tressider, who had just come from England to begin work on the British casualties from the retreat in Burma. They will forever remain my medical idols.

After being briefed by me as to my plight (in the usual Australian manner, coloured with plenty of colonial descriptions of my idea of the Indian and Austrian standards of medical treatment), and grinning at the demonstration of the flyswat technique of bone-length measuring, they both quietly looked at me and one said: "Not to worry old chap. We will fix all that this afternoon."

Sure enough, I was carted off to the operating theatre on a wheeled table, where Captain Tressider, having been told about the vomiting brought on by the previous anaesthetic, asked me if I had ever had a pentothal anaesthetic. My negative reply did not stop him from exploring my right arm for a vein with his hypodermic syringe, giving up because, as he said, "Your bloody veins are too hidden in this wing," and diverting his attention to the left arm where, after some probing, a positive result finally produced an, "Ah, gotcha. Count slowly to ten."

I slowly started counting, but went out like a light as I opened my mouth to say "eight". The next awakening was back in my hospital bed with a steel pin through the ankle bone, a stirrup on it with a wire attached, running over a pulley with a 14-pound weight on the end of it pulling like hell on my leg, against the resistance of the frame on which my upper leg was strapped. Captain Tressider was there to assure me that this would get me back to an almost full-length leg, but I would have to be tied up thus for at least three to four weeks.

The only joy I had out of this was, on questioning, that he assured me that I certainly did not need injections of calcium supplement and that the normal hospital diet would contain all that was needed. When the Austrian came bustling in with his syringe he was therefore smartly told by me to stick it in his own bottom. He thereupon rushed out in a high dudgeon and reported this to the registrar, who came down and started remonstrating with me until I pointed out the mess that the two of his hatchet men had got me into until Tressider and Leon had arrived. After this there was no further appearance made by either of the originals.

The next two weeks were spent writing letters, reading and studying the reactions of the others in the ward, and coming to the realisation that, no matter how much one felt sorry for oneself, there was the consolation that others were even worse. This helped me to become more patient and perhaps it was in hospitals that the word patience was originally derived.

A few beds away from me was a young Rhodesian whose Blenheim bomber had burst a tyre on landing, swung off the strip and hit a dump of full petrol drums, which ignited. He was burnt so much on his face that his eyelids had disappeared, he had hardly any nose left, or ears, and his limbs, where not covered by shirt, shorts or socks, were also badly burnt. He lay there quietly, smoking cigarettes between his thin lips through a holder held in his skeleton-like burnt fingers, without a word of complaint.

In contrast, across from me was an American Volunteer Group pilot who had been wounded in the raid on Magwe by a Japanese antipersonnel bomb, while he was sheltering in a trench. He had his jaw laid open and the break was wired up so that he could only take food through a straw, and his thumb was blown off. He did nothing but groan and complain day and night for a week until he died. It may easily have been that he was suffering from a massive infection – we were never told – but if so, the drugs then in use ought to have worked, but it did seem as though he had no willpower to ensure his survival.

At the end of three weeks my leg was back to its normal length and a plaster cast was put back on, even though by this time the wound was now infected, but

Captain Tressider assured me that it would come to no harm as it brewed up inside the plaster, other than getting very smelly. He and I got on very well together during the time I spent at Calcutta and, on reading through the saved correspondence of those days, I came across this letter, addressed to my father:

Directorate of Medical Services,
RAAF H.Q. Anderson St.
Sth. Yarra
Melbourne

7/8/42

Dear Mr. Cotton,

I am scribbling a hurried note to you on this paper because the letter is entirely unofficial.

I have just opened a letter from an English friend of mine who is now serving with the Indian Medical Services as a Major, Surgeon Specialist.

He mentioned that he had a most charming Royal Australian Air Force patient named Cotton who had a bad leg injury and that he had become quite friendly with him. He said he was the most cheerful patient in the hospital and that, although it would take some time before the leg would be completely better, he thought he was progressing favourably.

I am sorry that he had nothing more definite to tell me but of course he would not know that I would be writing to you. He, your son, has now been transferred to Poona according to my friend's letter and so of course he will not be able to give me any further news of him. Don't bother to answer this if you are busy because I thought you would like to hear a little further news of your son.

Yours sincerely.
J. Grayton Brown, Wing Commander.

Thus it was that I found myself on a hospital train bound for Poona, in the west of India near Bombay, along with numerous other wounded, including "Hookey" Russell, the burnt Rhodesian. We wended our way across India, collecting some bed sores and a lot of dust on the way, and finished up in the British Military Hospital at Poona on 15 March. We were sent there, not only to make room in Calcutta for the incoming casualties from the Burma retreat, but also because it was some 2,000 feet above sea level, and therefore more conducive for recovery to good health, since the monsoon was about to begin.

Next to me in the officer's ward was a very nice British lieutenant from 17 Indian Division, who had his femur broken by a Japanese Tommy-gun bullet. He was suppurating very badly, and had lost a third of the bone entirely, but, again, he was not complaining, even when he had to have it opened and drained without anaesthetic while still in his bed. A letter to home describes some of his experiences:

Letter, 27 April 1942

In the bed next to me is a grand Welsh laddie who has a very serious gun shot wound in the thigh. The femur is completely shattered for a third of its length and he has suffered, and still does at times, absolute hell from it. Nevertheless he is one of the gamest men I have ever seen and we have become very good friends now that we have been swapping our experiences in life and war.

He was telling me the other day that when he was in the hospital in Burma, his condition was so bad (having ridden on the tail board of an army lorry over 40 miles of paddy fields) that he was not expected to live and twice he actually felt himself sinking into the coma that precedes death, and was only able to come back by making himself think how awful it would be for his wife and children, should he decide to give up the struggle. I was never in fear of losing my life, once I was on the ground, so you can gauge from this that, comparatively speaking, I have had a much easier time than some of these army lads.

It was useful to be an Australian patient in this hospital, because one was treated rather differently by the administrative officers, who had their own army people thoroughly regimented. I had organised my corner of the ward exactly as I wanted it for writing and reading, and for the daily routine of shaving, bathing, exercise, and so on, with things readily at hand, either on top of my chest of drawers or hanging from convenient hooks on the wall.

Came the day when a visit by a VIP Army officer was to take place and all patients were given instructions to sit (or lie!) to attention, with nothing in evidence on furniture, floor or walls. The VIP duly arrived, came along the ward accompanied by a retinue of aides-de-camp and hospital officials, and took a look at me surrounded with my possessions and reading in bed. When told I was an Australian in the RAF he murmured, "That explains it," and moved on.

Hospitals are great places for thinking and writing and, apart from a constant stream of letters to home and girlfriends, I tried my hand at some poetry:

The glowing sight-ring superimposed.
Guns drumming in the wings, and
 the howling blast
Of wind, exhaust; terrible speed.

The curling tracers fanning out.
From the doomed enemy pieces flying and
    the black smoke streaming;
Betokening fire, destruction, death.

These I have seen many times, and felt
In my bowels the squirming, throttling fear
    that some day, I too,
Might be the streaking, downward falling torch.

Then in the awful melee above Rangoon,
One against ten I fight, to blast
    from the sky,
The enemy; viciously swerving, twisting, turning.

As the mad dance whirls and roars,
Confusing friend and foe alike
    the raging sun
Beats down oppressively, blinding hot.

With sweat pouring and hands shaking,
From constant days of fighting; sleepless nights,
    the nerves unstrung.
Is this what we were born for, educated, loved?

Then sudden, falling from the fight,
My stricken craft, shuddering, smoking
    from the furious impact
Of the streaming bullets, ripping metal.

Then, hellish, dreadful tearing pain;
Ah! Christ, the awful cries; not me?
    Must I die thus,
Screaming downwards to oblivion.

Flesh and bone torn and scattered,
Blood on the instruments, hands, everywhere.
    My foot jumping,
Shuddering off the pedal, falling, useless.

Controls firm locked! Then this is death.
Animal terror whirling the brain and then,
    the sudden calm
Of reason after panic, while yet a chance exists.

The giant hand of gravity pressing.
As from the fearful dive the plane
    slowly, ah, so slowly,
Straightens out below the fight.

Minutes later, with the senses darkening,
Hysterically shouting, singing, fighting pain,
    my 'drome is below,
I see the runway turn and straighten.

The boundary passes quickly underneath,
The earth gathers my craft gently
    to its smooth bosom.
The noise and fight is finished; and I live!

There is no point in recounting the details of the time spent in Poona, the joy of getting onto crutches, the infuriating itchiness of my leg in the plaster, the bravery and cheerfulness of all and sundry, other than to say that it was a real lesson in learning how to behave under adversity.

On 17 July I received a letter from Air Vice Marshal Pierce, Officer Commanding the Air Forces in India-Burma, congratulating me on the Immediate award of the Distinguished Flying Cross. My dad also received a telegram on 25 July from the Minister for Air in Australia to say that I had been granted an Immediate award of the DFC, and extending the congratulations from the Air Board. I dashed off a telegram home as follows:

JUST RECEIVED DFC CELEBRATE PLEASE LOVE MONT

When my old flight commander, Flight Lieutenant Batchelar (as he was then – now Group Captain), was visiting us recently he was insistent that I include in my book the citation accompanying the above award because, as he said: "People who read the book will want to know why and when you received it." This I do with some reluctance, but it at least officially explains why the award was made. The citation says:

This officer displayed great courage and devotion to duty during the fighting in Burma. On one occasion when his aerodrome was attacked by a strong force of Japanese aircraft, Flight Lieutenant Cotton took off and engaged the enemy alone. After shooting down a bomber his aircraft was attacked by ten enemy fighters and a burst of fire from one punctured both petrol tanks and shattered his left leg. Despite this, he succeeded in making a perfect landing on the aerodrome. Earlier on the same day, Flight Lieutenant Cotton distinguished himself during a raid by our aircraft on Moulmein aerodrome.

Amusingly enough, Bunny Stone had said my landing was a "corny" one.

While we are on the subject of awards, it is interesting to record that there were only two decorations and one Order presented to the members of the fighter squadrons during the whole of the first Burma campaign. Tex Barrick received the Distinguished Flying Medal (being a flight sergeant at the time) and I received the other medal. Our adjutant, Sam Crowthers received the Order of the British Empire, and Bunny Stone should have received a bar to his DFC, but he ran foul of the Old Boy, who refused to sign a recommendation put forward by Group Captain Seton-Broughall after the campaign was over. When it is considered that we did not lose a single bomber to enemy fighters it appears rather niggardly that more rewards were not made. Somebody said to me that retreats are not considered the appropriate occasions for compliments and maybe that had something to do with it.

The time came when I was able to get about with walking sticks and with an iron on the heel of the plaster, and, as a result of this mobility, was one day asked if I would like to apply for a job as an aide-de-camp to the then Duke of Gloucester, who was stationed at Poona at that time. Before this offer came I had been invited to an afternoon tea party with the duke and his retinue at their palace (I expect it was called) in Poona. I was so unimpressed with the fatuous behaviour of his entourage that it was very easy indeed to make appropriate excuses of refusal to the offer.

It never failed to make me as mad as hell to meet up with some of the asinine English fatheads who seemed to have congregated in India. Perhaps the Brits got rid of them out of their island, to India, in the same way as they used to send their convicts to Australia.

By August the plaster was off and I was mobile enough to be sent to an RAF station in the foothills of the Himalayas, called Chakrata. It was here that lots of physiotherapy was practised on my leg. Fortunately, I had tried continuously to flex the thigh muscles while in plaster, and this allowed me to get a reasonable recovery from the wasting which had unavoidably taken place.

Because of the monsoon rains, the road into and out of the place was one of the most hair-raising I had ever been on, owing to washaways and the decrepit state of the bus, but it was at least nice to get away from the hospital routine at long last. The small village of Chakrata offered very little in the way of amusement, and all one could do was to concentrate on getting fit by walking.

On the way to the rest house at Chakrata

The rest house, in the foothills of the Himalayas

By this time the monsoon was in full swing and a hill station was certainly the best place to get away from the heat and humidity of the plains. Now and again the rain clouds would break and give a view of the enormous snow peaks to the north and the lush terraced valleys below our 7,000-feet altitude.

In September I was informed that I was to report to the RAF station at St Thomas Mount (near Madras in southern India), and I spent some days on the train, travelling through stations where the signs of the famine that was raging were made only too evident by the beggars who thronged the tracks, opposite the platform, at each station where we stopped. My already poor impression of India, as a whole, was reinforced by the misery and the degraded lifestyle of the mass of the population, and I could not help but conclude that it would have to be, at that time, one of the worst countries in the world.

At Madras I was told that I would be the fighter controller for the area and I met up with the lads of No. 155 Squadron, who were flying American-built Curtiss Mohawks. These machines were, in effect, radial-engine Tomahawks, and were to be used in a ground-attack role when the squadron became operational after training at Madras. The job I had to do was very minimal as far as any fighter activity was concerned, because by this time the Japanese were

At Madras, I try out my camera in a mirror

concentrating on the battle in the Arakan, where our ground forces were having a rough time of it. The Japanese threat to our area by sea had also been reduced owing to the increasing scale of the battles in the Pacific, which drew their naval forces further to the east.

So 155 Squadron did a lot of strafing of ground targets which I attended, and also army exercises, where we watched artillery firing, tank attacks, mortar attacks and the like. I was not too keen on sitting in front of a lot of guns firing over our heads in case someone miscued and dropped one short, but I managed to calm down after a while and thanked my lucky stars I was in the Air Force, and particularly in fighters. All the Army people I talked to looked at me with sorrow when they discovered this, as though I was living on borrowed time, and it simply bore out the old adage of one man's meat being another man's poison.

At the end of September I began to sneak some unauthorised flights in a Tiger Moth, and after a few aerobatics I convinced Squadron Leader "Dimsey" Stones, the commanding officer of 155 Squadron, that I would not bend one of his Mohawks if allowed to fly it. This I did on 8 October and wangled more flights in the Tiger Moth and also a Hawker Hart, which was a light bomber used in the 1930s on the North-West Frontier as a replacement for the Westland Wapiti – affectionately known to its pilots as the "What a pity".

After talking to the St Thomas Mount medical officer and demonstrating to him that I could take off and do aerobatics in the Mohawk and land it safely, he agreed that I was obviously physically fit to fly. He arranged for me to go to Delhi for a medical examination and, if pronounced medically fit, a posting back to flying duties. The following extracts from letters to home say what happened:

Base Personnel Office.
Bombay,
INDIA

6/11/42

Dearest Family,

At the present moment I have just begun to settle into my room at New Delhi where I have come for my medical board which I sincerely hope will make me fit to go back to the squadron. It is unlikely that I shall finish this until tomorrow so I expect that later on in this letter I shall be able to tell you the result. I am waiting on a hot bath at the moment because the journey up was absolutely filthy and I feel that half the railroad bed is at present residing in my hair. However I would put up with a hell of a lot more than this to get back to where I belong for I was brassed off to a great extent in Madras and very glad to see the last of it, or perhaps I am speaking too soon!

On my last night in Madras I had dinner with Nic and Mrs Robinson of Melbourne, also her daughter Mrs Underhill and her American husband "Red". It was at the Madras Club which I will have you know is quite the most posh Club of India with absolutely no exceptions. We sat out on the lawn under the usual shaded lights and a background of sweet music and for a moment one could almost imagine that it was not India where we were, but perhaps a summer night in Aussie. Of course the illusion is soon broken when one turns around and is confronted by a few coal-black bearers (servants) and also when a breeze wafts the well known "Odour Of the East" (mostly generated by burning cow dung) towards one on the night air.

Actually we had a marvellous dinner and a very good natter (Air Force; "Talk") about whom we knew, and whom we thought we should not know, back in Aussie.

The evening before that I had dinner with a Mr Justice Wadsworth whose daughter Margaret was one of my nurses in the Poona Hospital. They are a very nice couple and altogether I have had quite a good social time while I was there.

8/11/42

Having passed my medical board and been pronounced fit enough to return to my squadron I am just waiting at the present moment to catch my train which will take me back to the boys. I find that since I have been away there are two new flight commanders in the squadron and thus I shall very likely have to revert to the rank of Flying Officer before I can be placed on the establishment. This seems rather hard I admit but when one considers that all that really matters is being in a proper job then it does not seem so unfair as at first sight. Actually I do not expect to be kept long as a Flying Officer because neither the Squadron Leader or the other Flight Commanders have ever been in action so it is certainly going to be rather incongruous when I arrive amongst them as a junior officer.

One cannot get away from this sort of thing because all acting ranks must revert to their original status when the holder has been out of action for more than three months, and in my opinion this is after all quite fair. The only catch in my case is that by now I should be a full Flight Lieutenant anyway, because of my length of service alone, but naturally this has not come through from Australia yet and until it does I am still a Flying Officer. It is all a bit silly but I think with any luck you may soon see me back on the job with perhaps more than two rings up, but that may be looking ahead a bit too far.

Now that I am going back to my old unit I am sure that it will be useless to expect me home at least before another twelve months, and maybe until the end of the war, because apparently the Australian Air Board do not seem very interested in what happens to their men overseas.

It does not worry me overmuch because I have an undying respect for the RAF as a whole and am only too proud to serve under them. I have heard that some of the chaps who have returned to Aussie from overseas have been disgusted with the amount of "bull" that flies around in the RAAF and have been breaking their necks to come back to the RAF again. I can well imagine that there may be a certain amount of truth in this rumour because, if I remember rightly, my own training in Australia was definitely much more rigid and with more petty discipline than the ways of the RAF.

It was by some very fast talking and lots of diplomacy that I was able to wangle back at all to the squadron because the big shot at Madras wanted to keep me back there in spite of my being fit, but I am rapidly becoming an "old sweat" now and know the ways and means of obtaining what one wants in the RAF. It says a lot for a service that does not have to abide strictly to all the rules and regulations that it lays down in the first place, and I expect that there is no finer service than the Air Force from this point of view, although at times they can still improve on their methods.

Well, I am afraid that this is not full of much news and is a trifle hurried but at least will be something for you to go on with until I can tell you of my further adventures in the Squadron from now on. Cheerio for the present and all my love,

Mont

The fact that my old job was not available to me was not a real worry when I turned up at Red Road to meet up with the gang. Even though Bunny Stone was no longer the commanding officer, the spirit of comradeship was still very strong among the others, and it felt like joining the family at home again. What a joy it was to be welcomed back by Tex Barrick, Jack Gibson, Hank Forde, Slim Lewis, Doug Cropper, Snooks Everard and the others who had survived the retreat from Burma, and also to meet up once more with our wonderful adjutant, Sam Crowthers, who was such a tower of strength and who was decorated with the OBE for his work during that campaign.

Back with 17 Squadron. The adjutant, Sam Crowthers (with hat), and the CO, Squadron Leader John Iremonger

I then met Squadron Leader John Iremonger, who had taken over from Bunny and who, at first meeting, looked, and was, a most impressive man, obviously destined to carve a name for himself in the RAF. I had already learnt that neither he, nor his two flight commanders, had been in any action, being all RAF India personnel since the outbreak of war. I wondered what lay ahead of the squadron from now on.

4 PROMOTED TO LEAD THE SQUADRON

Do what thy manhood bids thee do,
From none but self expect applause
(Sir Richard Burton, "The Kasidah")

The first thing I discovered on rejoining the squadron was that they had been re-equipped with Hurricane Mark 2cs, the same type of four-cannon machines to which we had been converted at Catterick and thought we were going to take to Russia. These machines indicated to me that we were in for a ground-attack role, so I wasted no time in taking one up and trying out the cannons on the air-to-ground firing range. A three-second burst demolished a pisé-type house in the range, specially constructed as a target, and it was quickly obvious that the striking power of this armament was awe-inspiring. It was no wonder they used them in the English Channel in 1942-43 for attacking German flak (anti-aircraft) ships, which they apparently sank in large numbers, but at a great cost in aircraft and pilots.

The next thing of some note which happened was that about six of the pilots from the first Burma campaign got me off to one side and said that, if the squadron was ever scrambled to intercept a Japanese raid, they would formate on me and let the commanding officer and the other two flight commanders go their own merry way.

As can be imagined, I was horrified at being put in the unwilling position of being elected as a number one in a mutiny, and immediately talked it over with Sam Crowthers, the adjutant. He told me that he had already heard of this proposal before I arrived and had taken steps at Group Headquarters to overcome it. He did not tell me what he had done, but within one week of being back in the squadron I was called in by John Iremonger and told that I had been restored to my rank of flight lieutenant and was to lead A Flight.

The Hurricane 2c, weighed down with cannons and 90-gallon, long-range tanks

No more was said about mutiny because most of the malcontents were on my flight anyway, and, like most commanding officers, John Iremonger could not fly as much as he wanted to and left a lot of the squadron leadership in the air to his senior flight commander.

One of the fascinating things about the squadron at this time was the aerodrome from which we were operating. Imagine that a runway had been built through the middle of Hyde Park in Sydney and it will give some idea of the situation of the Red Road, or Maidan (as it was known by the Indians). It was a long bitumen road, flanked by marble balustrades, along which the governor used to drive from Government House into the city, but was converted in wartime to a strip for fighter aircraft. In one take-off direction we literally flew between the tall city buildings and waved at the office girls therein as we climbed away.

Our aircraft dispersal bays were on a branch road which led to the main shopping centre on Chowringee Street, about 200 yards away. Our wing commander, Frank Carey, had worked it out that he could be on readiness in Firpo's Cafe on the above street and get sufficient warning of a scramble by having someone at the dispersal hut fire a red Verey light. By the time the rest of the aircraft had become airborne (only being able to take off one at a time down the road), he could be at the dispersal in his car and be airborne soon enough to take over the lead of the wing.

Although it was a useful emergency addition to the other aerodromes, sited to intercept any daylight raids on Calcutta, it was too dangerous to be used as

A Hurricane landing on the famous Red Road, in the middle of Calcutta. Note the marble balustrades in the background

a night-fighter landing field and, in fact, proved to be a bit too much for the less experienced pilots by daylight, let alone night. The main problem was the camber on the roadway. Everything was fine provided one landed and stayed exactly in the middle of the road. At high speed this took very nice judgement to prevent any swing, which, if not immediately corrected, would be aggravated by the cambered surface and, more than once, an aircraft ground-looped and slammed through the marble balustrade, with disastrous results to it and the aeroplane.

So we did a lot of fighter-night readiness from an aerodrome at Alipore, some 10 to 15 miles away, and it was from here that we set up patrol lines on 19 November 1942 to intercept Japanese bombers which were expected to raid Calcutta some time in December – according to our intelligence people.

We did a lot of practice at GCI (Ground-controlled Interceptions) and, sure enough, the Japanese sent over a raid on the night of 23 December. They got through three of the patrol lines (I was on one of them) but at the last line Jack Gibson caught one and shot it down. The squadron thus had the honour of shooting down the first enemy night-raider over Burma, and also the first in India, Bunny Stone having shot down the former over Mingaladon on 27 January 1942.

Before this, on 7 December, I was called in by John Iremonger to be told by him that he had applied for and been granted a posting to an operational squadron in England, and had recommended to our Air Officer Commanding,

Air Vice Marshal Williams, that I should be given the leadership of our squadron.

I was, of course, quite delighted that I had at last achieved my ambition, and at the same time was most impressed by John's altruistic, but sensible, decision. There was stacks of action over the English Channel and the continent, and he would obviously do better there in gaining the air-fighting experience he needed than by staying in the India-Burma theatre, where the war in the air was at a low level of activity while the armies slugged it out on the eastern borders of Bengal, and all we could do was become their airborne artillery.

I was duly interviewed by Air Vice Marshal Bill Williams, who was a wise and very helpful man. I thanked him for my appointment, which I pointed out I loved to accept, but also had to admit that my experience in the administration side of the RAF was virtually nil. He assured me that my adjutant would be able to be relied on for most of this and, in any event, if there was something that I really got stuck on, he would be happy for me to get in touch with him personally and he would advise me how to sort it out.

This was the first intimation I had of the close and direct liaison that often existed between the very top administrators of the RAF and their squadron commanders. It was not always the case (as Bunny's experience with the Old Boy turned out), but it was pointed out to me by the air vice marshal that the whole reason for the existence of the administration side of RAF was to keep a fighting man in a machine and in the air. All ranks above the leader of a fighting unit had to work to achieve that objective and not interfere unnecessarily in the carrying out of their tasks by the aircrew. It was very refreshing to realise that one was in such a responsible situation, and I gave it my resolve to see that our unit would make the air vice marshal proud of us.*

So I sewed the two and a half rings of my rank onto my uniform, flew my squadron leader's flag on the front starboard side of my personal car, and had my squadron leader's insignia painted on my chosen aeroplane, YB-G. YB were the 17 Squadron recognition letters and G the serial letter, which started at A and continued on to the sixteenth letter in the alphabet, P.

The next thing I did, which somewhat horrified the lads I had been with for so long, was to call them before me and give them an outline of the way in which we would train and work from now on. I pointed out to them that, regretfully, I was to be addressed in future at all times as "sir", and not "Bush". I knew that

---

* The rest of this chapter will be devoted to the joys and the problems of leadership and in the next chapter will be told the operations we carried out.

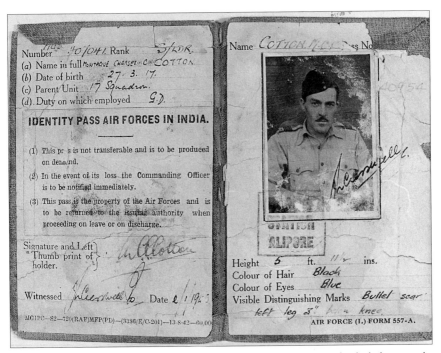

After becoming a squadron commander, I am issued with a new identity card, which does not take long to become tatty in the heat and humidity

if I did not insist on this from the very beginning that I would not be able to instil in them the sense of discipline that only comes from obedience to, and respect for, the team leader, which he would not be likely to get by being always referred to by his nickname. Naturally my promotion had to be reported to the folks at home:

Letter, 3 January 1943

About two weeks ago I was made a Squadron Leader and given command of my old Squadron, No. 17. You cannot possibly imagine the sudden extra amount of work that this entails and I find already that I am about back where I was before the war started, and working really hard again instead of being concerned only with flying. I now have a couple of hundred bodies for whom I am directly responsible and also a large number of pilots to be kept up to the mark at all times. However I am confident that I shall be able to cope as well as the rest of the squadron commanders around here and am in consequence very bucked about the whole thing. The biggest catch of all is that I find I have to spend a lot of my time in my orderly room (office), instead of being on the drome with the rest of the gang, and I have to delegate more flying than I would like.

I am just beginning to realize that in another few months it will be three years since I saw you and I am equally surprised to also realize that I have been able to survive so much in that time. It gives one heart to feel that, although it may be another year or so before I get back to Aussie, my chances of making it through to the end are now pretty good.

P.S. Did I tell you that I had received a letter from Pearl saying that she was being married soon? If I didn't then it hardly matters because it is just one of those things that happen in wartime. I sometimes feel that I was a fathead of no mean sort not to have asked her to marry me while I was in England but, there again, time will tell.

Training of new pilots and keeping the existing ones up to scratch, especially in gunnery, also made up a lot of our flying hours, and we started to use a new technique called shadow firing to teach deflection shooting. We used the wide, muddy waters of the Hooghly river, south of Calcutta, for this training which was carried out by having one of our machines act as target and fly about 1,500 feet above the water at noonday, so that its shadow would be almost directly underneath. The attacker would approach from the beam, ahead, and turn in and down on to the shadow on the water and fire at it. He could see his bullets striking on the water and therefore make immediate corrections to ensure they were hitting the target, and this way get used to the amount of deflection needed to lay off, at various speeds and angles.

I carried out quite a few of these practices and thought they were an excellent way of training until, one day, one of our sergeant pilots flew straight into the water while firing and killed himself. A court of enquiry found that on that particular day the air was more hazy than usual and the horizon not so definite as it normally should have been, and the pilot, through lack of experience of such a condition, could not properly judge his height above the water.

As it turned out, this was not the only tragedy which occurred while doing this or a similar exercise, because on 28 March 1943, "Bluey" Truscott, one of Australia's greatest and most experienced fighter pilots, suffered the same fate in the Broome area. In India we finally restricted its use to only those experienced pilots who were sent by the squadrons to the air gunnery school which was formed at Amarda Road later on in the year.

I then learned what a harrowing task it was to write a personal letter to the parents of my pilots who were killed in action or on active service. However can one make it seem worthwhile to them that their boy met with his death while training, rather than in the face of the enemy? The only thing one could do was to explain the details of the accident and the findings of the court of enquiry, and to offer one's sincerest condolences. I believe that this was one of the hardest of all the responsibilities that devolved upon a leader.

When I took over the squadron my replacement as flight commander was a Flight Lieutenant Eric Batchelar, who, of course, soon became known to all and sundry as "Batchy". He was about 6 feet 3 inches tall, a lanky character with all the aplomb and cheerfulness of the typical English fighter pilot, and was a delight to have in the unit. Extremely brave and quite unshakeable, he soon endeared himself to all and sundry, especially when he became totally lost over Bengal on a night sortie, ran out of fuel, and actually did a wheels-up landing on a paddy field and got away with it. When I asked him why he did not bale out, he simply said he hoped to save the aeroplane, as everything was so bright at full moon that it was better than a lot of daylight in England.

Flight Lieutenant "Batchy" Batchelar soon after taking over A Flight in 17 Squadron

Batchy served under me for eighteen months in 17 Squadron and, after the war, remained in the RAF to finally lead a crack jet squadron, No. 11. Before his retirement some few years ago, he had reached the rank of group captain and was in charge of the RAF Education Section. He and his wife Pamela are numbered among our firmest friends, and whenever Stella and I are in the UK we stay with them for a time to renew and extend our affection for each other.

After taking over the squadron, I got one of my pilots who knew something about jewellery to get an Indian firm to manufacture some silver 17 Squadron badges in the form of the mailed fist, or gauntlet – taking a leaf out of the book of experience I had gained in No. 43 Squadron. These were only about half an inch long and to be worn on the left pocket of the shirt or bush jacket. I had a lot of pleasure in presenting one to each pilot who had fired his guns at the enemy, including strafing, and the new pilots were ecstatic about it. It came to mean as much to them as the official decorations we earned, but never did receive, for the work that we did in the army-support role.

Soon after the squadron settled in at the Red Road, the officers were granted membership of a club in Calcutta called the Saturday Club. It was mainly a preserve for Army officers, and some of them were typical Colonel Blimps. We decided to take the mickey out of these base wallahs, and I got another of my chaps to hunt through the bazaar in Calcutta to buy some monocles with neutral glass in them, and adorned with thin black cords to hang around the neck. When we had got proficient at wearing them, about eight of us descended on the club one night, complete with monocles.

Putting on the most frightful Pommy accents we could muster, and talking loud drivel, we breasted up to the bar amongst the usual gathering of barrack-room warriors. It was not long before we became very unpopular and almost got into a bar-room brawl with some of them, before the impending fracas was broken up by the secretary of the club.

The matter was duly reported to our Air Officer Commanding, who hauled me in for a dressing-down. He grinned when told of our motives, but pointed out that it was imperative that we swallow our derision of the Army types we disliked and bent our energies to helping those soldiers fighting in the Arakan against the Japanese. He also told me to square it with the secretary, otherwise the Air Force might be blackballed from the club altogether.

I duly fronted up to the secretary and, when asked why we had behaved so outrageously, apologetically pointed out to him that our training, both on the ground and in the air, was based upon us being as nasty, cunning and villainous as we possibly could and, as we were so young and impressionable, it was sometimes bound to overflow, especially after a few Indian-brewed beers had removed some of our repressions. He looked at me after this and said: "Cotton, that would have to be the best story I have heard since I have been in this job. Congratulations on your inventiveness, but it doesn't mean a bloody thing to me. However, I accept your apologies and the undertaking that you will behave yourselves in future, so welcome back to the club, but please leave your bloody monocles at the aerodrome in future." We parted the best of friends after a few whiskies.

I was not prepared for the inordinate amount of work that devolved upon one in my position, particularly as I was notified that Sam Crowthers was to be taken from us to be promoted to adjutant in a new wing that was being formed under Wing Commander Athol Forbes (see Appendix C). Athol was a nice chap, but he started pinching some of my other highly experienced ground crew for his wing. I got as mad as hell at this, and rushed up to Air Headquarters one day and asked the secretary to allow me to interview the air vice marshal on an urgent matter.

I was ushered into a meeting where, lo and behold, Athol Forbes was there. When the air vice marshal interrupted the meeting to ask me what I wanted, I pointed to Athol and said, straight out: "He is trying to pinch all my good men." The air vice marshal asked Athol if this was true, and Athol, being a basically honest and decent bloke, admitted the truth of this and promised the air vice marshal to cease his poaching if he could at least keep Sam Crowthers, because Sam was entitled to the promotion anyway. I could not argue with this and agreed, provided the others were returned, which was done and everyone was happy again. This illustrated the significance of those of us who were leaders. It made our jobs so much more rewarding than higher rank, which, with no operations attached to it, simply made one a small cog in the big administrative wheel.

At about this time, while we were at Alipore, we were informed that General Archibald Wavell was to visit our squadron, and a signal came through advising the date and time of his arrival by air. Since all such visiting aircraft stopped at the control tower and the visitors were then taken by motor transport to the squadron dispersals (readiness huts), I duly installed myself in the control tower and waited on his arrival.

I noticed a lot of Indian coolies doing something to the bitumen runway, and was informed that they were sticking some loose hemp fibre to the surface with bitumen, and then spraying this with camouflage paint to make the strip look like ordinary grassland. This was fine until Wavell's aeroplane reported it was in the circuit area and I told the tower operator he had better get the mob off the runway. He advised that a red Verey light was the usual method of doing this, and moved out onto the balcony and fired one as Wavell's machine entered the circuit pattern. As the Verey light landed on the runway, it set the hemp alight, and this brought the fire tender rushing out to smother it.

After all the panic died down and Wavell's aircraft landed, taxied up and stopped, he climbed out and was saluted and greeted by me. With a twinkle in his eye, he asked if it was the usual thing to set the aerodrome alight for VIP visits and if so, was it a form of welcome or deterrent? He was a great man and immensely popular with those he met and talked to, and we felt very honoured to have him visit us. It was he who had borne the brunt of the defeats in Malaya, Dutch East Indies and the Far East, and it was he who had chosen "Bill" Slim to head the final part of the retreat in Burma, and then to command the 14th Army for the conquest of the Japanese, in the Arakan and the northern front, for the final reoccupation of Burma.

He thoroughly enjoyed talking to the squadron pilots and meeting up with some of those who had served in the first Burma campaign. He told us about the general plans that were being put in place for the reconquest of Burma, and how vital our task of army support was going to be. He also explained how some pilots from the ground-attack squadrons were being sent forward with infantry units to closely liaise with them and call on air-support by radio when required. This system was finally nicknamed the Cab-Rank method (by the Middle East armies), because it resembled in some ways the hailing of a taxi, but this time the hailing of a strike fighter or dive bomber, circling overhead, to hit a specific target, marked by the infantry with coloured smoke projectiles.

By mid-February 1943, I reported to the Air Officer Commanding that I felt we were as ready as we ever would be to go forward once more to the battle front, even though I was worried about the health of the ground crew, who had an awful time with sickness during the retreat up into China and across into India in 1942.

He told me that before we went forward he had plans for us to occupy a newly-made satellite strip in the jungle, some miles south of Calcutta, to test how we would be able to cope with conditions in East Bengal (now called Bangladesh). So on 4 March we moved to our new home at Acorn, which was a single strip of dirt carved out of rice-paddy fields. It certainly was a test of our resourcefulness and ingenuity, for I found myself suddenly confronted with all the problems of housekeeping for a few hundred personnel. These duties and their problems would normally have already been solved by the commanding officers of the stations which squadrons had moved into, but at Acorn there was no previous commanding officer, only me, whose knowledge of any housekeeping was literally nil.

A letter home tells some of the story:

Letter, 14 March 1943

I have been caught up with so much work recently that I have had little time to even eat, let alone write to you at any length, and I am afraid that this will hold for some time yet until I get some leave, or things slacken a bit. Our squadron has just completed a shift into the jungle and consequently we are all living in the raw trying to combat snakes, flies, heat, rain and stupid natives.

In view of the fact that the camp was hardly even started by the time we arrived then you can imagine what a hell of a time we have had trying to cook, eat and drink and also carry out our normal squadron flying duties. Everybody is living in tents and the other day it rained like hell and then blew about the same. We will draw a veil over what happened. Words could not even remotely paint the picture of the chaos that ensued so I shall leave it to your imagination to picture a bunch of tents on a perfectly flat, clayey piece of land, after being rained on and then blown flat.

Together with this I have become an inspector of works over the contractors who are completing the buildings on the place and, as they are all flat out to make money and give nothing in the way of a quality job in return, then we do not get on at all well together. They are now trying to offer me bribes with bottles of brandy which I have told them is a drink which is forbidden in the RAF and I expect the next thing will be either an offer of whiskey or straight-out money. If I can do so I will have great joy in tripping them up and hoping the RAF can sue them for a packet, or at the very least never give them any more contracts.

The letter tells only a part of what happened, for I finally did trip up the builders over the way they failed to honour their contract. On one of my tours of inspection I had noticed a square water-tank on a stand with the word "Sample" written on it, which had obviously been supplied to the contractors, by the RAF, as meeting the required specification. There was one alongside it (supplied by the contractors to the RAF) leaking like a sieve because it had half the number of rivets in its seams. Fortunately we had been issued with a mobile workshop and were able to weld up the faulty one; a phone call to the aerodrome-works people in Group Headquarters soon brought retribution on the heads of the shysters who were trying to rob the RAF. My already low opinion of Indians took an even steeper nosedive, especially at being so stupid as to leave the word "Sample" still legible on the good tank.

As soon as we had settled in at Acorn, I thought it would be a good idea if I called on the headman of the local jungle village to pay my respects and to assure him that we would not transgress any of their local laws or conventions, and would be happy to help in any way we could to prevent any disruption to their normal lifestyle by our presence and our noisy aeroplanes. The Bengali who turned out to be the headman was very flattered to be so treated, and invited me to dine with him next night. We duly consumed a very nice curry, washed down with a palm wine called *arrack*. This had a kick like a mule and quickly loosened our tongues, and turned the conversation to such topics as war, politics, economics and religion.

I was interested to hear that the village religion was the worshipping of one of the fertility gods, and my interest resulted in an invitation to visit their shrine. This I did, and I was fascinated to be taken into a darkened hut, wherein stood a massive human penis (called a *lingam* in their religion) about 6 feet high, carved out of what appeared to be a black, highly polished, marble-like stone, with offerings of fruit and flowers around its base and lighted candles on its top. The wax from the candles had, over time, run down the shaft in a most suggestive way, and it was explained to me that the young maidens of the village, before their marriage, were constrained to come and rub their genitalia against the stone to ensure their fertility, hence the high polish that a portion of the shaft had obtained over the years. The headman also pointed out to me that it was very necessary for women to be able to bear many children because most of them either died at birth (particularly if there was a famine raging) or before maturity, and the more offspring they had the better the chance that one would survive long enough to take on the traditional task of caring for the elderly parents.

Since average life expectancy in Bengal was then only about thirty-two years, I did not wonder that they had little else with which to amuse themselves other than a concentration on matters sexual, after their normal hungers had been satisfied. It was easy to see how the environment (fecund in the case of Bengal) had become the determining factor in their religion, as I believe it does with most religions of the world. As Lord Byron said in his poem "Don Juan":

What men call gallantry, and the Gods adultery,
Is much more common where the climate's sultry.

The extra work involved in squadron administration, together with the long-range operational flying we had begun to do over the Arakan front, was beginning to wear me down, and my early enthusiasm at being in charge of an RAF fighter squadron began to wear somewhat thin.

This was heightened one day when I welcomed a new flight commander to replace another, inexperienced one and, on looking at the new chap and his logbook, in spite of the fact that he had served in the Battle of Britain, I was not very impressed and would have much preferred to have appointed one of my own pilots to the job, particularly Tex Barrick, whom I had recommended for a commission and who was now a pilot officer. During my charge of the squadron I managed to promote most of the sergeants from the first Burma campaign to officers. In fact, I always felt that there should only have been commissioned officers in the flying ranks. If it was good enough to fly together and depend so much on each other it was good enough, I felt, to also eat together.

The new man hit the booze pretty solidly and one night, soon after joining us, got himself and one of the sergeant pilots as drunk as lords, and I heard him (from my hut where I was writing home) wandering about, saying they should each fly one of the Hurricanes. When the sergeant pilot said the commanding officer would be livid about this, the flight lieutenant let off a long string of abuse, including some doubt as to my legitimacy. I called up my engineering officer on the phone and told him to quietly immobilise all the aircraft by disconnecting their starter batteries, and after about half an hour or so of trying to start them, the flight lieutenant gave up and staggered off.

By 10 o'clock the next morning, I had written out an adverse report on him, particularly on his behaviour the night before, when he could have put someone else's life at risk, apart from his own. I recommended that he be reduced in rank and posted from the squadron for ground duties for a spell. He was told to report to me, called in and asked to read and sign the report before it went to Group Headquarters. On trying to excuse himself, he was told by me that he was not there to debate the issue but simply to sign the report as having been read by him. If he refused to do so, the adjutant would give evidence to that effect in any court of inquiry, and it would go very much against him.

As soon as he had signed it, I told him to pack his gear and report to the personnel officer at Group Headquarters, because as far as I was concerned he was no longer a member of our squadron. I then rang the Air Officer Commanding, told him what had happened and explained that I was sure that, to get rid of him, some other commanding officer of one of his previous units had the flight lieutenant promoted to make him surplus to their establishment and therefore have him posted away, rather than taking the harder option of reducing his rank unless his behaviour improved.

This sort of thing was fortunately not rife in the squadrons, but surely took place in some of the nonoperational units, and the Air Officer Commanding agreed that it was something that needed stamping out. He also agreed to my request for Tex Barrick to be made a flight lieutenant, which made Tex's promotion from flight sergeant to flight lieutenant about as quick as my own from flying officer to squadron leader. What it did for myself and the whole squadron, however, was to give us a great boost in morale, because we now had two flight commanders with experience from the first Burma campaign, and who could be given top responsibility, and the pilots had leaders in whom they had the greatest respect and confidence.

Tex Barrick becomes Flight Lieutenant Barrick, DFM, and takes command of B Flight

I had learned very rapidly that, although the Air Officer Commanding had told me the way to handle too much work was to delegate, what he had not stressed was that one cannot delegate accountability; that is, as the Yanks would say, "The buck stops at the top." In other words, if something goes wrong internally in a unit, such as a squadron, then the man in charge is accountable for it, even though he may not have been responsible. So if he wanted to delegate responsibility and there were not enough below him to handle it, then his only recourse was to do it himself, and then train others below him to accept it, or, failing that, replace them. This lesson, learnt so early in my life, stayed with me forever and, although one could do these things more rapidly in war than in peacetime, it was the only way to ensure the success of a team, and teamwork was a vital necessity on a fighter squadron.

While we were at Acorn, I found that a new unit had been formed at Amarda Road near Orissa in Bengal, called the Air Fighter Training Unit, which was headed by Frank Carey, with Barry Sutton as his second in command. I applied for some of my pilots to be sent there, and after their four-week course quizzed them as to its value. On learning how good it was, I smartly posted myself off to it as well, leaving Tex and Batchy to run the squadron. It was a highly intensive course of air-to-air gunnery, drogue firing, shadow firing and cinecamera gun attacks against all sorts of aircraft in all sorts of situations.

At the end of three weeks, when I was learning a lot of new techniques, a signal came for me to rejoin my squadron, which was to now move closer to the war zone. The squadron was directed by Group Headquarters to move to a place called Agartala in East Bengal. It was about 200 air miles from Calcutta and central to the main battle fronts at Imphal to the north in the Chindwin Hills, and Akyab to the south in the Arakan.

The aircraft and pilots moved to Alipore and were serviced there by another squadron until our ground crew arrived at Agartala, having left Acorn on 24 March; then we flew to our new home on 29 March. Although we were a little bit sad to see the last of Acorn, because we felt it was leaving the home we had created by ourselves, it was sensible to remove us because the monsoon was imminent, and had we stayed another week or two we would have been stuck in the mud for months – aircraft and all.

All the country to the east of Agartala became more and more mountainous, with elevations of up to 10,000 feet, and although we were taught the rudiments of survival, I doubt if anyone forced to vacate his aeroplane by parachute would survive unless fortunate enough to land in the middle of a friendly hill tribe.

This is what General Bill Slim had to say about it at his first sight, and it sums it up pretty well:

> We flew over the Arakan Yomas, and I had my first sight of the jungle-clad hills of Burma. Flying over them you can realize what an obstacle they are to vision, but you cannot really appreciate what an obstacle they are to movement. To do that you must hack and push your way through the clinging, tight-packed greenery, scramble up the precipitous slopes and slide down the other side, endlessly, as if you were walking along the teeth of a saw. I often wished afterwards that some of my visitors, who measured distances on small-scale maps, and were politely astonished at the slowness with which I proposed to advance, had walked to my headquarters instead of flown.

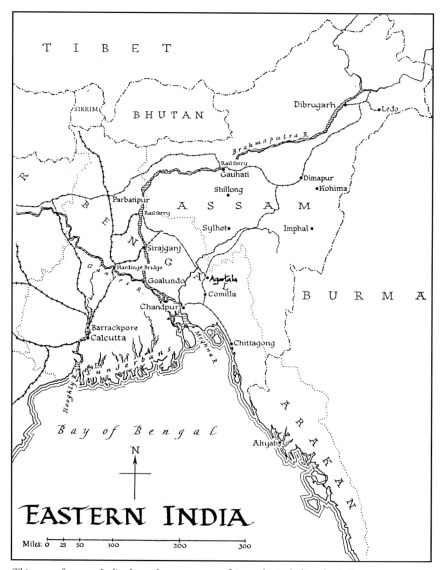

This map of eastern India shows the country east of Agartala, including the Arakan

Flying Officer "Slim" Lewis (a Canadian)
models the survival harness which we devised to
help a pilot who might be downed in the jungle

Some bright character in the RAF had devised survival packages for aircrew, which consisted of hermetically sealed tins of rations, medical treatment drugs and materials, water purifying and carrying gear, a jungle knife (in the form of a Gurkha kukri), maps, spare socks, and undershorts. What had not been devised was a method for a pilot to take all these bits and pieces with him if he had to bale out in his parachute. One of the first things we did, after flying a few sorties between Agartala and Burma, was to invent a special survival harness for each pilot, which fitted under the parachute. It contained all the above gear, plus a revolver. It may not have guaranteed survival if one was out of touch for many days after baling out in the jungle and landing safely, but everybody felt better wearing it rather than nothing.

Our jobs at Agartala were to stand-by on readiness as required and then, when not required, to do bomber escorts and long-range strafing – strategic (behind the enemy lines in Burma and the Arakan) and tactical, in-close support of the Army in both battle zones. We also had to carry out other escort duties, using 45-gallon drop-tanks under our wings to achieve the necessary distances over the mountains into Burma.

In chapter five I will relate the operations we were involved in after I took over the squadron in December 1942.

5 OPERATIONS IN THE ARAKAN

A pilot's part in calms cannot be spy'd.
In dangerous times true worth is only tried.
(Stirling)

Among my papers I discovered a copy, which was given to me afterwards, of an interview I had with a flight lieutenant, N.K. Welsh, of the RAAF at Sydney on 10 July 1945. I think he was an official historian. My memory and the study of my logbook today, which gives only the detail (because it was not supposed to have other than the barest record in the event that it fell into enemy hands) of the actual number of the aircraft used and its flight time, could never help me accurately recall now the full details of the operations we flew on during my time with the squadron. So I have set down the record made at the interview, which gives some indication of the work we did:

From the RED ROAD we went to ACORN, a few miles south of CALCUTTA and from there we used to go on forward flights equipped with long-range tanks, of six aircraft at a time, to the battle front in the ARAKAN and do sweeps over AKYAB and low-level strafeing.

On the 15th February 1943 we went on a "Rhubarb" (low-level strafe of enemy targets chosen by the Headquarters the night before) north of AKYAB on the MAYU peninsular. We strafed targets for the army and also set alight to some huts which we were told contained a Japanese radio station.

While we were at ACORN the squadron was moulded into an excellent fighting force, developing a true team spirit and we carried out many more long range operations from ACORN until we finally moved to AGARTALA.

On the 13th March Flight Lieutenant Eric Batchelar and Flight Sergeant Doug Cropper RAAF (whose commission I had recommended and which was later promulgated as from 4th February 1943) left for AKYAB on a strafeing operation, approaching from the sea at low level. When two or three miles inland, Batchelar received the message "I am right behind you". Batchelar carried on and strafed the target but nothing further was seen of Doug, who did not return to base. Subsequently we received reports from an Indian who had been in Rangoon after this, that he had met a Sergeant named "Crowper" but we received no confirmation. It was not until last night (10/7/45) that I learnt that Doug Cropper was safe and back in Australia.

On 29th May the squadron moved to AGARTALA and on the 1st June, twelve of us went to CHITTAGONG on army support control. On the way down we ran into an extremely violent tropical storm and I had to put the flights into line astern and fly as low to the ground as possible, without wiping the rear group off on the ground. The rain was so heavy that after we landed at CHITTAGONG we found that it had beaten the fabric off the rudders and tail planes of three aircraft which had to be re-doped back on before they could fly back to our base again.

We escorted Blenheim bombers over FORT WHITE on the 3rd June and on the 8th and 9th tried to get to CHITTAGONG again but the monsoon weather forced us back.

On 10th June six of our Hurricanes escorted Blenheim bombers to RAMREE ISLAND in Burma, the flight occupying 3 and $\frac{3}{4}$ hours. We strafed a Japanese occupied camp at the top of the island and a ship at the wharfs. Later we carried out another strafe at THAITKIDO for the army and shot up Jap supply dumps.

On 12th June, we strafed SINHO and on the night of the 14th I carried out a lone "Rhubarb" from DONBAIK to BUTHIDAUNG along the MAYU river and shot up the wharfs at BUTHIDAUNG for good measure.

We then received orders that all shipping on the rivers leading towards the front areas, behind the Japanese lines, was to be considered as transporting enemy supplies and destroyed.

From then on until 22nd June the weather prevented us from getting further than CHITTAGONG. Then we started doing dawn reconnaissances over the CHIN HILLS for meteorological purposes and for pin-pointing targets. These reconnaissances were always single aircraft.

With Pilot Officer Miller, I did a reconnaissance up the CHINDWIN RIVER and the MYITHE VALLEY on 22nd June. We got 15 to 20 sampans and it was the first time we saw trip wires across the river.

Next day Flight Lieutenant Batchelar led six Hurricanes up a tributary of the CHINDWIN and three of them saw a trip wire in time and pulled up over it; the other three had to go underneath. These wires were stretched across the river from poles on either side.

On 26th June we carried out a beat-up of the MAYU RIVER in very bad weather. There were only one or two sampans. There is no doubt that our activity in strafing all river craft had the desired effect of preventing supply to the Japanese armies, by this method, and justified the risk. By this time there were four Australians on the squadron – Flying Officer L.T. Rawnsley, Warrant Officer Nigel Bradbury, Sergeant J.J. Harrison, and me.

On 27th June Sergeant Harrison was with a flight which strafed some enemy positions in the hills. He ran out of petrol owing to a faulty fuel transfer line from his drop-tanks and was forced to land with his wheels up in a deep swamp north of the aerodrome. We searched for him but could not find him and gave him up for lost, but he thankfully turned up next day.

There was bad weather on the 28th and 29th June, but we got down through it past AKYAB on the 29th into HUNTERS BAY where twelve Hurricanes strafed shipping. That flight took three hours and 45 minutes.

On 2nd July I led six Hurricanes on a "rhubarb" up the CHINDWIN RIVER and we beat up more sampans. I carried out a dawn reconnaissance on the 6th July over the CHINDWIN HILLS and for 45 minutes was flying totally "blind" in heavy cloud. Next day we carried out a "Rhubarb" along the MAYU RIVER and strafed shipping.

Up till the twelfth July we tried unsuccessfully to get through to CHITTAGONG, but the monsoons were too severe.

At this stage the AOC sent us a signal congratulating and thanking us for the work we had done and advised that he had been asked to select a squadron for a rest, as fresh ones were now becoming available. He considered that we well deserved a rest and he was sending us to a southern posting for this and for re-equipment. Accordingly we were to move to CEYLON.

This was long overdue as we had been in the BURMA and BENGAL climate for more than 18 months and, although about 50 per cent of the aircrew were fairly fresh, the whole of the ground crew were very tired and in poor health owing to tropical diseases and heat exhaustion.

Other operations (not reported above) and some of the affects of operations generally were as follows.

On one of our ground-strafing sorties, Tex Barrick was leading a flight of six Hurricanes in the Arakan area in support of our Army, which was having a tough time against the Japanese in the Battle of Ngakyedauk. Tex was making his strafing run and, on pressing the gun button, one of his starboard cannons exploded and blew a great hole in the top surface of his wing. Anyone who knows about how an aeroplane flies will realise this destroyed a large percentage of the lift of that wing, because it is the top surface of a wing that does the lifting, not the bottom. Tex found that only by flying at full throttle, and at a speed in excess of 120 miles an hour, could he keep his machine in the air without stalling – and then only by holding the joystick fully to the left to keep the machine straight and level.

His nearest aerodrome was a strip at Cox's Bazaar, some 50 miles up the coast, and by the time he reached it his arms were just about giving out because of the strain. Needless to say, his landing was a superb piece of flying, in that he brought the machine down safely, using up every inch of the runway in so doing. It was never discovered why the cannon blew up, except that it was obviously one of the explosive shells, which were interposed between the armour-piercing and other ammunition in the gun belts, which had decided to explode as it was going into the gun.

At this time, we all began to feel the strain of flying and strafing in the monsoon weather and of the very long-distance trips over some of the most inhospitable terrain in the world. We also found that, because most of our operations were laid on the day before, we had time to not only work out the route to the target and the best and safest tactics, but also to lose sleep at nights going over everything in our minds before the usual dawn take-off. Letters to home started to comment on this:

Letter, 4 June 1943

I am snatching an hour or so off in the middle of the day to write this and in any case it is much too hot and sticky to try and do the least amount of work. I have just completed another move of my squadron and this time we are right in one of the forward areas of this front and are consequently quite near our arch enemy again. This has had the effect of making the lads much happier than they were formerly, even though we are under much more primitive conditions.

Our main jobs out here are bomber escorts and shooting up enemy ground targets. The latter is OK if one can find the target in this mass of hills and jungle but at the same time it is very dangerous because of enemy light ack-ack. It was voted as one of the most dangerous jobs in the last war, and still is in this one. The main catch is that one rarely gets a chance to smack down enemy aircraft and chalk up a score and consequently there is much less recognition for the same amount of flying and dangerous duties.

The climate here is quite what one has always read about in the tropics. One has only to walk about ten yards to cause a terrific sweat to break out. One suffers for so long with prickly heat that one can hardly imagine life without it. To prevent my arm from sticking to this paper I have to rest it on two pieces of blotting paper or I would never finish this off. Naturally in all this weather one has to be very careful when flying because, if a machine went into one of the big storm clouds it could be torn to pieces before it got out again, or become completely uncontrollable, causing it to crash.

Letter, 23 June 1943

In view of the fact that it is simply teeming with rain outside and it is useless for flying, I am relaxing again for the meantime to let you know how things are going with me and my lads. Up till about the 15th of this month I had clocked in about 20 hours of operational flying on bomber escorts and beating up ground targets. While I do not like it as much as air combat, it has not been without its moments of excitement. I actually did a ground-strafeing job by moonlight the other night and had a rather hectic time dodging rain storms and trying to navigate myself around without flying into the nearest mountain. I think now that nobody will ever be able to justifiably accuse me of being a "fair weather pilot" after flying at night in this monsoon weather.

Letter, 30 June 1943

We have had a fearfully busy month this time and the squadron has completed about 600 hours of flying which is pretty damn good for single seaters, especially as we have been unable to fly quite a bit because of the weather. Naturally I have more hours than the rest and I think mine totals up to over forty hours, which is nearly all operational. However, it is all a much bigger strain upon one than it used to be in the old days because we now go on definite missions, generally decided the day before, and we more imaginative ones don't get very much sleep that night, thinking about what might happen and planning ways to get a maximum result at minimum cost. It is really a very big responsibility having to lead six (sometimes twelve) aircraft around the sky for hundreds of miles in bad weather and to know that you will be held accountable if the weather closes down and the whole lot have to force-land somewhere.

I expect that you know that air-fighting is becoming harder for me to bear as every day goes by and of course the true test is yet to come as to whether one can go through to the bitter end without wavering in purpose. It seems that everything that has gone before has been more in the line of experience than hard work, for the time has come for a number of us when the fight seems long and dreary and the goal a long way off. To keep up the same enthusiasm and the same energy under these conditions, until the goal is attained is the real test of a man's fighting spirit and, by the grace of God I think I might be able to pull it off. I always remember some of the bad times in hospital when I am feeling shakey, and it helps considerably to feel that this strain can never be as bad as that was.

This of course is only the beginning of our fight back into Burma and I expect at the end of a few more months I shall really be in need of a rest and I do hope that, if ever this time comes, I will be allowed to come back to Australia for it.

And yet, it would be a very big tug at my heart strings to leave this grand bunch of lads, most of whom I have known for about 18 months and who are on the crest of a wave because they know that their officers are working for them the whole time. The change from gloom and despondency when I took over, to the quiet efficiency and happiness that now prevails, is most remarkable. This must cease now as I have just received news of one of my chaps having force-landed somewhere, so I must dash about and start collecting details. My fondest love to all.

The monsoon conditions were badly hampering our activities at this time. The problem of flying fighters in monsoon weather was one that had not been experienced by many squadrons, because in the 1942 monsoon season the RAF was in retreat, or back in India along with the Army, and had very few aeroplanes anyway. We wondered if, at the height of the monsoon period in 1943, we would be stood down for any length of time, but orders from above were that, "The RAF will maintain maximum effort during the Monsoon period."

On one occasion during this period, a Spitfire fighter squadron was returning from Imphal after being posted away from that area for a rest period. Its twelve aircraft flew into a monsoon cloud, where six pilots were killed and eight aircraft destroyed, owing to the enormous forces in the cloud which prevented the machines from maintaining their stability and either crashing into the ground or one another.

Today no aircraft flying in these areas, on military or commercial flights, would do so without a radar set which could pick up this turbulence ahead of the flight path and avoid it, but in our time there was no such thing. It was always a gamble, on entering cloud, that one might strike an active cumulonimbus embedded in the mass, and that could spell disaster. The prevailing winds are to the north-east in the Bay of Bengal in the monsoon season (summer months), and these pick up a tremendous amount of moisture and form themselves into huge cumulonimbus clouds. Sometimes the base of these clouds is solid rain, about 200 to 300 feet above the ground, before the cloud-base proper begins. From then on the cloud could extend up to heights exceeding 30,000 feet. The bottom of these clouds could be from 1 to 10 miles in diameter. In very bad weather, the huge clouds, together with layers of less turbulent cloud, practically touch one another, and consequently one could have an almost incessant wall of rain between oneself and one's destination.

In our day, there were two ways of operating aircraft in monsoonal weather. One way was to fly in the rain under cloud base, a few feet above the ground. This was all right if one was flying alone, or with a single section of four machines, because they could formate together on the one level. With a whole squadron it required the other two sections to tuck under and behind the leader's section in line astern and, with only 200 feet to play with, the leader had a job to maintain accurate height without wiping the lower section off on the ground. More often than not, any aircraft with exposed fabric on the control surfaces could have this beaten off in the rain, and this constituted a danger if allowed to persist.

The other way was to try and pick out the smallest cumulonimbus clouds and fly a variable course between them. That might be at any height from 5,000 to 30,000 feet, but the trouble with that system was that, even if we were flying a squadron of twelve aircraft, sometimes we had to fly in cloud. We would not know what we were heading into and might fly into the middle of a particularly bad one. When that happened, the only hope of survival was to turn over and bale out but, in spite of this, pilots in some instances were carried in their parachutes, by the updraughts, to heights where they either died of oxygen lack or froze to death.

Naturally, on some days the monsoon was less severe than on others, but one could safely say that there was no day which one could count on to be totally free of danger during monsoon weather. The only good thing about this sort of weather was that the Japanese were more sensible than we were and did not fly during most of it, and were therefore no real threat to us in the air while we went about our other tasks.

Although our lives were now a constant battle against the climate and the stresses of long-distance operations, it was not all so wearing that we did not find time to enjoy ourselves. My lads had somehow "won" a piano when they left Calcutta, and in no time had constructed a stage in one of the larger *basha* huts used for their eating area. The term *basha* was used to describe our dwellings, made from bamboo poles and beams, roofed about 12 inches thick with elephant grass and with walls of plaited palm leaves. None of them lasted much more than two to three years; the termites could be heard chewing at them from the time they were constructed.

A concert was finally staged and was a resounding success. One of the best numbers was a group of six airmen dressed up as Welsh coalminers, carrying hurricane lamps and singing some of the most beautiful Welsh songs in harmony. One of the things that amused me in listening to these lads, sounding like angels, was to know that they were normally the most bloody-minded lot of the whole squadron and it took a lot of hard work and persuasion to keep them in line. I sang "Waltzing Matilda" – as an extract from a letter to home reports:

> On the whole we are all very taken with our new jungle abode and last night we had a grand concert in the airmen's mess wherein the "Erks" (airmen) played all the parts and, although about 75% of it was definitely unfit for a presentation to the public at large, it was, notwithstanding, a scream from start to finish. We invited the station commander, Wing Commander "Jimmy" Elsdon, along and it fairly shook him because we haven't been here much more than three weeks or so. We are lucky to have him as our station Commanding Officer because I knew him well when I was going out to, and in, Rangoon last year. He was commanding one of the squadrons there and did a wonderful job together with Bunny Stone and Frank Carey during that campaign.
>
> Perhaps our concert was helped along by the fact that the lads drew their beer ration just before the show but it was so good that we will put on another one soon. I was prevailed upon to sing "Waltzing Matilda" for them and, though they all clapped like hell I am sure it was more out of politeness to their Squadron commander than to his dulcet tones. Next time, they said they want me to do a turn on the ukelele but I am adamant in refusing for I can't stand it myself, unless I am half stinko and then nobody but me can stand it!

At the height of the monsoon, we all suffered agonies from prickly heat and tinea, the latter usually attacking one in the crutch. The cure for this was a dressing called Whitfields Ointment, which, after application, made one's testicles feel as if they were alight. I am sure it worked on the principle that one often has to fight fire with fire.

There was no cure, however, for prickly heat, but some wag said that relief could be obtained if one stood naked in a monsoon downpour, soaped oneself with Lifebuoy soap, and allowed the rain to wash it off. It was as much as one could stand to see pilots and ground crew, not on duty, in the "wherewithal", going through the ritual. I felt that although there were no WAAFs in Bengal (and we used to beef about it), if there had been they certainly would not have been posted to Agartala. It was sometimes amusing to see the odd character caught out in a condition of full lather when the rain (as it often did) stopped as quickly as it started.

At one stage of our operations, we were required to do a daily weather reconnaissance flight to see if this would help in forecasting the severity of the weather for the day. I mused that maybe if we never returned they would assume it was no good, and thus establish themselves as the first foolproof weather forecasters in India. I used to do some of these, and once, while flying at about 20,000 feet and up-sun of a monsoon cloud, I saw a full-circle rainbow on the rain area of the cloud. It was absolutely beautiful and I longed for a colour camera to prove I had seen it.

The drop-tanks that we carried on our Hurricanes contained 45 gallons of petrol each and this weighed almost half a ton. Added to the weight of the cannons, it meant that one had to be very careful in manoeuvring the aircraft, to prevent high-speed stalls. On one strafing operation in Burma, along the Chindwin, I attacked a barge tied up under a tree on the bank across the river and, on pulling out of the dive, the aircraft mushed and collected the tops of a clump of bamboos, which adorned the wheel wells and the tail wheel until I landed back at Agartala. This, I swear, reduced my lifespan by a yet unknown amount.

Another of the antics we got up to, which at first convinced all our visitors that we were all "round the bend", was something invented, I think, by Doug Page (who was a great admirer of the whimsy of Lewis Carroll and others), together with a Flight Lieutenant Ley of No. 224 Group, during a boozy evening at our mess. I first encountered Doug's fantasy one evening when I fronted up to the bamboo bar in our mess to have a drink with him, to be told: "Look out, sir, you're treading on Joe the Camel's tail." He was pointing to the empty space on the floor between him and the next imbiber. From then on, there was always a space reserved at the bar for Doug's imaginary camel, Joe, and all visitors (no matter how high in rank) were warned to be careful and to avoid tripping over him.

If things got a bit crowded, Doug would lead Joe outside and tie him up to the verandah post and tell the Indian punkah-wallah to keep an eye on him. The nonplussed punkah-wallah was generally a young lad hired to pull a cord, going over an invariably squeaky pulley outside the building, which waved a plaited palm mat backwards and forwards inside the room, to create some air movement for the cooling of the sahibs. For further information regarding Joe the Camel, see chapter six.

Quite near to Agartala was the domicile of the Maharajah of Agartala. He and some of his retinue once came to the wing mess at the invitation of Jimmy Elsdon, and I was also invited.

His Highness was a very likable man. He was a great Anglophile, and in conversation, after many *chota pegs* (whiskies and sodas), he confided to me that he did not like the way things were shaping in India, as far as the aristocratic princes were concerned, and that was why he was raising and training his own army. He cogitated about whether he should also have an air force, and sounded me out to see, if he did decide to do so, whether I would be interested in heading it up. I played along with this idea to see what sort of aeroplanes he was thinking about, and when he said that he was sure there would be heaps of Tiger Moths to be had at the war's end, I politely declined, assuring him that I had already promised the RAF I would stay with them.

I show the Maharajah of Agartala and his entourage over one of our Hurricanes being serviced

When one was at readiness at Agartala, it was invariably a chance to lie back on a charpoy (a woven matting bed) and catch up on some sleep, in spite of the heat and the dopiness it invariably produced. I was in this state one day and was gradually wakened from my slumbers by the noise of the other members in the flight lustily singing one of our songs, from the squadron's repertoire, called "Please Don't Burn Our Shithouse Down".

The choir was in full voice at the back of our flight hut, and to silence them so that I could continue my sleep, I rose and walked around there. I was greeted by the sight of one of our lavatories going up in a mighty holocaust of smoke and flame. "Doc" Jackson, our medical officer, explained to me that, on his examination of the outhouse, he reckoned it was quite beyond being rendered properly sanitary and decided to burn it, as was usually the case.

The pilots, however, got into the act, and assured him that the best way to do this was not to just load lots of wood into it, but to also pour some gallons of 100-octane aircraft petrol down, retreat to a safe distance and fire a Verey light at it. They were so charmed with the result that they could not help bursting into an appropriate anthem of celebration.

Flight Lieutenant Fred ("Doc") Jackson was another of the squadron's unconventional characters. His prewar (and postwar) hobby was mountain climbing, and he lived for the day when the war was over and he could get back to his beloved hills. Being so close to the Himalayas must have been a frustration for him, but he managed to fill his and our days with amusement.

One of my official duties was to receive, and sign, the monthly reports and returns from my various senior administration officers. Fred's medical returns were quite important, and on the very first one I received from him I noticed under the column heading "Illness" the entry letters G.O.K. Alongside, under the column heading "Treatment", were the letters K.U.B. On enquiring of Fred as to what these letters stood for, I was told that they were used in cases of suspected malingering: "G.O.K." stood for "God Only Knows", and "K.U.B." stood for "Kick up the Bum".

On another occasion, I was leading a group of six Hurricanes on a shipping strike against Japanese cargo ships tied up at the wharf at Akyab. These had been photographed the day before by a PRU (Photographic Reconnaissance Unit) Spitfire, and we realised that the Japanese would very likely be expecting us, so we decided to hit them at midday, instead of the usual dawn attack, in the fond hope that they would be having lunch and might not be so alert.

We flew to Chittagong, refuelled, and then flew out to sea at low level to come in under any radar, and, on nearing Akyab, headed north as though we were going to strike the enemy army positions at Buthidaung from behind. We then swung inland, however, over the mountain range called the Arakan Yomas, where there was little or no settlement, and therefore, we hoped, no warning system to report our swing back to the west, and made our approach to Akyab down one of the rivers leading to the port.

Within a mile of the targets lined up at the wharf at Akyab, I gave the order to go into line abreast, lifted up from ground level to about 200 feet and blasted the bridge area of the first boat in line, then strafed an ack-ack site, which we had detected from photographs, on the top of a building. The others did much the same to their allotted targets, and we raced out to sea, again at low level, and reformed for the trip back to Chittagong. On my enquiring if everybody was OK, Batchy replied that he had been hit but did not think it was serious.

I got him to fly alongside me and, to my amazement, saw that he had a bullet hole straight through his canopy from side to side, exactly where his ears would

Batchy's bullet holes – the bullet entered just above the bar in the middle section of the canopy …

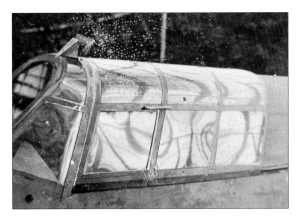

… and came out in the top left-hand corner of the opposite centre panel

have been. Apparently he copped one at the time he was leaning forward to look through his reflector sight as he pressed his gun button. The bullet took the buckle off the rear strap on his flying helmet; the rest of us, however, on landing, assured him that it was the vacant space between his ears that had saved him.

Near the end of our stay at Agartala, we were merrily absorbing our drams of spirituous and fermented liquors in the mess one night when the white-faced adjutant came racing in to say that, on the way back from the airmen's mess, he saw a bloody great tiger cross the track in front of him. We immediately armed ourselves with revolvers and whatever other firearms came to hand and set off back again. Naturally we were too late to see anything and went back to our drinking, only this time fully armed, as well as being primed.

It did not take long for me to start the ball rolling by objecting to the presence of a large tarantula spider on the wall and blasting it to oblivion with my Colt .45 revolver. This I then followed up by having someone place one of our less-liked records (that we used to play on the wind-up gramophone) on the wall and also blasting this into small pieces.

All sorts of bric-a-brac then took a fearful punishment at the hands of the smoking guns of the rest of the braves, until a frantic phone call from the airmen's mess, some mile away, asked if the officers would please fire in the other direction as the airmen were being enfiladed by the bullets. This put a stop to it, because the wing mess was in the other direction and we reckoned that Jimmy Elsdon might not be too happy about it.

Letter, 30 July 1943

I have just received orders (you will be pleased to hear) that I am to take my squadron to a back area for a rest, training and re-equipping with new aircraft – they didn't say what with.

Where we are going you will learn in due course and will be rather surprised too. Although it was a great relief to a lot of us it is a bit browning off to know that one is going to an area remote from enemy action but at the same time it is nice to know that we shall not be doing any more of these 250 mile ground-strafeing sorties into enemy territory. I have had to send three of my pilots away for a complete rest, because their nerve cracked on the job, but nevertheless our morale is still very high and I have a nucleus of experienced men still with me on the unit.

These last few months have in many respects been a worse strain on us than the aerial combats we were involved in during the first Burma campaign. Everyone says that the worst feature of strafeing is the unseen enemy on the ground and the knowledge that if he scores a hit then one has no chance of baling out but must crash land in the area. If this is survived and one is taken prisoner by the Japs then there is a good chance of being summarily executed.

We are however relaxing a bit more now and had some grand fun the other night when we shot up the mess with our revolvers, after we had come back from chasing a tiger which had been seen in the camp.

I received a very nice letter from The Air Officer Commanding the Group congratulating my squadron for the excellent work they have done and wishing us a well-earned rest.

6 NO ENEMY, BUT NOT MUCH REST EITHER!

Soldier, rest! Thy warfare o'er,
Dream of fighting fields no more;
Sleep the sleep that knows not breaking,
Morn of toil, nor night of waking.
(Sir Walter Scott, "The Lady of the Lake")

The "well-earned rest" we were to have turned out to be Ceylon. The signal accompanying the Air Officer Commanding's letter said that the squadron was to move to RAF Station, China Bay, at Trincomalee in Ceylon, but that I was required to remain behind for, among other things, some nonoperational activity for a short term at Group Headquarters at Chittagong.

I farewelled the ground crew and pilots on 3 August and flew my Hurricane, YB-G, to Chittagong and tucked it into the jungle until it was needed to fly me down to Ceylon to rejoin the squadron. The so-called "short term" turned out to be one month, during which time I did a lot of staff work in helping to determine operations for the fighter squadrons, and also liaising with the anti-aircraft section of the Army in coordinating the defence of Chittagong between them and the fighters. It was interesting, but my thoughts were always with the lads in Ceylon because the personnel in the Group Headquarters just did not have the same *esprit de corps*, although there were some fine chaps doing the organising so necessary to ensure the efficient use of the operational flying units.

I finally climbed into YG-B on 2 September and flew by easy stages down the east coast of India and, with a sigh of relief, landed at China Bay aerodrome, Trincomalee, where I was greeted with the news that a welcoming party was being laid on for me at the mess, and the Women's Royal Naval Service (WRNS) personnel from the Royal Navy base at Trincomalee were invited.

This base was only a few miles from China Bay, and the lads were delighted, as I was, to think that at last we were able to mix with some English girls. It was not that the Anglo-Indian lasses in Calcutta were not good company, but it was a bit off-putting to discover that their single aim in life seemed to be marriage to a Caucasian. The great percentage of the squadron pilots (whose average age was just over twenty) were, like myself, totally disinterested in marriage until they had survived the war (with a few exceptions) and were in any case basically married to their aeroplanes, but liked to make whoopee with the girls when off duty.

The party went off well and it was a delight to be able to dance again, after so many months in the jungle. I made a date for a picnic with a couple of lasses, and during the time at China Bay we had a few of these, and also enjoyed quite a bit of swimming and even some sailing.

A picnic on the beach at Trincomalee, with some Wrens (WRNS members) in their civilian dress

Another piece of news which delighted me was that we were to be re-equipped with the very latest mark of Spitfire, the Mk 8, at some time in the future, and the lift in spirits that this gave to us was the best tonic of all.

Letter, 5 November 1943

I am back with my lads again and we are having a grand rest down here. I have been able to do quite a bit of swimming (we are near the sea) and also some sailing and we have even been able to hold dances in the mess because there are some English Women's Royal Naval Service girls here. I don't know how long we are going to stay down here for our rest, or what they have in mind for us, but a lot of the lads want to get their Spitfires and set off back to the jungle again "toot sweet" as there is no action down here nor any prospect of some.

They have an admirable offensive spirit so I hope it will not be long before the Spitfires arrive and we can have a crack at the Jap again. However it is about time that most of us were out of the war because it gets harder each time we go back, but I would rather do this than sit in an office chair. I finished reading a very inspiring book about Major "Mick" Mannock who was one of our best aces in the last war. It is called *King of Air Fighters* and is written by Ira Jones. It is a wonderful tale of human courage and endurance and I am getting every pilot in the squadron to read it so that he can gain the mental benefit that I did. I feel that until we can all equal Mannock's fine record then we are not doing our utmost.

The book shows what wonderful companionships can be attained in a good squadron and how this automatically weeds out the boasters and self-seekers who are the "newspaper" aces.

Our billets and mess at China Bay were those of a peacetime RAF standard and it certainly was a wonderful change to get away from the heat and humidity and to dine and relax in comfort.

The officers of 17 Squadron at China Bay RAF station. Front row, left to right: Hank Forde, Shorty Miller, John Creswell (adjutant), Bill Buchan, self, Batchy, Neville Brooks, Doug Page, Ron Kirvan. Back row, left to right: Stapleford (engineer), Scottie Detlor, Ed Charles, Gerwing, Walton, "Widow" Dunkley (from New Zealand), Britten (defence officer)

There is, however, always a thorn with every rose, and ours happened to be the station commanding officer, a wing commander whose name now escapes me. This person had all the earmarks of a failed peacetime flyer – although wearing a pair of pilot's wings. His life in the RAF had been mainly spent in India. He had escaped being in any action against the enemy and I am sure was jealous of those of us whose whole careers had been the exact opposite to his.

This jealousy manifested itself in the enforcement of nitpicking regulations and insistence on working strictly by the book, which, while in peacetime may be acceptable, in wartime, even if we were remote from operations, was a fearful waste of time and effort, because we still had plenty of flying to do in training new pilots and in liaison with the Eastern Fleet in the harbour at Trincomalee. It made my life less attractive than it could have been, but now and again I managed to get even, although not always in ways that one could openly recount at the time.

The best example of how this was once achieved came about when I was called into his office one day and told by him that he had received an order from Group to hand over his Harvard aircraft (used for his private communication to and from Colombo for meetings) to us for training purposes. In lieu of this, he was being given a twin-engine de Havilland Dominie – a militarised

The de Havilland Dominie in civilian dress. It is the same as the one in which Batchy and I taught ourselves to fly twin-engine aircraft, with the kind "permission" of the station CO

version of the Dragon Rapide. He started questioning me about the flying characteristics of this machine, and I soon twigged he had not ever flown the Dominie, or any other twin-engine aircraft, and asked him straight out if this was the case.

He admitted that this was so, and asked me if we had any pilots who were proficient on twins who could give him a conversion course. I immediately told him that Flight Lieutenant Batchelar and I were both twin-engine pilots (with tongue firmly in cheek, both of us having hardly sat in one, let alone flown it), and we would check out his aircraft after it was delivered to see if it had any unusual characteristics. It duly arrived, and a dear little thing it was too. Batchy was very happy to play along with me and we quizzed the ferry pilot about its basic handling qualities. Then the two of us had the engines started (by hand-swinging the props, *à la* Tiger Moth), and we taxied out.

I explained to Batchy that my first civil instructor at Broken Hill, Dan Collins, had assured me that an experienced pilot should never have any trouble on a new type if he followed these basic rules:

1. If it was a twin, then use the two throttles in one hand and feed equal power to each engine to steer the machine on take-off until the rudder became effective, because there was no slip stream caused by the propeller – as is the case with a single-engine aircraft.
2. Hold the elevator neutral until it also responded. This too had little effect until flying speed had been attained.
3. After take-off, climb to at least 5,000 feet and practise all the landing configurations with engine-off and engine-on and note the stalling speeds.
4. Add at least 15 miles per hour to the stalling speed and approach with slight engine power. Do an engine-on landing with main wheels first, then cut the throttles gently to get the tail down and, as the machine slowed down, correct any swing with brakes, or engines (if necessary).

We duly set off and went through the recommended routine. After safely landing, we both agreed that it was, as far as we were concerned, a piece of cake. After we taxied in, the wing commander eagerly approached us, to be checked out, only to be told by us, with serious faces, that we were worried about the machine and the way it flicked onto its back near the stalling speed, and that was why we were doing wheels landings; we felt that it needed its rigging examined and should be test flown again by us until the problems were corrected. To our delight, he went quite pale, thanked us, and agreed that he must, of course, be guided by our recommendation. So we did about an hour's flying and half a dozen landings (usually called "circuits and bumps" in RAF training parlance), and found it was a delightful machine to fly, with no vices at all.

We spent the next few weeks fooling around in his lovely little aeroplane, taking some of the ground crew for joy-rides but telling the wing commander that we had them with us to track down the rigging problem, and should soon have it ironed out. It gave us almost a month of glee before we went through the routine of checking him out and finally handing it over, with him congratulating us at getting it into such magnificent trim. After this we could do very little wrong and our lives suffered from less irritation.

Not everyone in Station Headquarters was a stickler for protocol, and I had an interesting experience at China Bay, which bears recounting as it was perpetrated by the station adjutant, who was something of a practical joker.

Stationed at Trincomalee was a squadron of Coastal Command Catalina flying boats belonging to the Dutch Air Force. Their job was to go on long shipping patrols, lasting anything up to twenty or more hours over the Indian Ocean and Bay of Bengal. As they had been in Ceylon from the early days of 1942, they were well dug in and, like the Dutch generally, did not stint themselves when it came to the good things in life, such as food and grog.

The China Bay adjutant passed on an invitation to me and my two flight commanders to have a luncheon at the Dutch squadron mess on the following Saturday, and told me that I would have to get into training for it because the Dutch always downed a few Bols gins before lunch, and drank these straight down, without pause, after the word *skol*.

So Batchy, Tex and I duly fronted up to their very nice mess in a beautiful bungalow and, after smart salutes, introductions and greetings, were asked if we would care for an aperitif of Bols gin before lunch. This we agreed to, and to be polite, I raised my glass first. With an all-round gesture and a loud "*Skol*", I downed it. A slight pause at first from our hosts did not prevent them from doing the same. After a recharge of glasses, I repeated my performance, only this time the pause from the hosts was somewhat longer, and at the end of the third such episode the Dutch commanding officer said to me: "Tell me, squadron leader, do all Australians drink like you do?" to be answered by me: "Oh no, I am only doing it out of politeness and a desire to conform to your customs."

"Who told you that?" asked the commanding officer.

"The China Bay adjutant."

"That bastard; wait till I get at him. We never drink like that!"

Roars of laughter ensued, but by this time we were all a bit cross-eyed, and although the beautiful luncheon of *nasi goreng* and wines was appreciated greatly, so was the sleep we all fell into for the rest of the afternoon.

Soon after I arrived in Ceylon, I received a letter from the headquarters of No. 169 Wing at Agartala, signed by Squadron Leader Guy Marsland (who was a great friend and a character of no mean repute), applying to have Joe the Camel posted from 17 Squadron strength to No. 169 Wing. They were entrusted with his care when 17 Squadron left Agartala, and there was no firm indication when our squadron would return and take him back under our establishment. My reply to this letter was as follows:

8th Dec. 1943

From:- Officer Commanding,
No. 17 Squadron,
RAF Station,
China Bay.

To:- Headquarters, No. 169 Wing, RAF Station, Agartala. (For the attention of Squadron Leader Marsland)

RE:- JOE (THE CAMEL)

Reference your letter of 21st November 1943 in respect of the proposed posting of the above camel to the strength of NO. 169 Wing.

It is felt that since Flying Officer Page of our unit originally discovered and nurtured the aforementioned Camel (with the assistance of Flight Lieutenant Ley, No. 224 Group) then we feel it should be only temporarily attached to No. 169 Wing, pending the arrival of this Squadron back in Bengal again.

It is fully appreciated that the Camel will have to forego its Indian rates of pay while thus attached and, consequently, should its burden become too great (the last straw!) we will be prepared to waive the attachment.

Your views will be appreciated.

M.C.C. Cotton, D.F.C.
Squadron Leader, Commanding,
No. 17 Squadron R.A.F.

Unfortunately any further correspondence has been mislaid, so I have no idea what happened to Joe in the end.

We had not been long at China Bay before we were advised that we were not only to be re-equipped with new aircraft, but also that those pilots whose time on operations had reached the "tour" stage (twelve months on the squadron or 300 hours operational flying) would be posted, and we would be required to train their replacements. We therefore started the extensive training of new pilots in our usual methods of gunnery, formation flying, and so on.

In view of the fact that, in future, we might be doing offshore practice interceptions with the aircraft off the aircraft carriers HMS *Illustrious* and USS *Saratoga* (which were both in the harbour as members of the Eastern Fleet), we also trained ourselves to use the inflatable dinghies on top of our parachute packs. This we did by holding demonstrations off one of the air-sea rescue launches in the Trincomalee harbour. It consisted of throwing each of our pilots, one at a time, into the water with just the dinghy pack on and getting him to organise the inflation and use of the equipment, which proved to be most effective, but fortunately never had to be used by any of the pilots as a true emergency measure.

Trying out an inflatable dinghy in China Bay. The pilot is supported by his Mae West flotation jacket while he wrestles with the dinghy pack, on which he sits while flying

Safely on board after inflating the dinghy with the built-in CO_2 bottle

Farewelling us from the boat was Chico, our squadron mascot. I notice in my logbook that I had taken the Doc and Chico for a ride in the Harvard on 20 January 1944, and it strikes me that I should recount the story of Chico, because it is somewhat unusual.

Chico was a small Gurkha boy, then aged about four years, who was found by our ground crew near Calcutta in 1942, starving, homeless, obviously abandoned, and seriously ill with malaria. He was adopted by them and restored to health, and lived under the care of the warrant officer disciplinary, who was the senior noncommissioned officer of the ground crew. Having nursed and fed him, the lads then realised they had also acquired a responsibility. Everyone in the squadron chipped a weekly sum of money into a fund for him, so that when the squadron finally moved out of the East, and, of course, could not take him with them, at least he would have enough money to pay a guardian to take care of him.

While he was with us he had a great life. He had to attend a preschool, set up by the warrant officer, and was taught the three Rs by various airmen. He also had to play sport. One which he loved above all others being swimming off the air-sea rescue launches, and if he had been particularly good he was taken for a ride in the Harvard on someone's knee as a reward. He was a delightful little lad, much-loved by all, and, after being with the squadron right through the reconquest of Burma and into Malaya in 1945, was left in the safe hands of a family and educated at St Marks School in Butterworth, Kedah State, Malaya. He was given the registered name Jimmy Nutti, and the last news that most of the survivors of 17 Squadron have had since then has been that he finally joined the merchant navy when he was old enough, and was last heard of studying to be an engineer and hoping to join the US Navy.

It was soon after this that I was called to Colombo to be briefed by Air Headquarters on our future role in the re-equipping with Spitfire 8s and training ourselves and a lot of new pilots to use them. I was also told that we were to be used to test out some new equipment, still in its experimental stage, and, because of its secret nature, we would be moved to a new aerodrome near China Bay called Minneriya. While at Colombo, I met up with the usual RAF crowd who knew lots of the guys that I knew, and I joined them and some WAAF officers in a boozy party before flying back the next day.

Suffering somewhat from the results of this party, I took off in my Hurricane at Colombo and set a direct course for China Bay, which would take me near the high country in the middle of the island. Some clouds ahead did not look anything to worry about, so I set my blind-flying instruments and flew merrily into them. The ensuing five minutes became a nightmare. I had inadvertently flown smack into the edge of a cumulonimbus. I was picked up by the air currents as if I were a piece of tissue paper, and was thrown helter-skelter inside the cloud.

At one moment I would be doing more than 300 miles an hour in a dive and trying to level out, and the next moment doing about 70 miles an hour, obviously inverted, and whirling around like a top, completely unable to get the machine back to straight and level. I had entered the cloud at a height of 10,000 feet, and knew that the ground under me rose to 6,000 feet. I decided that if I got into another uncontrollable dive, then I would bale out at 7,000 feet and take my chances of being carried upwards, rather than dive into the ground. Sure enough this happened, so I slid the hood back, undid my straps and started to get ready to vacate the plane as the altimeter unwound itself and approached the 7,000 mark. Just as I was about to clamber out, the machine whistled out of the bottom of the cloud, on its side and pointing down into a valley. In a flash I was back into the seat and heading down the valley, back the way I had come. On reaching lower ground, I did what I should have done in the first place; that is, to have flown well to the north of the high ground and the clouds. I always prided myself on being good at instrument flying, but never realised how impossible it was to maintain even a semblance of control in a real cu-nim, and from that day on gave them a wide berth, particularly in Ceylon.

After this episode a letter home says:

Letter, 17 January 1944

The only news of any importance as far as I am concerned is that we have moved to a new place again and are back in a jungle camp, similar to the one we were in before we came here. The main difference seems to be that we have far more wild animals roaming about the place than formerly, but as soon as we have settled in it should be a good spot. I confess it gets a bit wearisome, all this changing about and settling in and generally getting a place in working order, only to leave it after it is complete. By a curious coincidence I am on the same aerodrome as another squadron which is commanded by Bunny Stone whom, you may remember, was my old Commanding Officer in our squadron when we came overseas from England.

You can well imagine how we bore everybody else to tears by recounting our exploits at Rangoon, in the first Burma campaign, at great length to all and sundry in the mess. He is still a Squadron Leader after nearly two and a half years, so you can imagine that he has not been very popular (he is pretty outspoken) but for all that he is a very nice, straightforward chap and I am looking forward to some good co-operation between our two units. Had a letter from cousin Professor Frank Cotton today. He and I are both interested in some special equipment and he is rather tickled pink that I am using the same thing in our fighters. Can't say more than this but he says he is well and fit.

Soon after the trip to Group and my tangle with a cu-nim, we received a visit from a Canadian officer to brief us on a development of an "anti-blackout" suit, which was the secret equipment our squadron had been selected to test for its suitability in the tropics and was why we were sent to our new aerodrome. The reason behind the phenomenon of blackout, which we all encountered on turning rapidly at high speeds in dogfights, is as follows.

If one spun a can of water around, attached to a string, then the faster it was spun the heavier it got, owing to centrifugal force. This was measured in units of a G force, which stood for gravity force. We are all subject, even when walking or sitting, to a constant 1 G, but when we hop into a Spitfire and start doing high-speed steep-turns, this force builds up until, at 5 G for five seconds, blood drains away from the brain. The first effect is loss of sight and then, if prolonged, loss of consciousness.

It stands to reason that as the top speeds of our fighters began to increase, owing to more powerful engines, pilots were increasingly disadvantaged by the blackout problem. The Allies apparently took this more seriously than the enemy, and a cousin of mine, Frank Cotton (who was the Professor of Physiology at Sydney University), as far back as 1940, when he heard about this phenomenon during the Battle of Britain, reasoned out a method of protection based on the following theory.

The problem is because of loss of blood from the heart into the large veins in the stomach and legs, which are flexible enough to expand and store it. The brain therefore becomes starved of blood. Its nutrients, on which it functions, become unavailable. The whole system of sight is the first thing affected, followed by unconsciousness if the force is prolonged. If the body is covered below the heart level, in a non-extensible covering, thus preventing the blood from draining away from it and pooling in the legs and stomach, then the heart is strong enough to pump the blood back to the brain against much higher forces than 5 Gs.

Accordingly, Frank Cotton developed a non-extensible, rubberised canvas suit which fitted the pilot from the heart level downwards, and put air bladders inside it at the points where the blood pooled. A special valve then pushed compressed carbon dioxide (held in special bottles in the aircraft fuselage) into the bladders at a rate calculated to compensate for the increasing units of G, so that the blood could not pool and the heart could get at it. To test out his theory on the ground, he built a human centrifuge at Sydney University, in which he could subject pilots, wearing the suit, to various rates of G, and he built up the data about the "5 G for 5 seconds" being the normal threshold for blackout to occur.

He proved that one of his suits could extend this threshold to 9 G for five seconds, and became the first in the world to record his data and to have built and used a human centrifuge to prove it. His suit was test flown by Squadron Leader Ken Robinson at the RAAF test-flying unit at Laverton, Victoria, and proved the theory, but the suit was too unwieldy to be capable of operational use. This research data was made available to all the Allies.

The Canadians found that they too had reasoned out the cause of blackout, but took another path to come up with a cure for it. It was explained to us by the Canadian officer who was visiting our new drome that their suits were much the same type as the graduated air-pressure suit of Frank Cotton, but they simply filled the internal bladders with water, and this, when under the G forces, automatically compensated for them and kept the blood from pooling. It did not involve the extra weight of compressed CO_2 bottles and the problem of recharging them.

We found this difficult to understand until it was pointed out to us that if in the laboratory one was to, say, put a mouse into a centrifuge (where extremely high G forces can be achieved) and spin it at full revolutions, then, on stopping, the poor mouse would undoubtedly be a small, compressed, dead blob at the bottom of the test tube. But if one filled the test tube with water and spun the mouse at the same G force as before, then he would come out alive (provided he did not drown) because the same pressure was exerted on the water as on the mouse, and therefore the G forces were cancelled out.

A selected group of twelve of our pilots were then fitted with the suits, which had to be done exactly. We found they were not very restrictive, when empty, as far as leg movements were concerned, and we could easily climb into our aircraft to test them. The system then used was as follows.

Before climbing into the machine, one undid small draining valves fitted at the bottom of each leg and then, once one was strapped into the aircraft, a ground crew member fitted a long tube to a similar valve on the top of the suit, to which was connected a water-filled rubber container shaped like a conventional hot-water bottle. He up-ended this and, as the water ran down into the suit, one closed the bottom valves, and the internal bladders filled, in about two minutes or so. Any air was forced out of the top of the suit through a non-return valve until the water flowed out, and the valve was then closed.

There was no doubt that the suits gave a good degree of protection, because on the accelerometers which had also been fitted to our aeroplanes, we were able to note the fact that we could pull 8 G and still remain in a proper visual state. Not only this, but we also found that we could do high-speed manoeuvres and aerobatics for a much longer period than ever before and feel much fresher after landing.

The implications for us were fascinating to contemplate. We reasoned that if we were equipped with G suits and our enemy was not, then, if we could somehow entice him into a continuous high-speed turn (say, in a spiral dive under full power) at anything above 5 G, he would black out; we would still be able to see him, and "splat" – one less enemy. Our delight can therefore be imagined, so we began to examine the whole idea with great enthusiasm. What we finally found out, however, was disappointing.

First, the suits became unbearably hot after a while on the ground, and this meant they could not be worn during readiness (which could be for some hours at a time) in the tropics. Again, they could not be worn on the ground when full of water because it slowed down our movements too much on a scramble. The excessive time of three to four minutes getting to, and into, the machine – plus the time taken to fill the suits – restricted us to only using them on escort duties and not on scramble interceptions, which was not much good in a real war, particularly if the warning was very short and the enemy appeared over the aerodrome boundary while the water was running in. The time of, say, five to six minutes taken to scramble (instead of the usual maximum of two) may not seem much, but, when a Spitfire 8 could climb at a rate of 5,000 feet a minute, this meant a great deal in climbing rapidly to intercept an intruder.

Second, our Hurricanes were simply not fast enough to take full advantage of the protection because we could not pull enough continuously high G for the suits to be really useful. Before we had finished our trials, however, we started to receive our Spitfires and, embracing them like lovers, we handed the suits back, thanking the inventors profusely and trusting they would be able to solve the problems of ground comfort and time loss.

Finally, towards the end of the war, the problems of the unwieldy nature of Frank Cotton's compressed-air filled suit were solved by the Americans. First, they made the suits of an open-weave nylon fabric to ensure maximum comfort. Then, instead of having a separate compressed CO_2 supply in heavy bottles, they plugged the suit into the exhaust of the vacuum pump (which drove the gyroscopic instruments in our planes; its exhaust was, in effect, also a pressure pump), and this had an automatic regulating valve to look after the graduation of the pressure into the suit.

I used one of these when test flying at the RAAF Aircraft Performance Unit (their unit for testing all new aeroplanes and equipment) in November 1944, and one hardly knew one was wearing them. It was as simple to quickly plug in as it was to do the same for our radio gear if one was scrambled. Further testing of the suit at Laverton disclosed, however, that the guns would not fire above 5 G due to the increased load imposed on the mechanically operated feel pawls for pulling the ammunition belts out of their boxes, and modifications to the whole system had to be made.

This was basically the same suit as worn by today's jet pilots. They have more sophisticated aerodromes to fly from and can air-condition the suits when on the ground, and this overcomes the problems which we faced when having to operate from strips in the tropics. Nevertheless, we wrote into our current squadron-training paper, on tactics and fighter-flying techniques, a section which gave an indication that we still felt they might come to something that we could put to good use when ultimately perfected. See Appendix D.

The model of Spitfire which we received was designated as the Mark VIII, or 8. It was easily the best aeroplane I have flown before or since. It was somehow a total thoroughbred, possessed of enormous speed, and yet was beautifully

The beautiful Spitfire 8s arrive. Ours had a 1,720-horsepower Rolls Royce Merlin, Model 66, engine, a maximum speed of 420 miles an hour at 21,000 feet, and a service ceiling of 41,500 feet. The Spitfire marked J became my machine. (Photograph spoiled by the tropics)

sensitive and responsive at almost all speeds. In flying it, one felt as though it became an integral part of one's very being, and, as a machine, it was everything the heart of a fighter pilot could desire. As an indication of ability of the Spitfire to immediately capture a pilot's enthusiasm, it is worth recording the time we went back to China Bay with them to carry out an exercise with the Grumman Hellcat fighter squadron from the US aircraft carrier *Saratoga*.

After we had duly intercepted them (they, acting as a fighter escort to the Royal Navy Fleet Air Arm, as the enemy) and had numerous camera-gun dog fights, we all landed our machines at China Bay to carry out a post-mortem on the affray. Batchy and I had parked our machines near our dispersal and watched as a Hellcat came taxying up on its long undercarriage and parked alongside us. Down from this tall machine climbed a US Marine, Major Bob Dosé (pronounced "Doesay"), their squadron commander.

The first thing he did was to make a beeline for my Spitfire, and when Batchy and I walked over to meet him and introduce ourselves, he was standing on the ground, looking into the cockpit, and in tones of some envy said: "Hey guys, what a dinky little ship. What's more, you gave us a hell of a time!" We introduced ourselves, and I found in him an immediate kindred spirit. I asked him if he would like to fly my Spitfire if he promised not to bend it.

His "Sure would" soon resulted in him being strapped in, shown the essential controls, and told about only using two-thirds throttle on take-off to avoid the swing caused by the 1,650-horsepower engine. We watched him take off and climb to about 6,000 feet and begin to tear holes in the atmosphere with his aerobatics, during which he called us up on the radio and asked: "Say guys, how do I get to join the RAF?" and added a few more superlatives.

The sequel to all this was an invitation for me to spend a weekend on the USS *Saratoga* in Colombo, where she would be a week later. I made an excuse to visit RAF Headquarters in Colombo on the Friday before that weekend and, after this, was met by Bob and told that because *Saratoga* was a dry ship we had best get a load of alcoholic fuel aboard ourselves at the PX before going out to the carrier. The PX turned out to be a shore-based canteen, and we duly sank a few rum and Coca-Colas, which was my first introduction to the potion, other than through the Andrews Sisters singing about it on the radio.

We giggled our way to the wharf, staggered into the liberty boat, arrived at the side of the *Saratoga* and climbed up the gangway, at the top of which I turned and saluted the quarterdeck, having remembered the protocol from previous visits to Royal Navy warships. This was received with great approbation by Bob and his ruffians who had accompanied us, and we were invited by him to have a drink in his cabin. When asked what I would like to have, I replied, "Whatever's going," thinking I might as well get used to a sober weekend. Bob pressed a buzzer, which later brought a knock on his door, and the head of an ordinary seaman appearing around it to enquire, "Whaddya want Barb?"

Bob ordered some split sodas and ice. When this duly arrived he locked his door, turned to a built-in wall safe fitted with a combination lock, opened it and pulled out a bottle of Jim Beam whiskey from the front of a line of them which filled the rest of the safe. I do not remember much detail of the rest of the weekend, other than games of poker, teaching the ruffians how to play "liar dice", being called "Lootenant Commander Cotton" by everyone (because of the two and a half rings of my rank), and being shown all over the floating city they called a carrier. I really loved those marines. All volunteers, as we were, and just as crazy.

Letter, 5 February 1944

We had a visit from a grand chap, by name Wing Commander Winfield, who is a flying Medical Officer, and has been decorated with the DFC and AFC during the war. He knows cousin Frank Cotton very well and we were all working on a special doo-dah so it is becoming quite a family concern as it were. He was decorated for work done on investigation of the use of Benzadrine by bomber crews, having used himself as a "Guinea pig" on numerous raids over Germany. Also he was one of the early researchers into the most effective design of our "Mae West" flotation vests. He used to have himself anaesthetised and flung into a swimming pool to see if they turned one up the right way, automatically, if unconscious.

We are on the eve of a whopping training programme for a lot of new pilots who have come to us as a result of some old hands being posted away, including alas, Tex Barrick. The rest of the "oldies" are getting tuned up to set some of the "new" boys on the straight and narrow with regard to air combat.

The above letter to home was one that gave some indication of the jobs that we were suddenly loaded with, after all the interesting work of investigation into new concepts. We were now thrust into a complete training program to be carried out with our lovely new Spitfires, which were, at that time of the war, the most advanced fighters in the world, with a straight-and-level top speed of more than 420 miles an hour, against that of our old Hurries of 240 miles an hour with their cannons and long-range tanks.

One of the sad effects of this program was that quite a few of the old guard, most notably Tex Barrick, were posted off for a rest period, and we were sent a large contingent of new pilots who had never been on operations. To properly carry out all the manoeuvres and practise them until they became second nature to everyone took a lot of flying and hard work, and it started to tell on me, to the extent that I became run down and fell prey to an attack of amoebic dysentery.

Letter, 13 February 1944

You will be surprised to learn that this is being written from the Hospital at Kandy. I am up here undergoing treatment for what is feared may be amoebic dysentery.

One bright feature is that I can now catch up on some reading. It would also be nice, in the event that I have to be treated for the above, to somehow wangle a spot of leave in Australia, but that is a dream of course. In any case the powers that be are going to find it rather hard soon to know what to do with me because I am now one of the most senior squadron commanders in India and Ceylon. If they take me off flying they will have to promote me, but if there are no vacancies then perhaps I might have to go back to Australia. However this would be grim indeed if I could not get a flying job back there because it is the only life worth leading in this war.

My new flight commander, replacing Tex Barrick, was a publisher before the war and he keeps us well supplied with reading matter. You will be interested to know that his name is The Hon. William Buchan, being the youngest son of Lord Tweedsmuir, otherwise known as John Buchan, the author. He is a grand bloke too and what is most important in this game, is a good flyer. My other, and senior, Flight Commander is still Eric Batchelar and we have been together now for fourteen months without ever having had a single disagreement.

Willie Buchan was telling me that his elder brother spent a lot of time in Canada amongst the Eskimos and said they just bump off anyone who gets too angry and disagreeable. Their view is that if a man is always angry then he must be insane and therefore might as well be dead as alive. Bonk! No trouble at all.

The dysentery necessitated quite a spell in the hospital in Kandy and, while recovering, I was visited by one of the Women's Royal Naval Service girls, Rae Hine, who was up there on a holiday. We took a mutual delight in each other's company and, on my return to the aerodrome, I decided that relaxing in her company was the best cure of the lot for flying stress, and took every opportunity to call for her in my jeep and go swimming and picnicking, followed up by dancing at the nice bungalow in which the RAF Operations Headquarters had installed themselves in at Trincomalee, where they held open house every Saturday night.

Before this, however, I was sent on leave to convalesce at a tea plantation as a guest of the manager, a sojourn that was organised by Bill Buchan, who seemed to know everybody who was anybody in Ceylon.

Letter, 16 March 1944

At the present moment I am staying in a beautiful bungalow in the hills at a place called Dickoya. It is the home of Mr "Nibs" Burnett and is 4,000 feet above sea level and I am here with one of my pilots, Flying Officer Douglas Page. He is an English lad and a most witty and charming bloke. His brother, [Geoffrey] Page, was one of Britain's top aces during the Battle of Britain and finished up with the DSO and DFC. Was badly burnt and had to go through 14 skin grafting operations. Finished up on operations again and finally scored 15 victories. Doug has very likely flown more hours actually shooting, but at enemy ground targets. Shot down no aeroplanes because there weren't any, and will get no medals. Which is all a bit sad, but I guess he is no worse off than many others and has at least not been disfigured.

Nibs Burnett was a fine chap indeed – a very strong-minded Scotsman, well spoken, well read, a good golfer, and a magnificent host. We became firm friends, mainly because of our mutual interest in agriculture and literature, and he was wonderful to Doug and me during our restful stay. In talks with him, I found he was due to visit Australia, before the end of the war, to investigate irrigation equipment and also to find a place to live when he reached the age for his retirement in 1946. I made him promise to visit us in Broken Hill if I survived the war. This he did at the beginning of 1945, and we were able to repay some of his hospitality.

Letter, 6 April 1944

There is no escaping the fact that, particularly after that disease, I am much too tired to go back into action again and do a good job of leadership. I don't think I would last for more than two months without packing in completely but if I am wanted badly then of course I most certainly will go back.

One never considers, at the onset of a career in a fighter squadron, that one will ever get to the stage where every take-off and landing becomes a mental hurdle, yet I have seen so many good chaps become "Tired" that I do not now consider this reaction is in any way connected with cowardice. About six months away from flying altogether can generally effect a cure but of course, as one gets older the cure becomes more difficult to achieve. These days we have found that the best age for squadron commanders is generally about 25 so I am already two years over the mark.

My old squadron commander (now Wing Commander) Bunny Stone is staying with us on our station for a few days. He is a staff officer in our Headquarters at Colombo and fairly loathes it. He keeps on telling me that he is trying to get me made a Wing Commander so that I will have to come and give him a hand, and I keep on telling him that he can keep the job. However, I can see the writing on the wall because one is only supposed to remain on an operational squadron for 12 months and I have been commanding this one for over 16 months.

No wonder I'm half way round the bend! Being part of the way round before one starts in this game doesn't help either. However the squadron has now been classed as the most efficient in the group and our ideas on tactics etc., are being recommended to others.

Letter, 15 June 1944

Talking about going "Nuts", we have one officer here who has been overseas from England for about 4 years and, in view of the fact that he was a school teacher before the war, he has got a slight lead on us and is now almost completely "crackers". The poor devil wakes up in the middle of the night swearing black and blue that there are snakes in his bed or in the room. Says he can see their eyes in the dark. The blokes alongside him talk him back to bed and next morning he never knows a thing about it. The curious part about it is that the poor blighter never touches a drop and is a very hard and conscientious worker.

Here is some news for you that I have just received this very minute. The RAAF liaison officer rang from Delhi to tell me that I should be home this August. This means that if I can survive till then I shall definitely be seeing you before Xmas. That is the best news I have had for many a day and I shall now go to sleep on it.

Not long after this, I received a signal to say that the Supreme Commander South-East Asia Command (SEAC), Lord Louis Mountbatten (known as SUPREMO), would visit the squadron on such and such a day, landing at 0900 hours. The signal said he wished to meet all pilots first, then the assembled squadron, and he required a box, 18 inches tall, to stand on. On the appointed day, his Dakota aircraft appeared in the sky, landed and taxied up to our squadron dispersal hut; the door opened and Mountbatten stepped onto the ground at exactly 0900 hours.

He returned my salute and said: "I note that you come from Broken Hill, Cotton. I visited there with the Prince of Wales just after the last war and went down one of the mines. What do your folks do there?" We chatted about the Hill for a little longer, and I was most impressed that he had taken the trouble to read up on me; I became a staunch member of his fan club from then on. I introduced him to the pilots, one by one, and he had something nice to say to each one of them, taking an obvious interest in their replies to his questions about their length of service on the squadron, how they liked their aircraft, did they have any problems, and so on, and of course, he collected another twenty more fans in his 17 Squadron Fan Club in the process.

He was then escorted by me to the squadron parade, formed up in ranks. He stood on his 18-inch box and told everyone to break ranks and gather around him as closely as possible. He started off with a couple of jokes, the first one being that soon after he got to SEAC he was told they were looked on as the "Forgotten Army", but, he found out after a while, that could not have been right because no one had heard of them in the first place. This raised a laugh, and he then went on to say that before we were finished the whole world would know about us and honour our deeds.

He then made the following statement: "I have come here especially to tell you that, together, we are going to retake Burma, and that you will be given a leading role, and I promise we will be back there before the monsoon begins next year." This was, of course, met with a rousing cheer, and he went on to tell us how he intended to carry out his promise by using Army, Navy and Air Force in coordinated campaigns. It was wonderful stuff to listen to and one could literally feel all spirits rising – mine certainly were. At the end of his talk, he was given an enormous cheer and was waved off in his aeroplane by all the squadron, lining the side of the runway.

I realised afterwards the psychology he used, in that when he said he would visit us at 0900 hours and stepped onto the ground at exactly that time, it was easy for us to also believe what he said about his retaking Rangoon at a certain time. I find it hard to describe what a wonderful sense of increased morale he left us all with and what a superb leader he was. No wonder everyone in his destroyer, the *Kelly*, earlier in the war, loved him. Fortunately, history has recorded all of his deeds, which bore us out in our assessment of him.

Another month went by before anything more was heard from the liaison office at Delhi, and finally I received a notification to proceed to the Bombay transit camp. Before this, however, I decided to take some leave that was owing to me. Rae organised to take some as well, and we duly arrived at a tea plantation near Nuawra Eliya, called Telawakele. Nuawra Eliya was the place where the tea-planters went to during the monsoons; it was higher than 6,000 feet above sea level and almost like England.

In fact the English, in their inimitable fashion when overseas, try to make their surroundings resemble "home" as much as possible, no matter where they are. Nuawra Eliya even boasted a trout stream and a golf course surrounded by heather. We stayed with a Bill Rennie and his wife and had a great time visiting other planters – including Nibs – going to their private club, fishing for trout and playing golf. I still weighed only 10 stone (63.5 kilograms), even after that sybaritic existence.

Towards the end of this break, I received a message to say that I was scheduled to leave the squadron within a few days and proceed to the RAF Bombay Reinforcement Depot for transhipment to Australia. This entailed some days of travel by train and boat, and pointed up the fact that I was no longer in command of a lot of aeroplanes which I could use for my own transport and, unless I was lucky when I arrived in Australia, I was destined to become "grounded" for at least six months, and maybe even until the end of the war.

As it turned out, I was immediately given a job of flying in the RAAF test-flying unit at Laverton because of the work we had done on the testing of the G suits in Ceylon, and was saved the awful fate of becoming a Shiny Bum, as our desk-flying friends in the service were called.

Letter, 9 August 1944

Base Reinforcement Depot
Bombay

The reason for the strange address which you see above is simply that I have finally left the squadron and am now "In Transit" on my way home to you. I am quite certain that the word "Transit" was originally derived from the verb "To Sit" because for the past seven days that is all we have been doing, while waiting for our boat. It was sad to leave the squadron but they gave me a great send-off and a silver beer mug with the words engraved on it:

"To Squadron Leader Bush Cotton. From the Officers of the 17th Pursuit".

Batchy was also posted away at the same time, so we went for a last "Thrash" together in our beautiful Spitfires and tore enormous holes in the atmosphere doing a special stunt we have invented called "Upward Twizzles". These consist of firstly diving at full throttle from 10,000 feet to ground level to achieve an airspeed of about 470 miles per hour then pulling up, using full throttle, and seeing how many vertically upward rolls can be executed before falling out at the top. Six complete ones is about as much as one can do, and that finishes almost back at 10,000 feet. Most spectacular.

Just for the record my total hours flown with the RAAF and the RAF are now as follows:

By Day:-	Dual.	57.55	Solo.	708.30
By Night:-	Dual.	2.00	Solo.	50.10

Total on Hurries & Spits:-	574.50
Grand Total:-	818.35
Operational Sorties:-	171

Please do not write any more letters if you receive this within 14 days. See you soon dear people.

The word "Pursuit" on my beer mug was a wordplay on the way our American pals spoke of a fighter squadron, and underneath the words is an engraving of the 17 Squadron crest, the mailed gauntlet. This is something of great value to me that I shall treasure for the rest of my days. It is almost impossible to explain how living for years with others, who would give their lives for you without a moment's thought, engenders a deep feeling towards them that lasts for all time.

It certainly has been truly said in the Bible that, "Greater love hath no man than this, that a man lay down his life for his friend", and this was exactly what we were always expected to do in any emergency in the air. One can never hope to meet with the same standing rule in a peacetime gathering, although there are obviously isolated acts of bravery in all walks of life.

I am indeed fortunate to have survived this experience, and even more fortunate to have learned the other lesson I was taught: "You can achieve anything you want in this world, provided you are willing to make the necessary sacrifices."

Their shoulders held the sky suspended;
They stood, and the earth's foundations stay.
(Anon.)

Book Two

THE MEMOIRS OF WING COMMANDER "BUNNY" STONE, DFC

Edited by Squadron Leader
M.C. "Bush" Cotton, DFC, OAM

FOREWORD

I served under (the then) Squadron Leader "Bunny" Stone as a flight commander in No. 17 Squadron RAF from 31 October 1941 to 27 February 1942, during which time the squadron was posted to Rangoon and took part in the first Burma campaign. I was wounded early in this campaign and was only able to rejoin the squadron on 11 November 1942. Very few of us knew at this time that Bunny was an accomplished artist, and when he left the squadron in mid-1942 in India he worked on some pen drawings, mainly depicting actions and scenes of the first campaign, drawn from rough sketches in an old logbook he had carried with him.

The next time I saw him was in April 1944, when he was a wing commander in RAF Headquarters in Ceylon, and our squadron was changing over to Spitfire 8s. We had been in the Burma-India environment throughout the campaign in the Arakan, and the ground crew and pilots were in very poor health. They were at last able to enjoy some leave at tea plantations, in the beautiful climate of the high country, and get away from the disease and privations of Bengal.

When Bunny went back to England in late 1944, he completed and lithographed a set of thirty-three of his drawings and, in the 1970s, also wrote a draft of his experiences during the campaign. He was then earning his living as a portrait artist in South Africa, but I have little further detail of his postwar life.

My wife Stella and I visited the UK in 1982 and called on Bunny and his wife at Yattenden, where we stayed the night and I read the draft of his memoirs and saw the finished drawings. He had sold the originals to the Royal Air Force Museum at Hendon to raise some money but had retained the actual copyright.

His efforts as a professional portrait artist since he had left the RAF had not been very successful, and it appeared that he had saved little or nothing in the way of cash or assets to ensure comfort in his later years. I suggested to him that we might collaborate on a book about our time together in the squadron – using my large collection of photographs, together with his drawings and both of our memoirs– but he was vague about it.

I discovered, in subsequent visits, that he had a problem with alcohol, which did not surprise me – the way he used to drink during the war years. Most of us over-indulged during the war, but, even then, he gave the impression that it had become a crutch, and this was not surprising when one considered what he had been through since the beginning of the war.

In 1984 we again visited the UK and found that Bunny's wife had left him, and he was quite fragile and staying with a relative near Patterdale in Cumberland. By this time he was penniless and under the care of the National Health Service, and I again tried to motivate him to publish his memoirs.

On my return to Australia, I decided it was high time I wrote my own story and, in doing so, I felt that some of Bunny's drawings and extracts from his memoirs would add an extra dimension to it, and wrote to ask him if I could buy both of them from him. The correspondence which ensued obviously rekindled a spark in him to finally have at least some of his deeds recorded, and we agreed that I would buy both his drawings and his memoirs, and he would grant me their copyright to enable me to use them in my book. This also ensured they would not be able to used by others, without my permission, before or after his death – which he felt was not far off.

His hard-to-read letters in shaky handwriting were elaborations (some unprintable) of his draft memoirs and the concluding remark on one letter was: "I remain just a playboy – Charterhouse and all that." On another he said: "Just been in hospital and dried out, I hope, for I have decided to fight and laugh again."

The end result of all this was the production of my own book, *Hurricanes over Burma*, which Stella and I self-published in 1988 under the name of Titania Publishing Co., and which has almost sold out at this date. I used a lot of Bunny's drawings, and some of his text, in my book, and I have therefore left most of these out of Book One in this volume and allowed Bunny to recount his full story in the following memoirs.

I will never know if it was a good thing to have given Bunny quite a lot of money for the copyright to his drawings and memoirs, because he had none of it left when we went to England again in 1989. It must have been mainly wasted on alcohol, and he was, by this time, in a nursing home at Salcombe in Cornwall, fortunately being visited and generally cared for by Commander Ronnie Hay, DSO, DSC and bar, Royal Navy (retired). They had fought together on the same squadron during the Battle of Britain. It was most moving to see how Ronnie obviously loved and cared for him during his last days.

It was sad to see that he was near his end, but, at the same time, trying to be cheerful and schoolboyish. He was at least able to down a few half-pints of beer at the pub next to the medieval Parish Church of Saint Michael and All Angels (AD 1200) at Stokenham, and to point out the plot of ground in the cemetery close by, where he would be able to see the pub and be in the company of his father whose deeds in World War I were honoured in the chapel inside the church.

He died not long afterwards, and it was only recently that I found the time to sit down to see what might be done to honour his memory. His single, roughly typed copy of his memoirs needed a lot of rearranging as to chapters, but what follows is Bunny's memoirs, with no modifications other than spelling and slight corrections of grammar.

Like so many young Englishmen, he was modest about his past deeds, and it seemed a shame to me that he, and so many others like him, are not given the credit due for the wonderful life that so many of us now lead under the democracy for which so many of them gave their lives, or their subsequent way of life.

Vale, good friend Bunny.

"Bush" Cotton

PREFACE

These personal anecdotes of my three-year tour with the RAF in the Far East are built around some thirty-three drawings in pen and ink which I started in India after the first Burma campaign, during which I commanded No. 17 Fighter Squadron. The original drafts were done by me, after any experiences worth recording, in an old logbook in Burma when I commanded No. 17 Fighter Squadron on Hurricane 2bs during the first Burma campaign and the retreat. I completed the set of drawings on my return to UK in 1944 while the events were still clear in my mind. The text was done later on, during the 1970s.

The first retreat in Burma was the longest in the war, fought against a ruthless enemy whose background and principles were entirely alien to Europeans, and fear of capture was uppermost in our minds. This was because, after the fall of Singapore, rumours of "the Railway" had filtered through. As distinct from the Battle of Britain we had enough pilots but could not obtain replacement aircraft and spares, though they seeped through occasionally. It was a war of improvisation at which the British troops excelled.

We suffered from long delays in news from home, the unknown territory and hot climate, plus being at the sharp end of frequent bombings, and the feeling of being forgotten. The one advantage was that one's squadron was completely self-contained, with an adjutant, padre and doctor, cooks, ground and maintenance crews and motor transport.

This is not a highly detailed history. Many names and sequences have been lost over the long period since the war, but it is an attempt to depict some personal experiences during World War II, particularly during the first Burma campaign.

I have therefore also included in the first chapter my beginnings in the squadron as a commanding officer.

Wing Commander C.A.C. Stone, DFC, RAF (retired)
1977

1 FROM SCOTLAND TO FREETOWN

We stood on the bridge of the *Durban Castle*, once a luxury passenger liner, now converted to a troopship – Frank Carey, Jimmy Elsdon and me. We were heading into a rising south-westerly gale. The ship started to pitch and roll in the increasing seas on our port quarter; the spume, whipping off the wave tops, stung our faces. We snuggled into the comparative warmth of our fur-collared flying jackets. It was bitterly cold. The date was 10 December 1941.

We had been two days out of Gourock in Scotland and were part of the largest convoy to sail to the Middle and Far East up to that time. The convoy stretched as far as the eye could see. The occasional glimpse of the huge bulk of the battleship *Ramilies* and some cruisers with attendant destroyers, sometimes disappearing in a welter of white foam, was reassuring. A Sunderland flying boat of Coastal Command droned overhead, appearing and disappearing, amongst the low, fast-moving, dark clouds. We envied the crew in their warm cockpits, and tried not to think of what might lie under the heaving seas beneath us. The Merchant Navy were the real heroes of this war, I thought.

I clapped Jimmy and Frank on the back and went below, throwing myself on my bunk. There were four of us to a single cabin; the ship was crammed with young subalterns and troops – reinforcements for the Middle East. We had only our pilots on board; our adjutants and administrative officers, together with the ground crews, travelled on different ships. Taking a swig at my nearly empty hipflask, I could not be bothered to join the "dole cue" at the bar, where one had to fight for a pint of beer. Ever since I had come on board I had felt numbed and unaware, as if enclosed in a free balloon pushed hither and thither between the earth and sky, with no control of time and space – a not unpleasant feeling of unreality which space travellers must experience at times. Now, with the whisky warming my belly, lulled by the increasing movement of the ship, the confused pieces of the jigsaw and the events of the last few months began to fall into place.

I little thought when I finally achieved my life's ambition in the RAF, of leading a fighter squadron, that it would turn out to be commanding one of the crack squadrons of the Royal Flying Corps – eventually the RAF. I had attained this childhood aspiration by being posted to command No. 17 Fighter Squadron, reforming at Elgin in Scotland at the beginning of August 1941 after serving in France and the Battle of Britain. This in itself was a good omen as, when I had joined No. 3 Fighter Squadron at Kenley (just south of Croydon) in 1938, No. 17 had been the other squadron also stationed there, together with 615 Auxiliary Squadron, which had Winston Churchill as Honorary Commodore. There was nothing funnier than to watch the great man, still with cigar, being pressed into the rear cockpit of a Hawker Demon after a good lunch at their mess. I took a photograph of this, but unfortunately lost it in my many wanderings.

Number 17 had just arrived from 11 Group in the south of England, under the command of Squadron Leader Count Czernin, a nephew of Dollfuss, the one-time premier of Austria. It was split into two squadrons. I, by good fortune, got No. 17 and Czernin the other. The latter was being worked up to send to Leningrad, where the suspicious Russians, who it seemed only wanted the Hurricanes, kept the pilots on the ground by the simple application of vodka – a useful deterrent to matters aeronautical. I learnt this later on meeting him in Assam after the retreat from Burma. When I took over 17 there was not a pilot I had known previously, but the ground crews had not changed much, one of whom was a certain flight sergeant known as "Chiefy" Guest – a large man of over 6 feet, and long experience of the service.

Number 13 Group at that time, beyond flying normal shipping patrols and being on readiness for immediate take-off, was engaged in training pilots, coming from Flying Training Schools based largely in Canada, who were to serve with fighter squadrons to replace the very serious shortage of pilots in the south. For this training we usually had a commanding officer, two flight commanders and two flying officers who were fully operational and had seen action against the enemy.

The poor trainees were usually given from five to ten hours only, on Hurricanes or Spitfires, before being hurled into the battle raging in the south. Contrary to general expectation, it took longer to train an efficient fighter pilot than any other type of airman due to the single-seater configuration; indeed, I was one of the lucky ones, being fully operational before the outbreak of war in 1939.

Casualties in 13 Group were high, and our main enemy was the weather, aided by the grim mountain peaks of the Highlands. Added to this, to appease the public, we had to carry out night readiness against the occasional Junkers 88s or Dorniers, which used to potter over from Norway and drop the odd bomb. If the Germans wished to annoy the Scots they certainly did, but perhaps not in the way intended, because our book, kept for abusive letters from the public, enlarged at an alarming rate.

When I was on night readiness, the troops, unaware of the thinness of the partition that separated us, used to take the mickey out of me. It also became a useful means of airing their grievances since, thank God, commanding officers and flight commanders no longer had the duty of censoring their letters – a duty we hated and which by now had been handed over to RAF Intelligence Officers. I was usually referred to in these conversations as "the ole man", or more often, "the effing ole man". This disturbed me somewhat, as I was only twenty-four, and sometimes I caught myself out, when shaving, searching the reflection in the mirror for grey hairs and other signs of general decay.

One of my pilots was a Czech, called Karl, who had managed to escape to England after the Nazi occupation. He was a good pilot, and a very likable character, aged eighteen. He greatly admired one of my dogs – a bastard bull terrier called Bleaker. Eventually, on his being posted to Duxford, I had not the heart to separate them, so Bleaker went with him. A month or two later I received a letter from a hospital in Cambridge which stated briefly: "I get shot down, I crash, I break my bloody head. Bleaker's head all right, and sends his love." What eventually happened to poor Karl I shall never know. I found, especially in flying, both in peace and war, that friendships are quickly formed and sometimes as quickly obliterated.

We were posted to a frightful aerodrome, and were the first and last squadron to occupy it. These aerodromes were apt to spring up all over eastern Scotland, and the "wise men" who built them at vast expense never appeared to consult the local farmers whose land they intended to use. One I remember was built on a marsh near Wick, so that the runway started to sink. Bearing this in mind, I drove down a day or two before the squadron was due to move in, and billeted myself on the local farmer, since I had, among other things, a wife to cart around – an added hazard in wartime – not, I hastily add, that I have any male chauvinists views about the opposite sex.

My host and his wife possessed the usual hospitality to be found in the Highlands, which they extended even towards a Sassenach from Devonshire. After an extremely fine dinner of roast beef, contrasting greatly by comparison with the ordinary wartime rations we were used to, I led the conversation around to the aerodrome. The result was indeed depressing, for he told me that this particular part of his land suffered in summer from dust storms and that the water for the field was taken from a rather contaminated loch just above a small village whose inhabitants, through the ages, had immune to the bacteria that thrived in it. He added rather drily: "For the likes of ye, t'will be guid whisky you will be wanting." The forecast of my friend proved to be only too true.

The next day on my arrival at the Station Headquarters I was met by the warrant officer in charge of the maintenance party, whose face bore an expression of stygian gloom, and, as we proceeded to his office, the few individuals we passed appeared to me not unlike those inmates I had imagined occupied that renowned establishment on Dartmoor, where in my youth my dear Mama had stopped for a while in her Morris Cowley to impress upon her son where "bad boys" inevitably ended.

When we arrived at the warrant officer's office, the WO, as if he felt some kind of welcome should be extended, suddenly said, "Like a cup of tea, sir?"

"Love one," I replied.

"Char, John," he bellowed, shaking the rather rickety structure in which we were sitting. Shimmers of golden dust in the shafts of the northern sunlight penetrating the dirty windows, rose from the many papers that covered his desk. A moment later a pale youth kicked the door open and arrived with two large white tin mugs relieved by surrealist patterns of black and red.

I noticed a change in the warrant officer's face, a certain sardonic twist of humour as he watched me raise the steaming purple liquid towards my lips – the same look I had often observed upon schoolmasters and others who used to beat me. Out of politeness I took a burning sip of this evil-smelling liquid, and fell into a fit of uncontrollable coughing. The WO opened his desk and produced a bottle of beer: "Try this, sir; never drink that there bleeding stuff – full of chlorine!"

After this he took me around the station. "Never mind, WO," I said. "The squadron will be here soon."

I think some strange metamorphosis must have taken place. He actually smiled, while my face must have shown my anxiety.

Shortly after we had settled in, I was on readiness one day with a gale-force wind blowing dust across the runway and reducing visibility to 10 yards. The telephone rang. I, by chance, answered it and a laconic voice from the Control Room in Inverness said: "Scramble. Bandit approaching at 25,000 feet."

"Not on your nelly!" I said. "I cannot see across the runway."

"What do you mean?" the voice said. "It's perfectly clear here."

"Well," I said, "I am not in Inverness," and put the receiver down.

I rang up the Air Officer Commanding, Air Vice Marshal Henderson, a very understanding man, much-loved by the squadron commanders, and explained the circumstances. What caused the greatest concern was that serviceability of aircraft was reducing at an accelerating rate, owing to worn pistons and valves, so I told our engineer officer to put in a requisition for desert filters. I do not think that such a request had been received before in the British Isles, for a day later the air vice marshal's personal assistant rang to inform me that Sir Archibald Sinclair, the then Minister for Air in Churchill's government, would be arriving for an inspection with the air vice marshal, the next morning.

I had met Sir Archibald on several occasions, official and socially, for at Wick, where we had been sent after being chewed up in France in early 1940, his two pretty daughters used to be much in evidence in the mess. I gathered that our aerodrome was his brainchild, so asked my adjutant, Crowthers, to smarten up our rather scruffy, bohemian bunch of desperados, for these excellent fellows, coming as they did from Australia, New Zealand, South Africa, Rhodesia. Canada, Texas, Poland, Czechoslovakia, Norway and even Britain, though highly disciplined in the air, were hardly of Cranwellian elegance on the ground.

The party arrived and, imitating the tactics of the warrant officer on my arrival, I took the party to the mess for a cup of tea – though served in cups and saucers. Sir Archibald drank the purple liquid, with every evidence of diplomatic enjoyment, before we set off on our tour. We eventually arrived at Flight Lieutenant Corkett's dispersal. It was cold, so we went into the flight hut.

Sir Archibald immediately engaged Corky in close conversation. I had already noticed several times in the past that the minister had the habit, when addressing one, of pushing his nose within a tenth of an inch of one's face. Poor Corky started to retreat slowly backwards across the full length of the crew room, towards the round red-hot stove at the far end. Air Vice Marshal Henderson looked a bit anxious, and Sir Archibald's private secretary, standing next to me, began shuffling. When Corky's bottom finally came into contact with the glowing stove top, he leapt into the air, and ended in a wild embrace in Sinclair's arms. I, having at the best of times little control over my emotions, let out a roar of laughter. Henderson tried to give me a frown, and the embarrassed private secretary stamped on my toes. The squadron was posted shortly after.

The last story I heard about Corky was when he was posted to Kenley in 11 Group. On his day off from operations he used to visit his family living nearby. He was sitting in front of the fire with his mother and two sisters, who were busily knitting balaclavas and socks for the troops. The air-raid alarm had gone and in the mounting noise and fury of the nightly Blitz on London, he heard the rising crescendo of an approaching stick of bombs. When the clicking of the needles could no longer be heard, his already taut nerves could stand it no longer, and he dived beneath the sofa. His mother peered underneath: "What on earth are you doing down there, Corky?"

Eventually, in November 1941, we ended up at Tain, and one morning I was called to Group Headquarters at Inverness to see the Air Officer Commanding. I flew in our communications aircraft – a de Havilland Hornet Moth – a beautiful little cabin biplane with an inverted Cirrus engine, and like most de Havilland aircraft, a sheer delight to fly, with no vices. Air Vice Marshal Henderson told me we were being posted abroad, he knew not where, and we were to report to Catterick in Yorkshire to convert onto Hurricane 2cs, equipped with four 20-millimetre cannons, desert filters, and with adaptions for non-jettisonable, long-range wing tanks. Furthermore, all my Czech, Norwegian and Polish pilots were to be left at home.

This was indeed a bitter blow, as they had proved to be some of my best aircrew, and when I gave them the news on my return, two of my Norwegians (who had escaped by fishing boat from Norway) broke down and wept. This, coming from such a tough Nordic race, amazed me at the time. I was left, however, with my two American sergeant pilots from Texas, who had crossed the border before America came into the war, and were accepted officially as Royal Canadian Air Force personnel. One, called "Tex" Barrick, proved an outstanding pilot. His companion Ken Wisrodt, was unfortunately shot down and captured later on. I was also lucky in getting a flight commander from that well-known fighter squadron, No. 43. He, an Australian, "Bush" Cotton (later DFC), was not only an outstanding pilot and administrator, but possessed that engaging direct wit and humour that so many from "down under" have.

My other flight commander was sound, but considered slightly old for fighters, being in his thirties, which is no reflection on him, but the average ages of a fighter pilot at that time ranged between eighteen and twenty, and I, who was approaching twenty-five, and Bush, at twenty-four, were both "pushing it a bit".

My memories of Catterick remain still depressing, coloured by my first flight in a Hurricane 2c. Weighed down with its long-range tanks, cannon and desert filters, it was very poor in performance. It seemed to me a quick form of suicide in any combat role. I quietly tried it out with two cannon removed but it seemed to make little difference.

I left most of the flying side to Bush. Organising for a complete re-equipment for overseas glued me to my desk. Besides other activities, I had an enormous waiting list of men endeavouring to get themselves off the draft. Cupid, all of a sudden, seemed to be working overtime. Some of the stories were indeed harrowing, and the help of my adjutant, an older man, was invaluable. In the end I could only let three men stay at home. In the middle of it all, my wife lost our expected offspring – twin daughters. The wife of Ken Hemingway, one of my senior flying officers, also lost her child after we had sailed; Flying Officer Hemingway had been a journalist and author in peacetime. During the war he wrote the first book on the Burma campaign, *Wings over Burma*. But with the thought of the courage of the people of London and other cities which were being heavily bombed at the time, our troubles, I suppose, were fairly small by comparison.

One day, Bush had stopped all flying, because the cloud was on the deck and visibility was down to 400 yards. Chatting on the tarmac, we suddenly heard the unmistakable crackle of a Merlin engine circling overhead, and we wondered what silly fool was flying around in that weather. The engine throttled back, and the ghostly form of a Spitfire loomed out of the mist to make a perfect landing. As the plane came to a halt, with the engine still ticking over, the pilot got out. Puzzled, Bush and I rushed over in my jeep. As we approached, Bush said, "Silly clot, bet it's one of your dopey pommy bastards."

"Wait, Bush", I replied. "Do you see what I see?" For a slight figure, dressed in a black flying suit, its back towards us, removed its helmet and, shaking out a mass of shoulder-length blond hair, obviously a girl, proceeded to stare into a small mirror and to fiddle with her face. As we drew up, she turned around; a smiling and beautiful face enquired: "Is this Catterick? I got slightly lost."

"Er, yes, it is," we said, with sails aback.

"Oh, good," she said.

There followed quite a party in the mess that night, with her holding her own with the rest of the pilots at the snooker table, and downing plenty of beer.

She, like many other women of the calibre of Amy Johnson, Amelia Earhart, Jean Mountbatten and others, had founded the trail of "women's lib" in the air in the late 1930s. On the outbreak of war they had joined the Royal Air Force Air Transport Auxiliary to ferry aircraft from the factories to the squadrons in the British Isles. They flew in all weathers, and every type of aircraft from Tiger Moths to four-engine bombers.

By an extraordinary coincidence, in 1947, when I landed at a small field in the middle of Africa on my way to the Cape in an Airspeed Auster, I saw a twin-engine Executive de Havilland Dove refuelling. Curious, I went over and there she was. "Good God, you! Disturbing the natives again I see," I said. She was the chief pilot of a large firm ferrying Executives and on her way to Johannesburg. She was still very feminine withal.

We were due to embark for overseas early in December at Gourock, still not knowing our destination. Rumour had it that we were also due to beat up German tanks in the Caucasus, which I think must have been true from reading Sir Winston Churchill's books on World War II. We spent the night in Glasgow and met our two fellow squadron commanders – No. 135, Frank Carey, DFC and two bars, DFM; and No. 136, Jimmy Elsdon, DFC – before embarking on the *Durban Castle*.

Frank I knew well, since he had joined us in No. 3 Squadron at Kenley after his promotion in No. 43 Squadron from sergeant pilot, DFM, to pilot officer, shortly before we were sent to France at the end of the "phoney" war. Short of stature (later in Burma-India to be known as *Chota* – Urdu for "Shorty"), with fair curly hair, a small moustache, and penetrating eyes, which were usually curled at the corners with humour, but which, if he was annoyed, took on the appearance of steel. He was a killer in the air, for he was a crack shot in his natural element, and wasted little ammunition. Even if outnumbered, he left a trail of wreckage behind him, sometimes to the consternation of his number two, if unused to his ways. He became one of our top scorers in World War II.

Jimmy Elsdon I had not met before, but I was to know him well later on. Rudely known as "Slug" Elsdon – I know not why – he was a man of almost square stature, with an enormous moustache which made one wonder how he ever encompassed it within an oxygen mask. I immediately nicknamed him "Marshal Budeonny", for he resembled that famous Russian general of earlier days. All I remember of that rather strange night, however, was our being introduced, by a friendly taxi driver, to all the lowest pubs in Glasgow, and being driven down the pavements, between unilluminated lamp standards, back to our hotel. The next morning we found ourselves aboard the *Durban Castle*, which, in happier days had transported so many great names to the Cape.

We man the twin Lewis guns on the bridge

I was disturbed from my reverie to face the night watch, a duty we had volunteered to carry out, on one of the two twin-Lewis guns – our only means of offence or defence on that large vessel – mounted on the wings of the bridge.

2 FREETOWN TO RANGOON

When we were only three days out of Gourock the Japanese bombed Pearl Harbour on 7 December and brought the United States into the war. This meant that Japan's ambitions towards the conquering of the Far East (already known to the Allies because of the cracking of the Japanese Navy code) meant that our destination was to be Rangoon, in Burma, and a state of emergency as far as getting the aircrew there was obviously declared. Thus our vessel was diverted to Freetown in Sierra Leone, and we anchored there on the day before Christmas while the rest of the convoy proceeded around the Cape.

Through the RAF grapevine we knew that "Killy" Kilmartin was stationed at the naval base HMS *Hastings*, which formed the reinforcement and assembly depot for naval aircraft supplying Gibraltar and the Middle East. Killy, by some means, also knew that we would be on the vessel. Both Frank and I knew him from days of old: a crazy Irishman with a DFC from the Battle of Britain. When resting his squadron in Scotland, he had committed some blue or other, and the authorities, not knowing what to do with such a hot potato, posted him to command the Hurricane flight at Freetown, to cool off, if one may use such an expression, since, lying near the equator, the damp heat never varies more than 7° Fahrenheit in the year at around the 100° mark. He was subsequently posted to the Middle East, where he again distinguished himself.

The anchor chains of the *Durban Castle* had barely rattled out when we saw a Hurricane appear low among the shipping. Having located us, it regaled us with a hair-raising display of low aerobatics, finally flying past about 10 feet beneath us. As we stood on the bridge, we gazed down on Killy's upturned grinning face. By now the captain was becoming rather agitated as to the safety of his ship, and Frank frantically signalled Killy with an Aldis lamp – "For God's sake piss off" – and he disappeared over the jungle-clad hills fringing the south of the estuary.

Half an hour later an, RAF launch arrived alongside with Killy aboard. After an hilarious lunch Killy wangled it for us and the flight commanders to go ashore. After lunch we said our goodbyes to the Old Man and the ship's officers, who had been very kind to us, and left for the rickety jetty, where an RAF lorry awaited us. We drove into the town in a cloud of red dust, passing dilapidated buildings with rusty corrugated-iron roofs, the corporal driving with his accelerator foot firmly pressed to the floorboards. One hand never left the wheel, which appeared to have no connection with the direction in which the bounding vehicle was travelling.

Our arrival at the centre of Freetown was memorable for the streets being jammed with a solid phalanx of laughing Africans, their teeth standing out white from their dark perspiring faces, their many-coloured garments forming a moving patchwork quilt against the dark interiors of the shops, where millions of flies buzzed and gorged on the meats, fish, fruits and the articles displayed. The damp heat congealed the different smells and stenches in layers. The well-accustomed driver in no way lessened his speed as we approached the crowd at frightening velocity. When mass slaughter seemed inevitable, they parted, only to close immediately in our wake.

Leaving the town, we climbed up through the jungle to the Royal Naval Air Service, HMS *Hastings*, where Killy's flight was stationed on the nearby aerodrome. That night we dined with the Air Officer Commanding on his veranda, set in a beautifully kept lawn, surrounded by the jungle beyond. The velvet darkness was lit by brilliant stars which looked as if they could be plucked from the night. The bullfrogs clicked and croaked and the fireflies danced, their bluish brilliance in contrast with the orange of the gas lamps which cast deep shadows on our companion's figures. It was memorable to us, so recently from the Northern climes. Conversation was muted, like a gentle tide advancing and retreating upon a pebble beach. It was there we learnt that we were to proceed to Rangoon via Khartoum, Cairo and India.

Next day we celebrated our Christmas lunch, held at the aerodrome and hosted by the Navy, who did us more than proud. It was interrupted by Killy being scrambled to intercept a Vichy French aircraft which had strayed into our territory. This he shot down, and then he rejoined us at the table to indulge in an even merrier celebration. We finished by cooling off with a bathe in a crystal-clear pool at the bottom of a small waterfall in a glade in the jungle, about 2 miles from the field.

Two days later we embarked in a Pan-American Dakota – that wonderful maid of all work, still flying in many parts of the world today – making for Takoradi near Lagos, the RAF assembly depot for single-seaters reinforcing the Middle East. We flew over mile after mile of low-lying steamy mangrove swamp: "A bloody awful place for a forced landing," I thought. There was no sign, on our arrival, of our Hurricane 2cs. I do not know what happened to them, but as events turned out, I was glad that we did not see them again. The next day we embarked again on an RAF Dakota and flew right across the heart of Africa, stopping for fuel and refreshments at Kano and Fort Lamy, to Khartoum, where we stayed the night before boarding a Canopus-class flying boat, the forerunner of the Sunderland, used throughout the war mainly for submarine search and destroy. The Canopus was, I think, the most comfortable passenger aircraft ever built.

We flew down the Nile at about 800 feet, and I was struck by the narrowness of the strip of cultivation which followed the bends and twists of the great river, in stark contrast with the desert beyond.

On arrival at Cairo, I telephoned my stepfather, who was in business there throughout the war. He recovered quickly from the shock of my sudden and unexpected appearance on the Cairo scene, and sent down his chauffeur to collect us. He put Frank and myself up in his very comfortable flat on Gezira Island, opposite the Gezira Club gates. The other pilots we managed to billet in various hotels in that noisy and crammed city. After a few days Frank, Jimmy and I, began to tire of the fleshpots. The Middle East HQ were not interested in the rapidly Rising Sun casting its shadows in the Far East. An expression I was often to hear in Cairo was; "Oh, the Japs; they cannot fly and are blind anyway – they all wear glasses !" – comforting at the time, but how mistaken! We began increasingly to think of what might lie in store for us. With no aircraft obtainable, we extracted permission to proceed on our way, each accompanied by a flight commander. Frank took Jimmy Broughton, DFC; I cannot remember Jimmy's, I think it was Barry Sutton; but I took Bush Cotton – leaving Carvel and the other pilots to try and obtain some aircraft from the Middle East HQ.

We took off once more in our flying boat, and landed at breakfast-time on the Sea of Galilee. The flying boat rocked gently on the turquoise waters of the lake, while the RAF refuelling tender went about its business. I gazed at the nearby shore, where the residents of a bright, white hotel, its green lawns extending to the shallows, sat indolently breakfasting under coloured canopies. Behind the hotel the ground rose through olive and orange groves, revealing white and pink stucco buildings. At that moment, war had not touched this place. On the other side, however, purple-grey mountains, ridged and forbidding, cast dark craggy shadows to the east.

That night we landed on the yellow waters of the Tigris at Baghdad. The hotel where we spent the night was stifling. The airconditioning had long been turned off, and I could not sleep. My thoughts turned to my father's bones far south, rotting somewhere in the banks of the river Hi below Kut, where he was killed, along with more than 1,000 others, in February 1917, when serving with the 45th Rattray Sikhs in General Maude's offensive. "What a bloody silly war that was," I thought.

The next morning we took off at dawn for Karachi, following that dreadful coastline of southern Arabia for mile upon mile without a sign of fresh water or habitation.

I remarked to Frank: "How did Alexander the Great ever manage to march his armies across it?"

Frank replied, "Our bloody engines seem all right. Stop flapping, Bunny," and drifted off to sleep again.

At Karachi, we were taken aback by the attitude of civil and service officials, which was a foretaste of the general lack of awareness that was to be found almost throughout the whole of the Far East at that time, and this *laissez-aller* was to continue until the arrival of Lord Louis Mountbatten and General Orde Wingate in 1943. We were eventually billeted in tents on the Air Force aerodrome, while Delhi endeavoured to find out who we were and what we were supposed to be doing. The old adage "How did Britain ever win a war?" loomed large in our conversations. Finally we received instructions to proceed to Rangoon by flying boat. With no aircraft available, as far as I knew, I left Bush and Hemingway behind to find some Hurricanes, sort out the muddle, and locate some of our pilots still supposedly in Cairo.

We descended upon the smelly waters of the Hooghly River at Calcutta. Next morning, having picked up a character called Wing Commander "Penny" Leigh, a former bomber pilot, we just managed to make the dawn take-off. Dark-haired and tall, he possessed a moustache comparable to Jimmy Elsdon's; thus, only the difference in stature could distinguish them from the rear view. Poor Penny was destined for a macabre death when, much later in the Arakan, after the fall of Burma, he commanded a Blenheim squadron. He force-landed after a raid, with a dead engine, in a glade by a so-called friendly village. He was extracted from the cockpit and cut up, alive, with pangas wielded by the furious natives, who obviously mistook him for a Japanese.

We took the coastal route, with the dense, tree-covered Arakan Yomas mountain range appearing blue in the distance to the north. Arriving at Rangoon and losing height, we passed over Mingaladon, the air base for the protection of the city, about 4 miles north, at a suburb called Insein (pronounced "Insane") – quite appropriately named as it turned out. The aerodrome presented a dismal aspect, with aircraft hangers looking like skeletons, burnt-out buildings and one or two fighter aircraft on the ground.

The pilot landed just south of the city, where the river was massed with shipping. An RAF tender put out from a small jetty on the west bank. As soon as we had transferred to the craft, the pilot of our flying boat turned around immediately and took off. We understood his haste, for at the jetty the air-raid warning sirens greeted us. The sergeant from Group HQ who had been sent to meet us looked at his watch: "Always on bleeding time them ruddy Nips, hevery day. 'Tokyo Express' we calls it. Ye're all right 'ere; 'aven't touched the place since Christmas. Hallways the drome, poor sods".

Encouraged by these words, we boarded an ancient 3-tonner, and bounced to a halt outside some forbidding gates. "You har to spend the night 'ere – them's my horders", upon which, we having disembarked with our parachute bags filled with all our worldly goods, he bumped of in a cloud of orange dust, never to be seen again.

Our residence turned out to be the local gaol – my first and only acquaintance, so far, with such a place. The morning after our arrival in Rangoon the welcome figure of my adjutant, Crowthers, appeared in a "Jeep". I was too overjoyed to enquire how he had found me in gaol.

I have never heard much said about these men, civilian adjutants, but I know that in the trying days ahead, I could not have managed without him. He was a tall man, with a wide-open face that immediately inspired trust among men and officers alike. In peacetime he worked in a London bank. When the Germans turned to the night bombing of London, commonly known as the Blitz, he immediately volunteered for the Auxiliary Fire Service, and must have witnessed the horrors of that time. He could not have had much sleep between that and his work at the bank. Being a man of about thirty-five, he proved a moderating influence on us much younger and hot-spirited fellows. Eventually he joined the RAF, took a short course in administration, and was posted to us with the rank of acting flight lieutenant. There were many like him, but he was outstanding. Later on in the war he was to receive the OBE.

As we drove to Headquarters to meet the Air Officer Commanding, I said, "How are things, Adjutant?"

"All right, sir. We have more or less settled in at Mingaladon and only two men deserted in Durban [a record for those days]. Of course, no aeroplanes, sir; I think they were sent to Singapore, and the pack-ups have not arrived [pack-ups contained all of our requirements for servicing aircraft]. I thought it better to disperse the men as far as possible, as the Japs bomb the aerodrome every day at about 11 o'clock. Just before we arrived, they mounted a large raid on Christmas Day on the aerodrome and Rangoon. Most of the dock area was badly hit. There were many casualties, so most of the Burmese labour evacuated the city, resulting in delay at the docks. From then on, they have entirely concentrated on the aerodrome. By the way, sir, I should be careful with Group."

I enquired after fighter defence and was informed that there was a squadron of the American Volunteer Group, the Flying Tigers; three of their squadrons were based at Chunking under General Clair Chennault, and one of these had been sent to Rangoon. There was also a flight of outdated Brewster Buffaloes, commanded by Flight Lieutenant Pymke, DFC, a former Battle of Britain pilot.

In due course, a Blenheim squadron, No. 27, arrived with some very tired Blenheims (a twin-engine light bomber) from the Middle East, where they had been due for a rest and refit. I must say, they did grand work under the circumstances, and their aircraft suffered from constant engine failures.

We arrived at Group, located in the untouched part of the city, in the one-time thriving European business-community area. The Air Officer Commanding, a bland individual who had commanded a light-bomber group in the UK during the invasion scare, we immediately nick-named "Old Boy", for he always addressed us in this manner. After No. 27 squadron arrived, which had at one time served under him in Bomber Command in the UK, he was also known to them as "the Butcher". We must have taken an instant dislike to each other, much to my later disadvantage, I having ignored the old Air Force saying, "You cannot fart against thunder."

Frank was posted to a field further north at Zigon, and Jimmy and I to Mingaladon, where our troops and ground staff awaited us. We were told to report to the fighter commander, a Group Captain "Seton" Broughall (afterwards always referred to as Seton). The adjutant drove us through the suburbs of Insein, which, incidentally, housed the local lunatic asylum, to the aerodrome at Mingaladon. The jeep drew up outside a bombed-out hanger. There were a few offices, showing the scars of recent bombing, on which was posted an informative but rather unprofessionally painted sign announcing "Fighter H.Q."

The adjutant said: "I'll just go and see if the group captain is there, sir".

A moment later he returned to say that the group captain was ready to meet us. The three of us followed him down a corridor, jumping over various holes in the floorboards, until we came to a door marked "C.O." Beyond the door, there was an open jagged wall which provided the simplest means of entry, so, stepping over a threshold we entered and saluted smartly. A figure bent over a desk at the far end, his group captain's hat lying on the table – he leaned back in his chair and said, in an unmistakeable Canadian accent: "Say, haven't you guys learned any manners? Come in through the proper door in the accepted way."

Beating a hasty retreat, we entered through the door and saluted again. By then the figure had stood up, a short stocky man in a sweaty shirt and shorts, with greying and diminishing hair, and bearing a marked resemblance to W.C. Fields. He burst out laughing, and extended a hand: "Nice to meet you guys; was wondering when someone would turn up. Goddamn shambles round here."

So we met Seton, who stayed with us to near the end; unforgettable, he was always ready with a wisecrack for the most difficult circumstance. He proved a useful cushion against the absurdities dealt out from time to time from the comfortably ensconced establishment in Rangoon. He had joined up in the Royal Flying Corps in World War I as a young man; obtained five confirmed victories on Sopwith Camels, before being shot down and taken prisoner. On his release in 1918 he had volunteered to fight with the RAF detachment operating with the White Russians against the Reds, and had remained with the RAF thereafter.

Frank went off to Zigon, where his men were waiting, and Seton left Jimmy and I to make our own arrangements, although officially Jimmy never received any aircraft at all. At that time, I happened to be the senior squadron commander. Later on, Frank was promoted to wing commander flying, on Seton's small staff, and Barry Sutton, DFC, took over 135 Squadron.

My adjutant had done much in the short time since disembarkation. The aerodrome possessed a main runway, running from west to east into the prevailing wind, which seldom had to be taken into account. Another, smaller runway led north-north-west from about the centre, to end up among trees to the north, where the American Volunteer Group were dispersed. The Buffaloes had their dispersal at the western end of the main runway. Our dispersal, and that of the Blenheim bombers, was to be down at the eastern end, where the aerodrome rose into a serrated escarpment. The watch office lay beyond us.

Aerodrome anti-aircraft armament consisted of about six Bofors guns and a few Lewis guns, manned by an assortment of Indians and volunteer Burmese, who with oriental logic, took cover when anything was happening, only to re-emerge after the all clear, sometimes to practise shooting on us as we came into land. Since their aim was not very accurate, no one suffered much from their presence.

Behind our dispersal there was a small *basha* (woven reed) hut which we used as a daytime mess for the pilots and officers on duty. During the day all necessary sections, such as motor transport, armoury and wireless, were dispersed for anything up to 3 miles from the field itself, and only essential personnel and aircraft were kept on the aerodrome.

The adjutant had already found permanent sleeping quarters for the officers, sergeants and men in Insein, grouped around a Roman Catholic nunnery. The sisters were for the most part American, and the novices Burmese. It had been decided to close the mission, since the violent Japanese bombing around Christmas 1941 had resulted in the disappearance of most of the novices. Hence on my arrival, only the mother superior remained, a dear old American lady from Virginia. Adjutant eventually managed to obtain a passage for her to America, and she bequeathed the sister's quarters to us for our officers' mess. It consisted of verandahed quarters, with sparsely furnished but comfortable cubicles surrounding a well-kept lawn. The main refectory was turned into a dining room-cum-bar, and after a hard, hot day of intense activity it was to prove a haven of relaxation spent mostly on the lawn, beneath the stars of the warm tropical nights, with the fireflies twinkling among the veranda pillars. After the old lady had left, I was given the mother superior's room, with its own shower.

My first experience of the almost daily visit of the Tokyo Express happened the day after my arrival. Although we suffered so many of these visitations, they scared the daylights out of me. I never got used to them. The troops, I noticed, treated them with far more indifference than we pilots.

The next day, the adjutant and I were settling into an office next to Seton's, when off went the wail of sirens. The American Volunteer Group and the Buffaloes were already taking off. About fifteen minutes later, we heard the drone of many aircraft approaching from the south east. Soon, high up at about 20,000 feet, we could distinguish the glinting silver against the dark-blue sky – two large "vics" (vee shapes) of about twenty-four aircraft, in perfect formation, followed by what seemed to be a cloud of cavorting gnats. The latter was the Japanese fighter escort, who seemingly never took up any battle formation.

Seconds later I heard the crescendo of diving aircraft, and the deep throated bark of the American Volunteer Group's 0.5-calibre machine-guns, against which one could pick out the staccato return fire of the lighter Japanese machine-guns. At that height, we on the ground were unable to see what was going on, except for an occasional orange-centred black trail of a burning aircraft, or dark mushroom against the blue of the sky as another fell victim to the fighters. Soon I heard a new noise, like the flutter of grouse wings, approaching the gun butts, growing even louder, and then with a thunderous roar, the aerodrome and its surroundings were obliterated in violent bursts of flame and orange dust. A strange silence followed, interrupted by the crackling of burning buildings or huts.

The black smoke rose into the calm sky. The kite hawks, our constant companions, as if by instinct, disappeared before these occasions, returning as soon as the all clear sounded to see what goodies might be left for them. The Japanese followed the American method of pattern bombing; that is, letting all their bombs go at the same time as their leader. This differed from the German method of stick bombing, which I had experienced to some extent in France in 1940. I found the pattern method particularly unnerving, as one could never tell where the beastly things were likely to land. In stick bombing, one could hear an approaching line of bombs, one after another. The fluttering noise was caused, I think, by badly made bombs, as the German bombs had a distinct whistle.

"That was nasty, Adjutant."

"You soon get used to it; it's the anti-personnel bombs that are the worst."

He took me into the adjacent hangar ruins, and showed me a series of pockmarks all around the crumbling, corrugated-iron concrete, literally flush with the cratered floor.

"Christ! Got to keep your arse down I see." I was still feeling shaken.

As soon as possible, I went round to see the American Volunteer Group, and inquired of one of the reclining forms, cigar in mouth and Coke bottle in hand (which made me feel that I had strayed onto the set of a Western), if I could see the commanding officer.

"Spect so … The name's Newkirk … somewhere over there, I reckon," he said, waving an arm in no particular direction. I wandered around, and finally stumbled upon Newkirk. He immediately put me at my ease, for by then I felt like a new boy turning up on his first day at boarding school. I knew that these men were seasoned veterans who had been fighting the Japanese for some time. He was tall, good-looking, fair, and blue eyed, with a quiet drawl, and was obviously a born leader – no side or bullshit about him. Also, he was polite, which was unusual because, at that time, the British and Americans did not altogether see eye to eye.

A moment later, the air-raid alarm sounded again. "Sorry," he said. "Come around and see me at our mess this evening."

He and the reclining figures, chucking away cigars, stamping out cigarettes and galvanised into action, had their P40s – with their evil-looking snouts painted with the eyes and the bared teeth of sharks – off the ground in under two minutes.

The American Volunteer Group messed in an evacuated colonial villa, 3 miles from the aerodrome. That evening I went around, and Newkirk introduced me to his colourful bunch, dressed in check shirts, some in high boots, with the inevitable slung cartridge-belts and a holstered Colt .45. They were largely former US Marine Corps pilots, with an average of 800 to 1,000 hours – as compared with our boys, with 250 to 300 hours, most of whom had never seen any action. Except for Frank and Jimmy, Barry Sutton, Bush and me, few of our pilots were experienced. Newkirk was extremely helpful. He was at the time the leading scorer in the American Volunteer Group, with about twenty-five confirmed victories to his credit, with more to come, until, much to my sorrow, he was later shot down and killed.

The American Volunteer Group had a superb and flexible command structure for the entirely different, almost guerilla-war conditions obtaining at that time. There were two commanders, General Chennault, with overall strategic command, in Chungking, and General "Pappy" Greenlaw, in charge of maintenance and supply. Pappy I later knew well, but I never came into contact with Chennault. For major maintenance, Pappy had instituted a factory at Loiwing, on the Yunnan border, about 500 to 600 miles north of Rangoon, with mainly Chinese labour, the whole outfit being known as CAM Co (Chinese American Maintenance Company).

Each evening the local squadron commander got in touch with Chungking by radio and delivered his daily operational report – enemy aircraft shot down, casualties, aircraft nonoperational, and so forth. Any strategic movements were delivered by Chennault. The fighter squadron commanding officer had no responsibility towards our own, in my opinion, cumbersome structure in Rangoon, where my reports would have to go through numerous hands before reaching the air commander.

The American Volunteer Group had a distinct advantage in that they mounted 0.5-calibre (half-inch) machine-guns, which gave a much greater punch than our .303s. When hit, their unarmoured opponents usually disintegrated. Newkirk warned me, however, not to mix it with the Japanese fighters, which were highly manoeuvrable, but to engage from a higher altitude and dive through them, a reversal of our tactics in Britain with the Hurricane and the Messerschmidt 109s, which we could out-turn and shoot down if they stayed with us, a mistake I was to make shortly afterwards, as will be seen.

Their principal opponents were at that time the Nakajima fighter (with a fixed undercarriage), the twin-engine Mitsubishi medium bomber – not unlike the German Heinkel and Dornier bombers – and a single-engine light two-seater bomber which we called Army Reconnaissance, or "Recces". With our two-stage superchargers in the Hurricanes, we were much more efficient at higher altitudes of around 15,000 feet than lower down. On the whole, the Japanese Army Air Force in Burma made unimaginative use of their superiority in numbers, compared with their naval service in the Pacific.

My visit to Newkirk provided much advance knowledge and food for thought, so, in return, since he had told me he was short of efficient ground crews, I offered him some of mine. There was no shortage of volunteers, because they were given American rations, and "never had it so good". The American Volunteer Group were mercenaries at that time. They were highly paid, and in addition received a bonus of $500 in gold for every enemy aircraft claimed. This was paid by the Generalissimo Chiang Kai-shek, who employed them. I knew of one Texan who bought a huge ranch back in Texas from his proceeds. Whether he lived to ride over his hard-won acres I shall never know. When my two Americans, Tex Barrick and Ken Wisrodt, arrived, they spent a lot of time in the American Volunteer Group mess, which helped overall relations considerably; previously, the American Volunteer Group had kept to themselves.

As bombing day followed bombing day, our frustrations increased as we watched the Americans and Buffaloes taking off. Added to this, loud and accusing noises came over the telephone from Frank as he, equally impotent, watched the battles raging overhead. Our eyes became glued to the western horizon, hoping for some sign of rescue for us from such an ignominious situation.

On 23 January we distinguished three Hurricanes, led by a Blenheim, trundling over the treetops. Jimmy Penny, who was by now our station commander, and I, with our few visible troops around us, burst into a storm of emotional enthusiasm. The witching hour for us had begun.

3 HURRICANES JOIN THE BATTLE FOR BURMA

I cannot remember who were the first pilots to arrive, as from then on they arrived in dribs and drabs from day to day. We never put more than ten aircraft in the air at any one time. Contrary to Churchill's remarks in Parliament, likening the battle over Rangoon to the Battle of Britain; it was, in fact, a complete reversal. We possessed too many pilots and not enough aircraft, removed as we were by thousands of miles from factories and proper maintenance facilities.

It often passed through my mind that with just thirty-six Gloucester Gladiators, now rotting in England, with the Hurricanes we eventually possessed and with the help of the American Volunteer Group, we could not only have shot the Japanese out of the skies, but also helped 17 Indian Division, where cooperation with the Army was virtually nonexistent on both sides. The Army and the Air Force appeared to be fighting different wars.

The three Hurricanes which arrived that day, however, turned out to be model 2bs, with twelve machine-guns, and fitted with long-range tanks which could not be jettisoned in flight. As they were refuelling, the usual air-raid alarm sounded, and Jimmy, Penny and I took off, with me leading. Shortly after, the American Volunteer Group and Buffaloes were airborne. Climbing to the west to gain height, since the enemy invariably came from their big base in Bangkok to the south-east, I found that at full boost we could only make about 1,000 feet a minute, less than half the usual rate of climb. The aircraft felt like lead in my hands. On reaching 10,000 feet, we turned back over the Irrawaddy estuary, to find the aerodrome smoking beneath us. The Japanese had come and gone.

When I landed I told the armourers to remove four of the Browning guns from the aircraft, and drove over to see Seton. I told him what had happened and asked if I could have the long-range tanks removed. He immediately rang Group, and after a long conversation with the Air Officer Commanding, he replaced the receiver.

"Sorry, Bunny, the old bastard said 'no dice' on any account; guess you'll have to get shot down before he changes his mind," and he burst into laughter.

This is exactly what happened, for the very next day Jimmy, Penny and I, struggling for height (although the rate of climb was slightly faster), were attacked from the sun by about twelve Japanese fighters at 15,000 feet. Jimmy and Penny summed up the situation and dived, for the Hurricane could dive much faster than the Japanese. For some reason – certainly not bravery, and contrary to Newkirk's warning, and my own experience – I decided to have a go. I probably lost my temper – dangerous on the ground, but usually fatal in the air.

The Japanese were delighted. Their first burst took the bottom out of my starboard long-range tank – luckily there were no tracer bullets. Another, approaching at three-quarters head on, at more than full deflection, took away

On my first encounter with the Japanese, I did not even fire my guns. The aircraft was finally cannabalised and blown up. Jimmy and Penny wisely dived away

my starboard aileron, allowing me to move only the rudder and port aileron. I could not manage to even get my sights on them, and boy, could they shoot. With bullets twanging into the aircraft, and clanging on the armour plate behind me, for an instant I panicked, when a little heaven-sent voice said, "Try the sun."

I climbed up straight into its brilliance, and for a brief moment my tormentors lost me, enabling me to do a stall turn to port, for I dared not spin, and I dived straight down at high speed to the estuary, among the shipping, leaving a long white trail of petrol vapour behind me. I landed like a distressed crab on the runway. What an aeroplane! More like a flying brick! As I switched off the engine, my final humiliation lay in my viewing the back of my A Flight sergeant, "Tug" Williams. On approaching me, he had observed that the canvas covers were still intact over the gunports in the wings, and the aircraft was holed like a sieve. He turned on his heel and walked away. It was indeed a very small rabbit that climbed out of that machine.

Seton, however, managed to get a reluctant Old Boy to examine the result, and our long-range tanks were removed.

That night, with much ribbing from my companions in the mess, we heard the dulcet tones of Tokyo Rose (the Japanese equivalent to Lord Haw Haw at home, and Lili Marlene in the Middle East) announce my demise. This incidentally proved somewhat embarrassing later when I met people I had known.

"Christ, you old bastard, thought you had bought it long ago."

The next day, however, some more Hurricanes had arrived, and we got our own back. Jimmy and I were in a more cheerful mood, as we had lost our long-range tanks. It was only three days since the first Hurricanes arrived, another three having landed the day after. We had four serviceable that day, and we took over readiness at dawn, with Jimmy and two of his pilots. I was to lead. As the sun rose, dispersing the morning mist, the sticky heat increased. The desultory conversations ceased, and we dozed in the long chairs surrounding our tented dispersal, each wrapped in his own thoughts.

We suddenly stiffened as the telephone rang in the bowels of the tent, and the operator shouted: "Scramble! Thirty-plus bandits approaching from the east."

The whole aerodrome coughed into life as we dashed for our aircraft a few yards away. My usual tension dropped away as I clambered up the side of my aircraft, the engine already running. My fitter, having started it, made way for me and helped me with my harness. Finally, clapping me on the back, he shouted, "Good luck, sir," and disappeared.

"They are a good bunch," I thought. I waved the chocks away, and taxied onto the concrete runway through clouds of orange dust ... the usual mad take-off, with aircraft appearing in all directions, some with their wheels already tucking up. To a newcomer straight from England, it must have appeared a spectacular way of committing suicide. For quicker take-off, we had arranged with the American Volunteer Group that they would climb immediately after take-off, and we would keep low as they crossed over us; we and the Buffaloes would each keep to opposite sides of the main runway.

The four of us made for height at full boost. At 15,000 feet I eased back on the throttle and started to sweep round towards the Sittang river in the east, up sun, and put the flight into battle formation, loosely echeloned up to starboard. It was one of those beautiful clear days with small bunches of snow-white cumulus clouds casting purple shadows on the yellow-grey paddy fields below, with the dark-blue waters of the Gulf of Martaban stretching to the light-blue sky on our right. It was good to be alive.

After ten minutes flying I spotted some dark specks ahead and below, and warned the others by radio. Increasing speed, I hastily switched on the reflector gun sight, turned the gun button to "Fire", pulled the booster plug and adjusted the pitch control. The specks quickly materialised into a tight vic formation of seven Mitsubishi twin-engine bombers, their red roundels standing out from the camouflage of their wings. We were in a perfect position for an attack, stepped up into the sun, and 1,500 feet above our quarry. I was somewhat puzzled, because I could not see any fighter escort; I put my thumb up against the sun to ensure that there were no fighters lurking above. I found out later that the American Volunteer Group were engaging them.

I yelled over the radio, "Going in *now*! Will take the far one." This tactic enabled us to arrive more or less together, confusing the rear gunners. I moved over into a dive, every faculty tensed and intent upon one thing; as I arrived at about 200 yards, I opened fire. The pungent and pleasurable smell of burnt cordite filled the cockpit. I felt a slight arrest of progress caused by 160 rounds a second speeding away. Now, nearly line astern, I altered my deflection and opened fire again, as I heard a clatter behind me. Red tracer-bullet smoke flashed past my starboard wing. Thinking that a Japanese fighter was on my tail, I broke violently up into the sun, with gravity pulling at my lower eyelids and cheeks. I just had time to see a Buffalo from 67 Squadron, which had appeared from nowhere, pulling away as the Japanese blew up in a shower of sparks and a mushroom of black oily smoke. Two others were falling, and another had smoke trailing astern.

Seven Mitsubishi bombers are shot down by 17 and 67 squadrons while attacking Mingaladon

This left three Japanese bombers, still in close formation, heading for the aerodrome. I could not help admiring the discipline of our opponents who, as one of their comrades fell, merely closed up on their leader to fill the gap, pushing on towards the field, now almost within bombing distance.

Finding myself alone, I attacked again, taking the bomber nearest to me. After I knocked chunks off him, he started to turn away, tilting on his port wing. I turned my attention to the leader, whose rear gunner I could see firing at me. I realised I was closing far too quickly in my excitement, and just managed to slither past him to be confronted by a Japanese 97 fighter, coming at me head on.

We both fired at each other and missed. I distinctly remember wondering, as we approached each other, whether the Japanese knew the rules of the air, so decided to carry straight on. The Japanese pulled up over my head as we reached each other at about 500 miles an hour. We continued this incongruous joust until all our ammunition had gone. As he turned away for home, and a drink of saki, I flew up alongside and made a rude two-fingered gesture, which he returned likewise, to my astonishment. "At least some of the Japs have a sense of humour," I thought, as I flew back over several funeral pyres littering the earth below, with dark columns of smoke rising vertically in the still air.

The score was seven fighters shot down by the American Volunteer Group, with the loss of one aircraft, and seven twin-engine bombers downed by the British. This action must have disturbed the Japanese high command; for some time the Tokyo Express ceased, and they resorted to only the occasional fighter sweep.

My aircraft appeared undamaged compared with the day before; it even brought a smile to Tug Williams' face. Upon closer examination, however, my fitter found a bullet had passed right through one of the blades of my propeller. It hit absolutely square on the thin leading edge, passing through to leave a small hole in the trailing edge – a chance in a million – and must have come from the rear gunner whom I had killed. Luckily, the propellor taken from the aircraft the day before – which had been so badly damaged that it had to be cannibalised – replaced it.

Without our pack-ups, and replacements being hard to come by, we resorted to this method of obtaining spare parts early on. Adjutant and my engineering officer had told me that the railway workshop was nearby, and together we visited the engineer in charge, who readily agreed to do anything he could to help. Without the use of his heavy equipment, I do not think we could have kept an aeroplane in the air. The Japanese never bombed the workshop, no doubt not wishing to destroy what they so confidently felt they were about to shortly acquire.

The Japanese increased their bombing by night, but only came over in moonlight. One night we had lost a Blenheim and a Hurricane on the ground, so Group decided that all aircraft should be dispersed at nightfall and brought back to the aerodrome at dawn. The American Volunteer Group gladly fell in with this suggestion. To the north of our drome a series of paddy strips had been constructed by a Scots tea-planter, who at one time had been a pilot during World War I in the Royal Flying Corps. In his honour, these strips had been nicknamed after various brands of Scotch whisky – John Haig, Highland Queen and Johnny Walker.

The bunds, which retained the water when the rice was growing, had been removed, but the strips were very rough. I do not think that Spitfires, with their lighter undercarriages, could have used them, but we had no trouble with the Hurricanes and the P40s. Even the Blenheim bombers suffered from broken tail wheels. Maintenance parties, mainly from Jimmy's squadron, were placed on the strips, for it had early been discovered that the aircraft petrol tanks had to be topped up before nightfall in the tropics, otherwise the water condensation which occurred resulted in engines cutting out on take-off.

We, and the American Volunteer Group, used John Haig, about 40 miles north, and the Blenheims used Highland Queen, to the north east. The only disadvantage was that after a tiring day, we had an hour's dusty drive back to the mess and, in the mornings, we had to get up before dawn to drive back in the mist, missing bullock carts and Indians by inches, as they started to evacuate the city in increasing numbers.

Towards the end of this time I had a painful experience when we came across an old Indian standing in the middle of the road while, nearby, his family sat on their worldly goods in an old cart, pulled by two half-starved bullocks. I stopped the jeep, and the old man came up with his hands raised in supplication.

"Sahib, sahib, please help me; we shall all be killed."

He pointed to the trees by the roadside, where I could vaguely see, through the mist, Burmese lurking around with pangas (bush knives). There was nothing I could do other than to tell the boys with me to spray both sides of the road with Tommy guns as we proceeded down the road. Thousands of Indians were murdered, or died of cholera, in the retreat. It took me back to those early days in 1940, when the roads beneath us were crammed with French peasants retreating before the Germans. This surely is the ultimate folly of war – it still makes me sick to think of it.

The night bombing started to build up, and I asked Newkirk if he had considered attacking the night bombers. He told me that they had, earlier on, using car headlamps to light the runway, but he had lost two aircraft in the ensuing landings. I thought we had a slight edge on the American Volunteer Group here, as most of our more experienced pilots had flown under blackout conditions and foul weather at night in the UK, long before ground-control radar interception was brought in.

Jimmy and I discussed it with Seton and he received permission from Group to try, provided we used only one glim lamp placed in the centre of the runway for take-off and landing. At the next period of the full moon, the Japanese turned on their usual nightly display for everyone's entertainment, as we used to watch the fireworks in comfort from our mess lawn. We decided to have a go the following night. Jimmy was to patrol up to 20,000 feet, with me above and beyond.

As all the other aircraft took off for their nightly dispersal, we two were left. Night fell quickly. We felt strangely alone with just the subdued voices of our ground crews and the croaking of the frogs, while the almost-full moon rose to light the runway, pale against the dark silhouetted trees, and glinted on the two Hurricanes, their wings casting dark shadows beneath them. I looked at them

17 Squadron Mess at Insein, in the old American mission. Drinking on the lawn while the Japanese carry out their usual on the aerodrome

with affection. I had spent more than 500 hours of my young life in these grand machines – ever since I had been a pilot officer in No. 3 Squadron at Kenley before the war, for we were the second squadron to be equipped with them. Slow compared with the Spitfire, but extremely rugged, a steady gun platform, with a splendid view from the high cockpit, it was a lovely aeroplane to fly. Hawker's had always produced good aeroplanes, the finest perhaps being the Fury biplane, as near-perfect a flying machine as a pilot could wish for.

We turned in early, for we were tired, using our parachutes as pillows. We were soon asleep, and it seemed but a moment before the air-raid sirens started. We took off together, and then split up. I circled south and south-east of the field at full boost, clambering for height. The city stood out quite clearly, with the great Schwe Dagong pagoda dully gold, the shipping quite visible in the estuary, and the Irrawaddy, with its twists and bends, looking like a silver reptile beneath. The Japanese command must have possessed an almost paranoid hatred for us, which was in its way flattering, as there were so many targets for them to spend their energies on instead of just our aerodrome.

At 25,000 feet, I flattened out. It was cold at that height, since I had to open the canopy for better visibility. We had no night-flying deflector plates to cover the bright red and blue lights from the exhausts, which made forward vision difficult. After about 20 minutes, away to my port side, I saw the flashes of

The Buddhist Schwe Dagong pagoda at Rangoon. Covered entirely in gold leaf, it made a splendid navigation landmark for fliers – including the Japanese

bombs sparkle across the field, whose runways were quite visible in the moonlight. From their pattern, I guessed that the bombers had circled and attacked from the north-east, and would now be on their way home.

I adjusted the reflector sight and turned the gun button onto "Fire" on the spade grip on the joystick. I looked until my eyes were streaming. I suddenly saw what appeared to be a shooting star on my port quarter; on investigation, it appeared more orange-coloured, and was crossing slightly beneath the horizon below me.

"Those are the bastards," I thought, and went into a shallow dive.

On closing I could make out eight distinct red lights from exhausts. I thought they must be two twin-engine Mitsubishis in close formation. The rear gunner of the starboard aircraft spotted me and opened fire. Blue tracer curled towards me. I gave the source of light a burst, and it stopped. Getting closer, I opened up on the twin exhausts of the starboard engine of the port aircraft, hoping to get the two of them in one burst.

Semi-blinded by my own tracer and exhausts, I saw this aircraft flick over to port into a steep dive, so following him vertically I gave him a long burst until he finally exploded into flame, throwing off an exciting display of fireworks, to crash in an orange glow by a bend in the Irrawaddy. I climbed back to try to find his partner, but, seeing nothing, flew back and landed, feeling rather chuffed with myself. When I was getting out of the cockpit, however, there was a furious

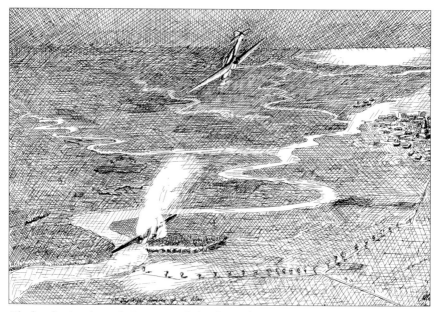

The first shooting-down of a Japanese night bomber in the Burma campaign

Jimmy, with moustache quivering. Using one of Seton's expressions, I said, "What in the fuck's up, Jimmy".

"You silly bastard, you nearly shot me down".

Apparently Jimmy had spotted them at the same time when at 19,000 feet, and was about to open fire when my first burst at the rear gunner passed closely over his starboard wing, which must have been upsetting to say the least of it, and, moreover, I was in his patrol area. Being the nice fellow that he was, he forgave me in the end. That night there was a great celebration. I was called down to Group, where Old Boy introduced me to General Hutton and the Governor, Dorman Smith, and other VIPs. He waxed so enthusiastic, indeed, that one would have thought that he had shot the damned thing down himself.

I think that I must also have shot down the other one, since a Mitsubishi with the crew dead inside it was found near the Syriam oil tanks the next day, but of course it may have been from a previous raid. There was a great write-up in the last edition of the *Rangoon Times* the next morning – I think by Gallagher of the *Express*, whom I had met previously. In his later book, in which he described this incident, he referred to me as an "old" night-fighter pilot, which added to my complex about age.

Two strange incidents occurred during the next few days. After a battle overhead, an American Volunteer Group P40 landed and pulled off to the verge of the main runway. The pilot, badly wounded, had just been taken to hospital when what appeared to be a Buffalo came in to land – they looked similar to the Nakajima fighters with their undercarriage down. Suddenly, on seeing the P40, it swerved towards it and opened up with its two machine-guns, and attempted to ram it but missed, taking away only the P40's rudder.

He ended up in a ball of flame just beyond – he had bullets through his stomach, knew he must have been mortally wounded, and would have died just at the last moment. I went over and inspected the wreckage. The aircraft was of light metal-alloy monocoque construction. There was no armour plate, no self-sealing tanks, and the control surfaces, to my amazement, were constructed out of balsawood, as used in model aircraft. The armament consisted of two machine-guns firing through the propeller with an old-fashioned Aldis sight. No wonder they could turn like a butterfly.

This confirmed my opinion that the Gloucester Gladiator, used by 17 Squadron during the between-wars years, would have been an excellent weapon at that time in the Far East – even *Faith*, *Hope* and *Charity* (the three Gladiators which first defended the whole island against the German 109s) proved their worth in

Our first experience of Japanese harakiri, not to be confused with kamikaze later in the Pacific war

Malta against far more modern adversaries. This was easy to think of at the time, but then we were only individuals without responsibility for global considerations of supply and demand.

The next day the same thing happened to a Blenheim parked in a pen down by our dispersal. After the all clear had gone, while we were in the *basha* mess, about 200 yards away, a Japanese came in and attempted to ram the Blenheim. It missed its nose by a foot and piled up just beyond. The Doc told me that this Japanese pilot also had some 0.5 bullets in his stomach and must have passed out at the last moment – obviously a victim of the American Volunteer Group. This behaviour should not be confused with the actions of the kamikaze pilots much later on in the war in the Pacific; but this was a form of suicide which concerned me, remembering my friend with whom I had jousted with so recently. I am certain that if I had wounded him he would have flown straight into me.

This is all that remained of a Japanese Army 97 fighter which contained a wounded pilot who aimed his machine at a Blenheim bomber on the ground and missed

The saga of the long-range tanks, although it had seemingly receded into the background, was suddenly revived by Group. The message came down to me that we were to refit three aircraft with them and strafe the airfield at Bangkok, some 350 miles away. By my calculations, we would be over the field for a maximum of three minutes, provided we were very careful with our fuel consumption on the way there and back. We would, in any event, be sitting ducks for any Japanese fighters because of our inability to jettison our tanks. Even if we did survive any combat, the chances of getting back to base would be nil, because of the fuel used and the time taken.

Headquarters persisted in their request that the operation be carried out, in spite of my advice to the contrary, but agreed to my request to allow me to nominate the pilots I wanted. My choice, apart from myself, was Squadron Leader Frank Carey and one of the flight commanders. As soon as someone in Headquarters realised that there was every chance of losing the three most experienced RAF pilots then in Burma, no more was heard of the request.

The Japanese were equipped with beautiful silk parachutes – much in demand at home – but they seldom used them. I only witnessed one occasion. We were watching a fighter battle overhead, and a Japanese fighter pilot took to the silk about 2 miles away. I sent our medical officer over in a jeep. He was greeted by some of the American Volunteer Group just putting their smoking Colts back in their holsters. One of them drawled, "Guess you're too late, Doc. Reckon he's dead." He was indeed, with about twenty revolver bullets in him. This may sound barbarous now, but the American Volunteer Group were shot on sight if captured, and we had little time for the Japanese as a race because of their frightening barbarity towards the vanquished. Apart from the strangeness of the country, we were fighting with this added fear of capture.

It was now the beginning of February, and the Japanese had taken the port and town of Moulmein. Number 17 Indian Division were engaged in bitter fighting on the far side, and we spent a lot of time escorting the Blenheims to bomb the port and railhead. It was about a forty-minute flight over the Gulf of Martaban to the east, and then up the Salween river estuary. I never met any air opposition on these occasions. After the Blenheims had dropped their bombs, we would go down and beat up machine-gun posts on the jetties, or any small boats we could find, or the railway station, before escorting the Blenheims home.

I had noticed during our beat-ups of Moulmein that the town appeared highly inflammable, so thought why should we not relieve the monotony slightly by burning it down. I found that we could fit two of the Blenheim's incendiary bombs into our Verey pistol tubes. My warrant officer armourer fixed up an ingenious release device whereby one pulled a looped piece of bent wire in the cockpit. We became quite efficient at dropping these contraptions on a target set up in the paddy near the aerodrome, and the resulting flames and smoke were indeed spectacular to us, unused as we were to this method of warfare.

Seventeen Indian Division were then on the opposite side of the Salween river, so I asked Lieutenant Penton, our Army liaison officer, if he could get one of his pals opposite Moulmein to give us a report on the results. We arranged a day, and six of us took off with twelve whole bombs. I had also increased the amount of incendiary ammunition in our gun belts, and I thought the results should be spectacular. Arriving over Moulmein, we peeled off from 5,000 feet near the docks, dropped our bombs and machine-gunned the area. Beyond a little return machine-gun fire, there was no opposition. Towards evening, Penton came into the office. To my eager enquiries, he replied that Moulmein appeared much the same. I felt like a frustrated inventor.

About this time the few remaining Buffaloes, together with a few Blenheims, were moved to Toungoo, a permanent aerodrome situated to the north-east, near the Thailand border, for the Japanese were showing increased activity on the ground and in the air. After the Buffaloes had gone, we occupied their dispersal at the end of the main runway, leaving the remaining Blenheims at our old one. This fine squadron, No. 67, had carried out magnificent work in outdated aircraft, but with mounting casualties and lack of maintenance facilities, they had been whittled away over the weeks to about four aircraft.

After one of our escorts one day, we were all in the hutted mess having a drink; casually looking round the corner towards the trees, I saw twelve Japanese fighters approaching at treetop level. I shouted, "Christ, look out chaps, bloody Nips". There was a mad scramble for the slit trench beside the hut. Frank Carey dashed over to man the anti-aircraft Lewis gun outside, and drinks and hats flew all over the place. I was last in, just as the Japanese opened up. Unfortunately,

Bags of "twitch". Don't look now, but ... Army 97s hit Mingaladon

I landed on top of dear old Seton. Above the clatter of the Japanese machine-guns, he shouted: "Bunny, you clumsy bugger, you've spilt my pink gin."

One day in February I was at dispersal when we were visited by a particularly nasty Tokyo Express. The American Volunteer Group, 135 Squadron and our boys had already taken off, and were scrapping overhead at about 25,000 feet. The old mess had been hit; the watchtower had received a direct hit, killing the duty pilot and two airmen, and a parked Blenheim lay burning at the far end of the runway. The sound of falling bombs had nearly ceased when I saw a Jeep hurtling across the runway towards us. It disappeared momentarily in a cloud of orange dust kicked up by two antipersonnel bombs which straddled it, only to emerge miraculously, bouncing to a halt by our slit trench, into which the large figure of the driver hurled itself head first.

It was Chiefy Guest, who was greeted by roars of relieved laughter as he recovered his dignity. Indeed, this was the only occasion I had seen him at all put out. Neither he nor the jeep had a scratch on them. Chiefy, however, was not amused at our hilarity, and drawing himself to his full height, fixed the nearest airman with a steely eye: "Jones, take that bloody silly smile hoff your face; come and see me in my hoffice." And then, eyeing me equally fiercely: "You, sir, har wanted in the CO's hoffice immediately ... sir!"

4 A FORCED LANDING

The burning sun rose high into the sky over Mingaladon, sucking the last of the morning dew from the crusty orange earth surrounding our dispersal. It was 23 February 1942. Our few Hurricanes, with wet sacks over their gun compartments on top of the wings to cool them, seemed to vibrate in the heat. Another day, I thought, and wondered what would turn up. Suddenly the phone rang.

"For you, sir," the operator announced.

I grabbed the phone. It was our group captain, Seton.

"Say, Bunny, I want you to get off right away. Take another pilot with you, and escort Generalissimo Chiang Kai-shek and his wife from Lashio, where they will be calling on their way to Delhi, via Rangoon, in their Sikorsky amphibian, OK?"

"OK, Seton."

I detailed Sergeant Cropper, one of my Aussies who happened to be standing nearby, to take an aeroplane and to have mine run-up. I hastened into the watch office to find a map. Eventually, from under a pile, we extricated some ancient maps which I had no time to study properly. We would have to refuel at Toungoo. From there it was about 450 miles to Lashio, in the extreme north-eastern corner of Burma, near the Chinese and Thai borders.

We took off and reached Toungoo in about an hour. Throttling back, I did a circuit and noticed a few Blenheims parked up one end with one or two Buffaloes of 67 Squadron, which had just come up from Rangoon. I landed and taxied up to the watch office at the far end, followed by Cropper. A fitter came up at the double.

"Hurry up, sir. The Nips is nearly overhead."

I switched off and, hastily undoing my straps, was out of the aeroplane like a cork from a champagne bottle. The three of us dived into a slit trench nearby. I hated diving into slit trenches, as I always thought of falling on a snake, but my fear of Japanese bombs was greater.

Meanwhile two Buffaloes, actually the only two serviceable, roared off in a cloud of dust. A moment after, a Tiger Moth with civil markings came in and landed opposite. It taxied rapidly off the runway.

By now we could hear the beat of the Japanese bombers, and picked them up as they glinted like diamonds in the deep blue of the sky, flying their usual perfect vics at about 18,000 feet. They came in from the east and then turned into their bombing run. A moment later came the usual accelerating flutter of the bombs; all at once the aerodrome erupted with a roar, hurling great orange clouds of dust into the still air, luckily up at the other end, where the Blenheims were parked. The Tiger Moth, in the meantime, hurrying to escape this rude welcome, tried to take off with some chocks still in front of its wheels, and gracefully tipped on its nose, leaving its fuselage and tail pointing disapprovingly in the direction in which the predators were now retreating. This somehow cheered us.

It would take some time to refuel, because the petrol had to be pumped by hand from 50-gallon drums, so we went to investigate the damage. One Blenheim had a bomb land under its nose which, miraculously, had left it completely undamaged. A sliver from this bomb, however, had slightly holed one of its companions parked about 50 yards away; otherwise there was nothing but a large number of holes in and around the tarmac.

The fitter pronounced my aircraft unserviceable, with a glycol leak. It was not my day. I told Cropper to return to Rangoon when my plane had been repaired, and I flew on in his. Flying at about 10,000 feet, and not long after take-off, I could see nothing but jungle-clad hills, often capped by white pagodas poking out of the low mist. Map-reading did not disclose a village, a road or a lake, which were supposed to be visible on my track. I discovered that the map's scale was in metres, and that large areas were marked "Unsurveyed". My anxiety grew because I was flying on the compass, which might have been anything from 20° to 30° out. I did not relish the thought of baling out in such terrain.

Eventually I had to switch over to my gravity-fed tank, the main tanks showing empty, but suddenly, on the horizon, the sunlight shone on a strip of water to the north-north-west. I breathed again. After another quarter of an hour's flying, I found a large river which could only be the Irrawaddy, but whether to the north or south of Mandalay I did not know. With only about ten minutes of petrol left, I decided to put down as soon as possible. Shortly afterwards, I found a small village with a golden pagoda jutting out into the river, with a large concave sandbank in its lee. I went down to have a look at zero feet. The sand looked perfectly smooth, whether soft or not I could not tell, but I decided to try landing with wheels down.

Bringing her in with fine pitch and plenty of throttle, and with full flap in a semi-stalled condition, I laid her gently down on the sand and cut everything. She trundled nicely towards a halt, and I was beginning to congratulate myself when, just before stopping, she hit a small ridge of loose sand. The undercarriage collapsed, and the warning horn blared.

"Hell! How am I going to laugh this off?" I thought.

There was no one in sight at first, and then a colourful crowd began to collect on the dazzling yellow sand about a quarter of a mile away. They edged towards me, but would not come too close. I saw, with apprehension, that some were carrying nasty-looking pangas. I slipped to the ground, unwrapped my gun and placed it on the wing, advancing towards them with my hands up.

"Me British," I said.

I felt foolish. They appeared to understand, but I could not speak a word of Burmese, nor they English. After much attempt at powwowing and nodding of heads, they sent a man back to the village. He returned with an Indian doctor, who, I was relieved to find, spoke English. They were frightened, he explained, and thought I was Japanese. On hearing I was British they relaxed, and made a concerted rush for the aeroplane, which was soon engulfed. To my horror, a Bhuddist priest was playing with the gun button. I told the doctor to get the crowd away and to not allow anyone in the cockpit, and please, could he get me a screwdriver. I quickly disconnected the battery to stop the maddening noise of the undercarriage horn, and unloaded the guns.

After this I was treated with great respect, and the crowd assumed a festive mood. I was introduced to the village dignitaries. The headman was a youngish Burmese with a kindly manner. He had a smattering of English. His number two was a tall old Sikh who had fought for the Raj in the 1914-18 war. He was delighted when I told him that my father had served in a Sikh regiment. The village policeman was a small but important-looking little Burmese. The postman, getting on in years, was of academic mien, as befitted a man with a lifetime of filling in important "O.H.M.S." forms and tapping them out in

Morse to any village that might be interested. Last, but not least, was the travelling Chinese trader in a battered topee, who peddled his wares around the upper reaches of the Irrawaddy; some of these wares I was soon to taste from the beautifully labelled bottles of Gordon's gin and various brands of Scotch, camouflaging more lethal distillations.

By now, as if by common consent, the whole affair had turned into a fiesta, with much laughing and shouting, and clashing of anything that could be clashed together. Attractive naked young children weaved their way in between the stamping feet, and I was borne off to the headman's house.

The policeman mounted a guard on the aeroplane, which he delighted in doing. We left it surrounded with ferocious-looking men armed with pangas and ancient and lengthy flintlock guns. I had soon forgotten the aeroplane, or where I might be, lost as I was in the gaiety and scenes around me – an everchanging pattern of colour; good-looking girls with high breasts; chickens squawking and fluttering under one's feet. The odd pig, infuriated by all this noise, charged across the dusty road, squealing. We arrived at the headman's house, behind the temple, where I was to spend the night. It was built on stilts, with a veranda surrounding the living quarters, topped by a low roof thatched with banana leaves. The space underneath the house provided shade and cover for fowls and pigs, and also served as a general rubbish dump and sewage disposal for humans and otherwise. After clambering up the wooden steps, we entered, through bamboo curtains, a comparatively cool and dark main room. It was furnished with mats and spittoons, the latter used for the eternally chewed betel nut, accurately spat with a clanging noise into these receptacles.

A council of war was held, squatting on mats presided over by my host.

The policeman said a telegram must be sent. Everyone agreed. After much deliberation and many feats of composition, a message was taken down on official paper by the postman, using a frequently licked stub of old pencil. The message apparently had to be first stamped by the policeman, who kept it at his house, thence to be taken to the postman's house for transmission to the next village down the line. I was at Tagaung, a small village about 250 miles up the Irrawaddy from Mandalay. The headman said I was in luck; the Irrawaddy steam paddleboat would be calling the next day and, by changing boats halfway, I would be in Mandalay in about two and a half days. I was indeed lucky but of course, he said, I had three gods working for me – God, Allah and Buddha.

At supper we were waited on by one of the Sikh's sons, a nice-looking lad of about 16, and obviously half Burmese. The meal was excellent – course after course of different dishes served on banana leaves, assisted by the high-octane liquid concealed in the Chinese trader's bottles. From behind the bamboo curtains leading to the kitchen and the chief's quarters, there came the constant chattering and tittering, and the occasional glimpse of dark, inquisitive eyes. After the meal was cleared I realised that the going was likely to be hard, since one's glass never appeared to be empty, but I was determined to hold my own. The conversation centred on events down south, and so as not to depress these cheerful and welcoming people, I had to lie, as I knew their way of life would soon be disrupted. I personally gave Rangoon about another three weeks, and could see no hope of us holding Burma.

As time wore pleasantly on, the potent liquor began to take effect. Our host was the first to succumb with oriental grace, from the lotus position to the horizontal, to be quietly removed to his family behind the curtain. Our Chinese friend followed, as if caught in mid-sentence, with a grin on his face; he suddenly stiffened, his eyes opaque, as if gazing upon a disaster which overcame his many previous reincarnations. After the postman and village policeman had gone their happy ways, I was left with the old Sikh who, on religious grounds, was not supposed to drink anyway. He had now gravely decided that his son, as his father before him, should become a soldier for the British Raj. My defences being somewhat weakened, I promised the old man that I would take on his son as my batman. I subsequently regretted this, as the poor boy was terrified by the bombing, and in due course I sent him home just before Rangoon fell.

The old man eventually departed with great dignity on shaky feet, assisted by his son, and I fell into a dreamless sleep using my parachute as a pillow. The next morning I awoke to the clanging of the temple gong reverberating hideously in my sore head, summoning the priests, who came out of the temple gates in a long yellow line with their begging bowls to be filled by the villagers. The headman appeared, beaming as though nothing had happened; he asked me if I wanted anything, so I begged a cup of coffee and some shaving water. I went out to the veranda, brushed my teeth and swilled out my mouth on a large pig below, which took no notice. I presumed the pig was used to worse things, and I emptied my shaving water on to the desiccated chickens, which set them off clucking and fluttering with rage.

Quite soon there was a loud tooting upstream, and a rear-wheeled paddle-steamer appeared round the bend of the river, making fast just beyond where the poor old Hurricane lay. I told the headman I would send someone up to remove it, and thanked him for his hospitality. I did not have a rupee on me, but luckily was able to present him with a silver swizzle stick I had bought in Cairo, with which present he seemed highly delighted.

The Irrawaddy Flotilla Company paddle-steamer to the rescue

The steamer was out of *Alice in Wonderland*, built with the mechanical genius of Heath Robinson. The lower deck was filled with logs surrounding a long boiler, surmounted by a chimney which penetrated the middle and upper deck, to end 6 feet or so above the bridge and European quarters forward. There was a direct drive by twin cranks to the paddle aft, with room for the rudder, which was operated by chains from the bridge wheelhouse. An iron gangway reached up to the second deck, where squatting Burmese endlessly smoked their long, green, uncured cheroots, talking and spitting among the goats, pigs and fowl in wicker baskets. Ashore, trading was going on full swing. Another iron gangway forward led to the bridge, captain's and pilot's quarters, and room for about four first-class passengers, with a saloon served by a small galley.

These steamers, belonging to the Irrawaddy Flotilla Company, formed the connecting link via the arteries of the Irrawaddy and the Chindwin, between upper Burma and the south as far as Rangoon and the outside world. Unfortunately most of them were not destroyed during the general evacuation, and had to be sunk later on by Beaufighters with cannon and rockets. I said goodbye to my friends of the night before, and with much salaaming from the old Sikh, midst his tender farewells to his son, went aboard, among the curious stares from the deck passengers. Pushing past the pigs and goats, I reached the upper deck, my only luggage being a washing bag, helmet and oxygen mask, goggles and parachute, borne proudly by the boy behind me.

I met the captain and the pilot. I felt rather smelly. The captain, however, lent me a sarong later, while his servant washed my clothes.

With a couple of blasts from the whistle, we were off downstream, the paddle churning up the yellow waters. Every boat carried a pilot. I learned it took years of experience to be one, simple as it looked on the wide waters; but the unseen sandbanks moved from day to day, shifted by the swiftly running stream, with its many convolutions indicating the riverbed to the practised eye. I noticed that the pilot and skipper kept a constant watch on the flow of the river and on the river banks.

I found a tremendous peace and contentment while relaxing to the rhythm of the paddles and the subdued noises from the decks below. I realised how wound up I had become over the past two months. It was wonderful to have someone else in charge, and to absorb the strange sights and sounds of this unsought journey. The next day I changed boats. My first one turned round to chug back against the current. A teak wallah joined at the next staging post. He had been in the teak forests for about two years, and was surprised to learn about the Japanese war. He had a bottle of Scotch and, mercifully, cigarettes. The day before I had been so desperate for a cigarette, the captain and the pilot being non-smokers, that I had tried a green Burmese cheroot which, after a couple of puffs, nearly scraped my mouth out, and I hurled it into the river. It reminded me of my childhood, trying to smoke dried beech leaves wrapped in newspaper.

I could have listened to this man for hours as we lay comfortably in deck chairs under the awning forward. He was unmarried, and content with his own company. His love of his job was manifest, as was his love for the men who worked for him, the wild creatures that surrounded him, and, above all, his elephants. I was happy to listen as he quietly unfolded this new world of the jungle that had looked so menacing to us, flying above it.

He spoke very highly of "Elephant Bill" (Bill Williams) who, not so long after, saved many civilians trapped in upper Burma, taking them out with his elephants on the great trek over the Arakan Yomas to safety in India, so well described in his book *Elephant Bill*, which he wrote in England after the war.

We stopped at nearly every village en route to Mandalay. Everywhere adorable naked children played, women washed sarongs, and the men squatted on their haunches gossiping or discussing business, spitting, smoking their long pipes or their horrible green cheroots. The smell, like incense, hung mistily in the bright sunlight. At one stage, we ran into the chief of police from Kathar, who was touring in his steamer. I went aboard to tell him about the Hurricane.

I had a cold whiskey and soda poured out by his charming young wife, who was dressed in a white shirt and blue slacks. She was like a being from another world, totally unexpected; I did not know what to do with my hands. Her husband, noticing my reaction, was somewhat amused. He said he would be in Mandalay before me, would tell the Irrawaddy Flotilla Company that I would be coming, and would lay on a float for the aircraft.

Thanking him, I took my leave. His wife gave me a farewell kiss. Rather shaken by this unsolicited gesture, I returned to my boat and some chaff from the teak wallah and the captain. On arriving at Mandalay, I bade my farewells, feeling sorry for my teak friend, whose world would soon be shattered. I went straight to the Flotilla Company office, and found that the chief of police had been as good as his word. I told the Flotilla Company I would send a ground crew up to contact them.

We then took the long sweaty journey to Rangoon on the train. For me it had been a bright interlude, except for the loss of an aeroplane, which at that time was worth its weight in gold.

5 OPERATIONS OVER RANGOON

As we neared our destination, I was suddenly roused from my fitful contemplation of the last few days by the sight of the burnt out wreckage of one of the 67 Squadron Buffaloes, lying in a field near the line – poor Pymke, killed the day I left. More and more wreckages appeared, mainly Japanese I was pleased to see. Feeling somewhat ashamed, for this was the first and only aeroplane I had ever crashed, I reported to Seton.

"Say, Bunny, where have you been?" he asked, in his Canadian accent. "Thought you had been shot down. Anyway, the goddamn Generalissimo didn't turn up at Lashio either." He laughed.

Frank Carey was, by now, consumed by impatience, and telephoned to ask if he could come down and take over some of my readiness. I was only too pleased, since I was carrying out as much flying as the boys, as well as the ordinary administrative duties of a squadron commander. The latter I shortened slightly by tearing up much of the vast amount of irrelevant information in triplicate that appeared on my desk from Rangoon. It was good to see Frank's cheerful but frustrated face again, and on his first sortie he shot down a couple of Japanese fighters, just to get his hand in. Shortly after this his squadron was moved down to join us. I must say that it was hard on some of our more inexperienced pilots, since we were unable, owing to the shortage of aircraft, to give them enough flying.

I was pleased at the arrival of Hemingway, Tex Barrick and Ken Wisrodt, and, at last, Bush Cotton turned up, fuming at Delhi. He had found, while at Karachi looking for Hurricanes (which he eventually found at Shuaiba up in the

Persian Gulf) that a certain station commander on the North-West Frontier, which was quiet at the time, had retained some.

For recreation, Adjutant had formed swimming parties. The sergeants and troops went to a small lake near the Schwe Dagong pagoda, and, for the officers, there was a swimming pool which belonged to the Rangoon Club. On my arrival I had also used this for the sergeant pilots. This pool was always empty of people except for an officious little secretary. Most of the local community had left the city. I was down at the pool one day when this little man came up to me and complained about sergeants using the pool. There was quite a battle proceeding at the time high up to the north. I pointed up, saying, "And what do you think these sergeants are usually doing?" I ordered that no badges of rank were to be used on our swimming parties in future. This fixed him.

The Army, in the middle of February, had been forced back to the bridge over the river Sittang, and affairs on the ground were looking very grim. We had carried out several low strafes on some areas around the Sittang, and had once even been sent to look for elephants, which 17 Indian Division had reported the Japanese were using for transport (which I think was questionable). We used to go down and strafe areas in the jungle where from the air, at treetop level, we were unable to observe anything but dense foliage. Further up from the Sittang bridge, there was thick jungle which only gave way to the open paddy fields to the west towards Rangoon. Even in the paddy fields I never saw a single Japanese soldier on the ground, and even if they were there, they never opened up on us when we were flying at ground level.

About 23 February the Sittang bridge was enfiladed by the Japanese and, tragically, was blown up by the Army too soon for the bulk of one brigade to retreat over it. They had to abandon their guns, equipment and vehicles and swim the river, losing many of their troops in so doing. Added to this, our Blenheim squadron was given the wrong aiming point from Army Head-quarters in Rangoon, and they bombed and strafed a collection of transport which turned out to be ours. Penny Leigh was acting as a forward Air Force liaison officer at the time. He dived for cover, in company with a colonel, as a Blenheim passed overhead at about 200 feet.

"I'm sure that was a Blenheim," the colonel said.

"Yes," said Penny, with tongue firmly in cheek. "The Japs captured some of our Blenheims the other day."

I had shortly before discussed with our liaison officer in the Army, Penton, the possibility of the Army providing ground-to-air radiotelephone links and operators to service them, plus donkeys or mules to carry them, so that we could properly communicate with each other. This would help avoid our misidentifying troops on the ground. Penton was enthusiastic, but, although we contacted Headquarters, nothing more was heard. This kind of liaison was adopted much later on in the Arakan battles after the retreat into India.

The Japanese, experienced in jungle warfare, were very successful at moving through the jungle around any point of resistance, and setting up roadblocks to halt our vehicular traffic and ambush our troops, who stayed on the roads all the time. This resulted in a series of retreats with no idea of how to combat the Japanese technique. Things improved slightly when General Alexander took charge of our forces in Burma, just before the fall of Rangoon. I remember distinctly, even among us junior ranks in the Air Force, how we thanked God that he had come.

I say all this because I believe we were responsible for considerably delaying the Japanese advance on Rangoon, and could have done a lot more had there been better liaison between the two services. In any event, however, the major problem was that 17 Indian Division was quite green; its lack of experience, in particular its lack of appreciation of how to make the jungle an ally instead of an enemy, and its consequent lack of morale, told heavily throughout the campaign.

On the morning of 25 February, I took off with six Hurricanes to carry out an offensive patrol over the Moulmein-Martaban area. As usual, Sergeant Wheatley was my number two. We had come to know the Moulmein estuary well over the past few weeks, and hoped to find some shipping we could beat up. We cruised at about 5,000 feet, with the formation stepped up into the sun, undulating slightly, in loose line abreast, etched against the pale-blue horizon; the sun sparkled on the dark cobalt waters of the Gulf of Martaban as we left the coast and headed for the estuary.

I opened the hood, relaxed by the beauty of the day, but I kept a wary eye around the clock, and I knew that five other pairs of eyes were doing the same. I knew these lads well by now. They were all from different parts of the world – Bush Cotton from Australia; Sergeant Pilot Tex Barrick, one of my star pilots, from the deep south of America, who joined the RCAF before Pearl Harbour; Guy Gibson, another US citizen (also in the RCAF), festooned with cameras; and others from Rhodesia, New Zealand and South Africa.

The only other Englishmen on the squadron were Ken Hemingway, and my B Flight commander, Flight Lieutenant Alan Carvel. I had made it my policy, when circumstances permitted, that my number twos were pilots who were particularly friendly on the ground, with the best pilot leading each pair, regardless of rank.

As we approached Martaban, then occupied by the Japanese, situated on the north bank where the estuary broadens into the gulf, we spotted a large river boat, with one smokestack forward, steaming on a course to the west of the Sittang river. We were in a perfect position for strafing. I closed my hood, and turned on the gun button and the reflector sight. I went into a shallow dive, increasing speed; I told the others on the R/T to follow in line astern. I went in to the attack.

As I descended, a cannon, mounted on the top awning just forward of the funnel on the top deck, winked at me. Waiting until I was in range, I opened up on the cannon, whose crew promptly collapsed, one falling over the side. I kept my finger on the button and raked the boat from stem to stern. Pulling out of my dive, I swept over the boat at about 10 feet and saw at a glance that the boat was full of Japanese troops in full war-gear. I watched Sergeant Wheatley going in as I circled up and around. The boat appeared to burst into a white sheet of flame from the funnel to the stern.

The other chaps went in, and smoke started to billow up, casting a long shadow on the glassy waters beneath. As I went in for the second time, figures appeared like fleas, disturbed by powder, jumping from a dog's fur. Some disappeared beneath the water, others popped up to be extinguished by the

We estimate that there were up to 200 Japanese in this boat

spray kicked up by eight guns delivering 160 bullets a second from each aeroplane.

My imagination told me they were not my guns and the dots on the water were not human beings, but like the puppet figures of a miniature rifle range at the circus, whizzing round on an axis when hit.

When we had no ammunition left, I called the boys together and we made off home as fast as possible at sea level, leaving the boat still burning, but afloat and not moving. The Blenheims went in shortly after and sank it. I was sure that these Japanese troops intended to cut the road towards Pegu, behind the lines of 17 Indian Division, which was then fighting further on towards the Sittang.

Captain Penton, our Army liaison officer, drove to dispersal in a hurry one day soon after. He had his wings, and had carried out a few hours on Hurricanes, although most of his flying hours had been on Lysanders. Apparently, Army Headquarters wanted a report on the Sittang area. My aeroplane was the only one available. I lent it to him with some reluctance, since it was my most prized possession. I had made it about 10 knots faster than other aircraft in the squadron by blocking up all the holes and gaps, a practice I had used since my first joining the squadron at Kenley as an acting pilot officer on probation. I saw him off with the comforting words, "Take care of the old lady, Penton".

About an hour later, Bush and the boys returned after escorting some Blenheims to bomb Moulmein, but they had seen nothing of note. After two hours I started to worry, and when a further half hour had elapsed, I borrowed another aeroplane from Bush and went off to search for any sign of Penton. Flying at 100 feet, I covered the whole area, and saw nothing but the odd bullock cart or a village with a few peasants working in the fields. One never saw a Japanese; they did not fire at you, and if they were there they melted into the landscape like grouse, crouched still among the autumn leaves, only moving when nearly trodden on.

There were plenty of burnt-out wreckages dotting the countryside, grim reminders of the many battles fought almost daily in the sky overhead during the last two months. It was hot in the cockpit, even with the hood open. I was on the point of returning when I spotted what appeared to be a Hurricane on the ground near a small village. I dropped to zero feet, and there was my dear old Hurricane on its nose in the middle of a paddy field. On closer inspection, I saw that the hood was open and the Sutton harness hung over the side. The prop was chewed off and the machine appeared full of holes. I thought, "Poor old Penton, probably been caught by the Japs." I pulled up and returned for home, very depressed.

Penton rapidly abandons my beautiful Hurricane

Two days later, Penton returned, having been smuggled through the Japanese lines by a friendly Burmese in a covered bullock cart. He had been set upon by about a dozen Japanese fighters, and eventually belly-landed with a dead prop. He ran for the nearest cover – the village, with the Japanese hastening his passage by peppering him all the way. He was lucky, and I was very glad to see him; I forgot the loss of my Hurricane.

The general outlook was grim, despite our feeling at Mingaladon that we still retained the upper hand in the air. Although outnumbered by the Japanese, their losses had proved much higher than ours. The American Volunteer Group and the Hurricane pilots were superior in air tactics, armour, and guns and armour-plate protection. The civil administration in Rangoon was gradually disintegrating. Civilians were leaving in increasing numbers, and dacoity (banditry) was increasing rapidly. We began to feel the effects of this breakdown of law and order at the aerodrome. The inmates of the lunatic asylum were let loose, and many of them used to amuse themselves by taking pot shots at us as we drove from our mess to dispersal. We responded with our Tommy guns, which we now carried in our vehicles.

Large numbers of half-starved stray dogs collected around our dispersal to feed on scraps discarded by the troops. I became anxious over the possibility of rabies, which could have put the squadron out of action for a fortnight from inoculations, so I published a routine order that stray dogs were to be shot on sight. This resulted in the only near-mutiny I ever experienced.

At the dispersal one day, surrounded by these pathetic creatures, I ordered the men to shoot them, for by now I had issued arms to all the men. A deadly hush occurred, and no one stirred. I felt embarrassed and, plucking up courage, I ordered two of the officers present to follow me. Drawing my Luger pistol, I marched forth, I hoped with a steady step, and we shot five of these poor creatures. The rest ran off howling into the surrounding bush. The looks on the men's faces, usually so friendly, had turned to belligerent distaste. That night I got Chiefy Guest to muster all ranks for a lecture on rabies from my medical officer. We had no further trouble.

The adjutant pointed out to me that we were disastrously low in motor transport, which was vitally important at that time, for Rangoon was a long way from the aerodrome, and it seemed most likely we would be having to evacuate to another area before long. Luckily, I knew that near the docks there was a large vehicle park run by the Americans. Their job had been to provide the Chinese with motor transport, via Mandalay, Lashio and the Burma Road (known as the Road). Most of these assorted brand-new vehicles, incidentally, never reached their destination, since they were driven by Chinese. They were the most polite and inscrutable race on two feet, but when put behind a wheel they become raving maniacs.

Nor did they seem to consider that these vehicles had need of more than just petrol to reach their destination. Many vehicles seized up on the Road for want of oil or water, and lay abandoned. I digress, however. On consideration, I decided there was only one man on the squadron who could produce the desired result, so I summoned Chiefy Guest.

"Chiefy," I said, "we want as many motor vehicles as possible. There is an American car depot by the docks …"

"Yes, sir, I am aware of that! See what I can do," he said, and left.

Two hours later a large column of motor vehicles arrived, led by Chiefy in a brand-new Dodge saloon. Getting out, he announced: "This 'ere is for you, sir; 'bout time you 'ad a staff car."

I asked no questions, but there were jeeps, 3-tonners, and even a heavy loader for an aircraft fuselage and wings. I did, however, notice a swelling black cloud of oily smoke rising from the direction of the docks, and assumed Chiefy had arrived just in time to convince the Americans to give him all his needs rather than burn them, which they realised had to be done to avoid the Japanese getting them. He was one of that rare breed of soldiers who would be able to raise Lazarus from his grave if asked to do so, but not if you were watching.

So that the transport be properly allocated and controlled, I appointed a Canadian pilot, Rick Chadwick, who was quite inexperienced in the air, to be the motor transport officer from then on. We lost only one motor vehicle, with a burnt-out coil, in more than 800 miles of retreat. We had all the vehicles numbered, and marked with occupant's names, stores, spares, ammunition, wireless, and so on, so that with several drills the whole squadron, intact, was able to move in less than an hour.

Chadwick told me that Chiefy had gathered all the drivers from the Group Headquarters motor transport section, concealing them in one of the few remaining 3-tonners. He drove down to the American vehicle park, and, having gained admittance past the American guard, he wandered down alone to see the officer in charge, a small, worried-looking captain with gold-rimmed spectacles. Chiefy was able to sum up anything from an elephant to an earthworm, and gradually he led the conversation round to the present situation.

"My commanding officer tells me the Nips will be 'ere in about three or four days."

"Gaard! What do you reckon I ought to do with this lot?" the American asked, indicating the rank upon rank of transport.

"I'd burn it," said Chiefy. "No good letting the bleedin' Nips 'ave it."

The captain looked like a man upon whom reason had suddenly dawned. He lost his furrows and beamed.

"Guess that's just what I'll do."

Chiefy, thinking that he had overstepped the mark, hastily enquired if he could take a few before setting the remainder alight.

"Sure," said the now-determined captain. "Take anything you want."

Before all this, the arrival of Bush had been a great help and a fillip to general morale. During my absence at Tagaung, he and the boys had done very well by day, and also shot down another two or three at night. Hemingway got one, and so, I think, did Tex, but because all records were later lost, it is hard to say; not that I think much of claims in the air unless you see the enemy break up or crash.

On the big day in the Battle of Britain, I think 160 Germans were claimed, but after the war, when the German records were checked, the figure for losses for that day turned out to be nearer forty-five. The really good fighter pilots were soon apparent to their companions in the air and were not assessed from others' reports.

What had upset us at one stage was that Old Boy had ventured to tell us that our claims were too high compared with the American Volunteer Group. Since the bullet holes in the wreckages can easily be checked for 0.5 as against .303, this had annoyed both 135 and 17 squadrons. The squadrons had no part in the reporting of victories to the press or others. We finally believed it was the work of someone in Group trying to justify their existence. Since most of the battles took place near Rangoon the Japanese had a long way home over the dense jungle to Bangkok and, of course, there was no check on how many damaged aircraft failed to return there.

My A Flight commander, Bush Cotton, was the obvious successor if anything should happen to me. I had told Seton this and he agreed. Therefore Bush's loss from the squadron came at a very awkward time. The only other two I could consider were Hemingway or Tex Barrick, both of whom survived the war.

At dawn on 26 February, Bush was at readiness at John Haig with Frank Carey and four other pilots from 17 and 135 squadrons. Frank decided to conduct a sweep over Moulmein as soon as the early mist lifted. They took off when this cleared and flew a loose battle formation at 15,000 feet towards Moulmein, little realising that a squadron of Japanese Army 97 fighters had earlier flown over Mingaladon, were on their way back to their base at Moulmein, and were in a landing pattern, with one or two already touched down and short on fuel.

Frank and Bush dived down through the upper group in the circuit and each nailed one on the way down. Bush pulled up and fired at another, while Frank did the same, and both dived to avoid any dogfighting and to see what they could do before hightailing it for home. Frank joined behind one as it was landing, and his burst caused it to swerve, in flames, straight through a hangar. Bush strafed one as it touched down – it pulled up in a cloud of dust – and they set sail for Mingaladon. They caught up with each other on the way back and counted the bullet holes in each other's machines, but there were no serious ones. Bush said, on looking back, he counted five pillars of smoke over the drome area. One of our six failed to return, and there was no idea as to how he was lost.

While they were doing all this, and were on their way back, I had taken off with the remaining Hurricanes from Mingaladon to escort Blenheims for a raid on the Sittang area, leaving one aircraft behind because it was unserviceable owing to a failed radio. On our return, there was visible evidence that the Japanese had left their usual visiting cards. The Hurricane we left behind had disappeared.

After Bush had landed from his fracas over Moulmein, he found the unserviceable machine and correctly, as senior officer, told the ground crew to take Tex Barrick's gear out of it and replace it with his, because his own machine needed refuelling and rearming. I taxied up to dispersal to find that Bush had already taken off alone, to intercept the Japanese raid, in the Hurricane with the unserviceable radio. When the air raid sounded he took off in hot pursuit, much to Tex's disgust. The American Volunteer Group dashed off and left Bush to his own devices. Shortly after my arrival, the American Volunteer Group came back in, but twenty minutes later, there was still no sign of my aggressive flight commander. By then we were all rather anxious, when a Hurricane appeared.

After a normal circuit, it put its wheels down for a slightly erratic landing. It turned off the runway and pulled up short of our dispersal; something was obviously wrong. I raced over in the jeep to find a very much alive Bush, with his right foot jammed under the starboard rudder bar while he clutched his left knee, stained with blood. The cockpit instruments had also copped some damage and were covered in blood and bits of bone.

His language then was much more graphic than the epithets he sometimes reserved for us "Bloody Poms". We had considerable difficulty in removing his tall and badly wounded frame from the cockpit, since by that time he was in

Bush is lifted out of his shot-up Hurricane

great pain. The medical officer injected him with morphine and took him off to the Rangoon hospital. When I inspected the aircraft, I saw that it had been shot up almost vertically from underneath, right along the port side.

The next morning, the adjutant had managed to get a Hudson communication aircraft laid on to have him flown back to Calcutta. With this welcome news, Hemingway and I went to the hospital. We found Bush with one leg in the air, wrapped in plaster, and still cursing volubly. I managed to extract his story.

He had not been able to catch up with the American Volunteer Group, so flew to the south of Rangoon, where there was a large column of smoke from the burning warehouses and vehicle yards, set alight to prevent the Japanese from getting anything from them. He hid behind this at about 20,000 feet and watched the aerodrome erupt from the bombing. This allowed him to pinpoint the group of twelve Mitsubishi bombers as they turned for home.

He also saw a group of fighters being chewed over by the five AVG, and obviously out of his range, so he flew to the starboard side of the bomber group and let fly, downing the outermost one (later confirmed by the American Volunteer Group), and climbed up again, knocking bits off another one on his next attack.

He saw the fighters were nearly on him and commenced a turn to port to have a shot at the topmost one. His adversary, using his high speed and rate of climb, stood on his tail, and a burst from his guns punctured Bush's Hurricane from underneath. It was one of these bullets which broke both the bones in his leg, just below his knee joint. The others tore into his instrument panel, but the machine still flew, so he dived through the group in a full-engine spiral turn, simulating a spin. Finding his left leg quite useless, he jammed his right foot underneath the rudder pedal and managed to make the field after ten minutes of flying.

Later on in 1942, when he finally recovered, he commanded the squadron from 9 December 1942 to 23 July 1944 in the Arakan campaign, and then in Ceylon, where the squadron was re-equipped with Spitfire 8s. I was not to see him again until he, by now, a highly successful businessman, and a well-known glider pilot in Australia, arrived with his lovely wife Stella in our small cottage in Berkshire in 1982. Apart from his language being quite commendable, he had not changed.*

---

* EDITOR'S NOTE: Bunny actually caught up with me when we were down in Ceylon, at Minnerya, in 1944. See *Hurricanes over Burma*, part two, chapter six.

I drove back to the aerodrome in sombre mood. The Japanese by now were hotly engaged with 17 Indian Division, by Pegu, a strategic town and rail centre connecting Rangoon to Mandalay and Lashio, where the Burma Road winds through the mountains to Chungking, over the Yunnan border.

By chance, I had recently carried out a low reconnaissance to the east of Rangoon and observed, far to my right, a cloud of orange dust rising. I went over to look, and found a large number of covered bullock wagons trundling across the paddy in a north-easterly direction. Curious, since I had never seen so many in that area before, I went down to about 15 feet, and the drivers appeared to be Burmese peasants. I could not shoot, so I returned and reported it to Penton.

The next day, I think it was, the Camerons were overrun, and we heard that some of the prisoners had been crucified – true or not, it was not out of keeping with Japanese behaviour. If they had been Japanese in those carts, we could easily have wiped them out. A similar thing happened about this time when, returning from a patrol, we spotted a considerable number of vehicles and tanks in a clearing among the trees. We reported it on our return, but nothing was done, and we were informed that they must have been our own. Nobody really knew.

Towards the end of February Rangoon became undefendable. Old Boy came and parked with us in our mess, waiting for a ship to take him and the larger part of Group Headquarters to Calcutta. The breakdown in the life of a city induces a dream-like detachment; the only reality was our own squadron troops and fellow pilots, and the relief of finding oneself airborne and free from earthly considerations. Fortunately the Japanese showed little activity in the air at this time.

At the end of February the retreat started.

6 THE MOVE TO MAGWE

We were sent, together with the Blenheims, to Highland Queen, while the American Volunteer Group went up to Magwe, a permanent aerodrome on the banks of the Irrawaddy, 250 miles north of Rangoon, which, in peacetime, served the Burma Oil Company. Our move to Highland Queen was achieved smoothly. The paddy strip was set among dense trees, the single take-off runway running west to east, with a short taxiing strip constructed at right angles, where the Hurricanes and Blenheims could be secreted beneath the overhanging foliage. We slept and ate underneath a great tree in the open and, although we carried on with intensive flying, the Japanese never bothered us there. It was not unlike a *fête champêtre* after the rigours of Mingaladon.

Unfortunately, my shaving kit and toothbrush had been lost in the move, and due to lack of washing facilities in that climate, I began to smell a bit. I comforted myself by thinking of what the poor bloody Army was going through. Having to wear unwashed clothing undoubtedly leads to a loss of morale and, not being able to shave – because of the prime necessity for a fighter pilot to constantly twist his neck from side to side to search the skies – not a few of us had extremely sore necks from the rubbing on dirty clothing.

General Wavell turned up a few days after we had settled in, flown in with Old Boy from Calcutta, plus a retinue of immaculately dressed gentlemen, red tabs, creased trousers and polished buttons, in distinct contrast with our scruffy, sweaty mob. At the time I was disappointed with the cold, rather distant reception we received from this great man, who appeared little interested in

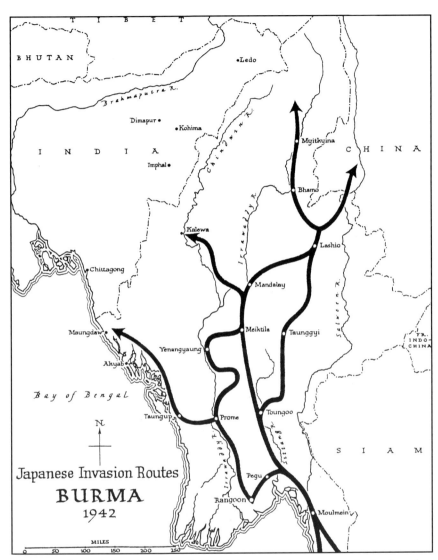

This map indicates the line along which the British Army carried out its retreat. It also shows the route up into Loiwing (not named on the map, but above Lashio on the Chinese border) along which 17 Squadron evacuated its aircraft, later coming back to Lashio and then up to Myitkina with their ground personnel

matters aeronautical. I realised later, however, that he bore an intolerable weight on his broad shoulders.

Dacoity, which we would now call armed robbery, murder and rape, was proliferating in the disjointed society around us. To suppress this, within the limits available, we had attached to us a company of Karens, commanded by a pleasant, diminutive, Karen captain. The Karens resembled the Ghurkas. Being a hill race, they had little time for the lowland Burmese, who were the chief offenders in dacoity at the time. The captain came to me one day and said he had surrounded a village, about fifteen minutes' flying distance away, which contained the most wanted dacoit in the area. He said the dacoits were heavily armed, and asked if I could assist. Naturally, we were only too keen, and I said by all means.

I rang up what was left of Group Headquarters, who were away up at Zigon (100 miles north), who informed me that Wavell had issued orders that we were on no account to attack any Burmese villages. I did not want to let down our popular captain, nor did we wish to see him killed unnecessarily, so went into a huddle under the tree that night to see if we could do a successful "Nelson Job" – a telescope to the blind eye.

We decided to attack at dawn the next morning, and I would lay on all the serviceable aircraft I possessed – about six. From the captain's map, we saw that the village was thirty miles to the south-ease, lying among paddy fields, circled by scrub about 500 yards distant, where his troops were concealed.

I had all the aircraft loaded with mainly tracer and as many red and green Verey lights as we could carry. I gave orders that the boys were to only shoot when pulling out of their dives, so as to shoot only above the rooftops, or into the open paddy nearby. The next morning was great fun, rather like one of the old Hendon air displays.

That night the little captain came back beaming from ear to ear. He had not lost one man. The dacoits were so terrified that they did not fire a single shot. He told me the booty they recovered from them was immense. From which he gave me a Queen Victoria half-sovereign on a gold chain. Unfortunately, returning home after my tour in 1944, I had this stolen with all my other kit at Karachi. I did not inquire into the fate of the unwanted dacoits, but I guessed that they suffered summary justice.

Unfortunately, by now we had no air-raid warning system, because it had been overrun by the Japanese. We had to revert to World War I tactics and put one machine into the air at 18-20,000 feet at all times to report back if sighting any bandits, which consumed valuable aircraft hours. We called this "Jim

Crow", and took it in turns. Beyond this, we spent a considerable time on Blenheim escorts, and tactical reconnaissances as far as Toungoo and around the Prome area. One day we went to beat up Kaykto aerodrome on the Sittang, but found no sign of Japanese aircraft.

General Alexander had broken the roadblock just north of Rangoon and 17 Indian Division were retreating. We felt very cut off from events. Finally we were sent up to join the others at Magwe.

I must admit that I felt filthy and very low in morale. When I landed on the one concrete strip at Magwe, I was met by the Blenheim squadron commander, a very nice young New Zealander, who must have instantly summed up my condition. He took me in his jeep to his quarters, laid on a hot bath, and lent me his razor and a freshly laundered kit of his own clothes.

After a dreamless sleep in his bed I felt considerably better.

That night, Old Boy paid one of his few visits from Calcutta, and at a dinner in the mess, Seton, Frank and Barry Sutton were all present when Old Boy started quoting Kipling's poem "On the Road to Mandalay" in a disparaging

Pilots dig slit trenches at Magwe

manner. Beyond a laugh from his personal assistant, there was a horrible silence. I had been born in India and my mother had spent thirty years of her life there, and had more or less brought me up on Kipling; I wondered if the author had ever meant his poem for such an occasion.

I had noticed on landing that the aerodrome only possessed the one concrete runway in the usual west-east direction, with all the main buildings positioned at the western end. There were no revetments and all aircraft were parked as far apart as possible along its length – a sitting shot for a sneak raid. The field was surrounded by more or less flat desert, covered with small cactus and scrub. It seemed to me that it would be fairly simple, at the eastern end, to clear a sufficient take-off run and dispersal. So we set all hands, including pilots, about this task. It proved highly successful and was more or less unnoticeable from high up in the air. It also happened to run along a raised *kud* on one side, which proved useful cover for men and aircraft. Some low-flying Japanese fighters, later on, were the only ones to find us there and, after one pass, disappeared, having done no damage beyond scaring us.

Pilots and ground crew take shelter in a ditch (known as a kud *in Burma) from the Japanese raids on Magwe*

The Syriam oil factory, just south of Rangoon, goes up in smoke

Together with the Blenheims, we kept a close watch on Toungoo and our old aerodrome at Mingaladon. Day after day, there was no sign of Japanese activity, puzzling at the time, and making us wonder what beastliness they were brewing up. One day I flew down to Rangoon. At 10,000 feet I was met by a dense cloud of oily smoke about 2,000 feet thick, casting a long purple shadow on the yellowish paddy beneath, and still rising from the Syriam oil factory, just south of the city.

Mingaladon had not a single aeroplane on it.

One day a Blenheim came in, but continued to circle the field at about 3,000 feet. It was behaving in an erratic manner, sometimes diving and rising, or dropping a wing. It suddenly dropped a parachute and then another billowed out. After this it came in with its wheels down, landing with one or two bumps.

I heard afterwards that it had been sent on a low reconnaissance of the upper reaches of the Sittang river. While it was flying down at 100 feet, a chance bullet from the river bank mortally wounded the pilot, who fell forward over the controls. The navigator, who had never before flown an aircraft, grabbed the stick and pulled it back. At the same time he managed to drag the inert pilot away and properly take over the controls, and to get the plane more or less stabilised.

On his arrival at Magwe, he had consumed most of the fuel, but had suffi-cient time to attach a rope onto the release handle of the dead pilot's parachute and push him out. He also told the rear gunner to bale out, and decided to try to save the aircraft by landing it. This man, I thought, deserved the VC, but in the chaos that was soon to come I do not know if he was even mentioned in dispatches.

Later on I went with Sergeant Wheatley, my constant number two, on a recce to the same place. Whatever situation one found oneself in, he was always there, which created a great bond between us. (I heard later on in the war that he had been shot down on the Arakan front and killed.)* We had orders to shoot at any boat seen crossing the Sittang. It was Sunday. Just by a couple of small villages, opposite each other at the water's edge, I witnessed a small boat paddling across. Something stopped me opening fire and, passing over it, I saw an old Burmese at the stern with his family. On pulling up, I heard a burst of fire. I looked back and saw Wheatley blow the boat out of the water.

I was consumed with an almost ungovernable fury, and returned immediately to our strip at Magwe. I descended from the cockpit, telling my fitter to ask Sergeant Wheatley to come and see me. I gave him an awful dressing down. That night I could not sleep for thinking of the incident; after all, he must have seen me dive on the boat and could have thought my guns had jammed. The next morning I called him in and apologised for my behaviour. I do not know why this incident should have remained so long with me, but the sense of guilt on my part is still there.

Seton gave me and some of the boys two days of leave at the hill station, nearly a 400-mile drive away, in the hills at Maymyo. His parting words were: "Say, Bunny, bring me back a blonde or I'll have you court-martialed."

Most of the roads were not tarmac. The dirt roads were narrow, which made our progress interesting, since bullock carts make fast travel exciting. We arrived, however, at 4 o'clock in the afternoon, covered in orange dust. Quarters had been arranged for us not far from the swimming pool, into which we soon hurled ourselves. After the dusty cactus-strewn plains, it was a beautiful part of the world, with great trees standing in green, well-kept lawns with masses of bougainvillea, hibiscus, roses and flowering shrubs. The only thing the place lacked was female company, for evacuation of the white community was uppermost in people's minds.

---

* EDITOR'S NOTE: Wheatley was shot down and captured by the Japanese, and survived the war.

Long vistas revealed range after range of timber-covered hills disappearing into the blue of the horizon. It was hard to think that this beauty would soon be outraged by the Japanese. The station was mostly occupied by teak wallahs and the oilmen from the wells of the Burma Oil Company.

I was surprised and delighted when I ran into my old teak friend, whom I had met on the Irrawaddy after my forced landing. He asked me back to his bungalow and laid on a party that night for us at a friend's house. His friend was a Scottish engineer, whose wife turned out to be a rather stunning blonde of about twenty-five years of age. Her husband said he was worried about evacuating his family to India, as he also had two young children. He had to stay, since no decision had yet been arrived at as to the fate of the oilwells. Most of the remaining people were eventually taken out by Elephant Bill.

Already the Americans were sending aircraft to Magwe to evacuate their nationals. I suddenly remembered not only Seton's fond farewell, but also that the Blenheims were now operating from India and refuelling at Magwe on their way home, so I confidently told him that I could probably do something provided his wife was able to move the next day. The boys were not unhappy with this arrangement, of course, despite the overcrowded conditions; there were, however, difficulties. She, not unaware of her attractions to the opposite sex, possessed great determination.

Arriving at her bungalow the next day, I found that I had not only the two children, but also the Burmese nanny to be embarked, together with an enormous gilt mirror, over which I had considerable argument, for I could not see how we could carry it in the car, let alone in a Blenheim. In the end, this priceless object, wrapped in blankets, was strapped to the roof. Our drive back to Magwe was lively, and the dear young lady did not seem overconcerned at leaving her husband behind. When we arrived at Magwe, I reported to Seton.

"Hello, Bunny. Have a good leave? By the way, did you get that blonde?"

"Yes and no. Anyway, come and see what I *have* got for you," I said, leading him out to the car.

I introduced her, and the nanny, and the children ... and the mirror.

"Over to you, Seton," I said, and disappeared.

Seton somehow managed to pack them into a Blenheim returning to Calcutta the next day, and the poor Blenheim pilot was nearly court-martialed by Old Boy, who, by chance, was carrying out an inspection of Dum Dum just as the dreaded mirror, followed by the blonde, the children and the nanny, emerged from the rear of an operational aircraft.

On 19 March we carried out a fighter sweep of Toungoo, which was by now in Japanese hands, but saw nothing. That evening, however, a Blenheim came in and reported that Mingaladon was filled with Japanese fighters and bombers. Götterdämmerung had arrived. After a conference with Seton and Frank, I was ordered to take off at dawn the next day, meet the Blenheims at 25,000 feet just to the west of Mingaladon, and, after they had bombed, to go down and create as much trouble as possible. We were quiet in the mess that night and most of us turned in early.

The next morning I was down at dispersal before dawn. We had eight aircraft immediately available, and I decided to lead the first flight of four; Tex was to take the second. At first light we took off through the mist and, tucking up our undercarriages, set course for the south, climbing slowly. At Rangoon I commenced circling, looking for the Blenheims at 25,000 feet. We were dead on time, but after about ten minutes I noticed dust rising from our old airfield. The Japanese were beginning to take an interest in us. There was still no sign of the Blenheims. I thought the whole ruddy lot would be airborne in a moment and decided to go in.

I ordered Tex to take the old American Volunteer Group dispersal from the north-east, and I would attack the main runway from the west. Descending in

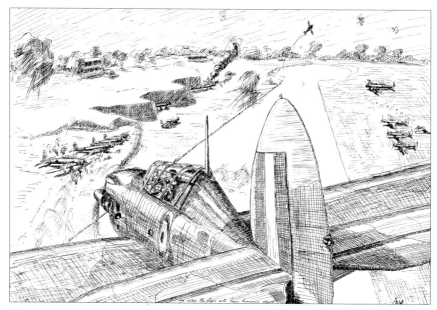

We catch the Japanese with their kimonos down at Mingaladon after the fall of Rangoon

a dive of about 400 miles an hour, we were met with light flack, mainly from our old Bofors guns, which the late owners had failed to destroy. The aerodrome appeared packed with aircraft, mainly fighters and Army Recce light bombers. I took a tanker and some Army Recces parked wingtip to wingtip. I looked back as I swung to the north, and there appeared to be a nice little fire starting. I broke to port at treetop level, having given strict instructions that on no account was a second attack to be carried out, since everyone would then be waiting for us.

A moment later, bombs from the Blenheims, now arrived on the scene, erupted across the field. As I weaved north, still at treetop level, I spotted a Japanese fighter to port, going the other way. I turned towards him and gave him a squirt at full deflection, but missed. He was on my tail in a flash. The only way to avoid him was to run for it, because if I climbed he would have undoubtedly shot me down. Pulling the booster plug, I weaved madly among the trees. He gave me several bursts but, thank the Lord, he proved as bad a shot as I was, and I soon out-distanced him; he turned back, and I began to climb for home, when I noticed the oil pressure was dropping.

I just managed to land at Prome with the needle nearly off the clock. On inspection, the fitter found that a bullet had passed right through my oil tank – luckily about 3 inches above the bottom. I told him to put a couple of corks in it and took off again for Magwe about twenty minutes later. As I circled to land at our concealed dispersal, the aerodrome presented a dismal sight, for aircraft were burning along the main runway, several dispersed petrol dumps were aflame, and black smoke from the headquarters and living quarters at the western end made it look as if a certain amount of demolition was in progress.

As soon as I landed I told the fitter to check the corks, refuel and rearm. Meanwhile I went along the main runway in my jeep to see Seton. Strangely enough, the runway was little cratered, except at the ends. I had noticed this in many former raids at Mingaladon and elsewhere. Since the Japanese bombed on the orders of their leader, I wondered if he took the runways as his aiming point and flew down the middle of them; this could account for it.

I arrived at Seton's just as the alarm went, and there was another big raid coming in for its bombing run from the east – probably Toungoo or Thailand. They were high up, at 20,000 feet or so, and we had no proper warning system for the aerodrome, which was the cause of the following disaster. Telling Seton I had better get back, I dashed down the side of the runway and met a Hurricane with a dead propeller, which had just landed. I yelled to the pilot to get in the Jeep. About 100 yards on I found a fitter and rigger working as if the rising sound of engines overhead was of no concern of theirs.

"Snooks" Everard looks at the town of Magwe going up in smoke during the raids on the aerodrome

I had to leave the jeep to order them into it, and they climbed in with superb indifference. One could see them thinking, "Windy old sod; wot's up wiv 'im?" I knew of a small tunnel underneath a road near our dispersal, and stopped underneath as the field erupted in the accustomed manner. I felt ashamed, and thought, "Christ, that couple have got guts," as the dust fell from the roof upon my cowering head.

As soon as the worst was over, I bounced over to our dispersal, where a couple of Hurricanes were just taking off in a fog of dust – Hemingway and another pilot. The Japanese fighter escort came down and shot up anything of interest, including us – of which I took a photograph – but they did no damage. Hemingway claimed a fighter on his return. After that raid was over we discovered a wrecked Japanese fighter. The wallet we extracted from the dead pilot proved interesting, for it contained a photograph of his family – his wife, a quite ordinary woman in spectacles, with numerous children – plus several photographs of more glamorous females (geisha girls?) and about four brothel tickets from Rangoon.

The Japanese dropped 147 tons of bombs on Magwe in twenty-four hours, and virtually wiped out the RAF and AVG

Since, as far as we knew, the Japanese had only landed the night before, he must have been a fast worker. To cap it all, there was a graphic ink-and-brush pornographic painting on rice paper. I was given this and intended to have it framed for the squadron records, but unfortunately this was stolen with my other kit at Karachi on my way home.

Summing up this disastrous day, it was reckoned that approximately 147 tons of bombs were dropped on Magwe and our air opposition had virtually ceased in Burma. Nearly three-quarters of the American Volunteer Group were lost, mainly on the ground, which caused angry ripples in Chungking, Delhi and Calcutta, so we squadron commanders and Captain Penton were ordered to send confidential reports to Old Boy in Calcutta.

I do not know how many of Barry Sutton's 135 Squadron were lost, but I had one shot down on the dawn raid. In reports I have subsequently read, I consider our publicly reported claims on that day were overrated. Tex shot down one fighter after it had taken off, which was seen to crash, and one of his section another. I claimed two Army Recces on the ground, a probable third and a tanker. I think we probably destroyed about six altogether. By that evening Brooks, my Rhodesian pilot, had not turned up.

He arrived late the next day with an interesting story. Having mixed it with some fighters north of Rangoon, he had to bale out. This occurred near a small Burmese village with a temple. The locals, gazing at this globe descending from the heavens – equivalent perhaps to us in these days as the sighting of a UFO – rushed out with any arms they could find to where Brooky was disentangling himself from his parachute harness. Thus surrounded by this rather terrifying horde of fierce-looking men, he naturally submitted. They must have been equally astounded to find that the object was but an ordinary white man. He was led off to the local temple and handed over to the Buddhist priests, amid much excited chatter.

By this time Brooky felt that he was about to become a sacrificial pig. After certain rites were performed over him in the temple, however, he was given to understand that he was now an honorary priest – the only pilot I know who has ever achieved such an honour. He obtained a lift most of the way back to Magwe on a 17 Indian Division tank.

After this eventful day, what was left of the American Volunteer Group went off to Loiwing. The remaining Hurricanes were to be split between 135 Squadron and us. They were to go with Barry Sutton to Akyab, in the Arakan, and my lot to Lashio and then Loiwing. Barry suffered a heavy raid shortly after his arrival at Akyab, and his ground crews and pilots were evacuated by small naval craft to India. He later gave me a photograph of all his boys in the nude on the small deck of one of these boats, underneath which I had written: "Give us the tools and we will finish the job." Unfortunately I cannot regale the reader with an enlargement of this, since it was eaten by my labrador when I returned to the UK.

I sent the few Hurricanes to Lashio and decided to accompany our remaining officers, pilots and troops with my adjutant, on the long haul by road to Mandalay at the end of March.

Like all retreats, there was distressing evidence of human and animal suffering; the trail of burnt-out and twisted remains of abandoned vehicles, usually stripped to their frames, became more frequent on the dusty roads. Our squadron had wisely been inoculated against cholera by our medical officer. The stench of rotting corpses from the land around Mandalay, mainly Indians, dead from this vile disease, was unforgettable. Our men, so recently from Europe, and most of whom had never been outside England, were deeply shocked; we pilots longed for the clean air high above.

We seldom saw Europeans, since General Alexander was extracting 17 Indian Division towards the west and the Arakan. Most of the resident European population had already left. Currency had broken down, and I was only too pleased that we were overstocked with rifles and ammunition; this placed us in the millionaire class, which did not displease even our most left-wing members.

I remember passing through a countryside, mile upon mile of which would have made even Salvador Dali rise from the coffin which he is reputed to have occupied from time to time. The flat rusty earth was covered by huge phallic erections, some 30 feet tall, which looked as if they had been carved by some long-lost civilisation. They were termite hills, but more interesting in shape than much of our modern architecture.

We eventually arrived at the railhead and the hills of Lashio, more attractive and cooler than some of the country through which we had passed. To my delight, there was Seton.

"H'ya, Bunny. Have a snort." I willingly accepted.

Our mess and station headquarters were built on a green clearing overlooking the concrete strip some 800 feet below. Our *basha* mess and sleeping quarters were built on stilts, underneath which we could easily hide our motor vehicles.

It was here that I met our Chinese liaison officer, a certain Captain Wong from the Generalissimo's headquarters at Chungking, which was apparently his home town. Everyone took to Wong. He wore wings, although after close acquaintance I imagined that he would have been a danger to himself and to others in an aircraft. On the ground, he possessed an engaging personality, and we became great friends.

7 ESCAPE TO INDIA

Lashio was the beginning of the Burma Road, which connected Chungking on the Yangtse to northern Burma and Rangoon and Bassein – the only road, rail and river routes to supply Chiang Kai-shek's armies in Burma, beleaguered by the Japanese. The only alternative was by air over what became known as the Hump, across mountains rising to 20,000 feet into Assam and India. Except perhaps for the South American air routes over the Andes, this was the most dreaded air route in the world, particularly during the monsoon when, from beneath the dense jungle and tree-covered peaks, the fermenting cumulus clouds rose to 30,000 feet or more. It must have claimed more victims over the years than any other air route.

The Hump was flown by Dakotas with American aircrews, or Chinese trained by the Americans. The Americans that I met on this passage were a pretty fearless bunch, but they made a lot of money as well, on the side. Anything from a broken-down wireless set to a car radiator cap could be sold in Chungking. At one time there was not a wristwatch to be bought in Calcutta, all having been acquired there and sold in Chungking.

The Burma Road was a magnificent feat of engineering, built by Chinese labour, not with bulldozers and mechanical equipment, but with picks and shovels, wielded by thousands of people. Hewn mostly out of the solid rock of the mountainsides, the debris was removed, on their heads, by women with small wicker baskets which appeared to carry about 2 pounds of material. Thousands must have died. I spoke to the American Volunteer Group doctor at Loiwing, and he told me that in his experience, further north, the Chinese could make an aerodrome as quickly, or more quickly, than they, the Americans, were able to do with modern equipment.

It displays the immense fortitude and disregard for death of which this race is capable. I drove many miles over the Road between Lashio and Loiwing, and it always proved romantic, exciting, frightening and always different. It needed a Beethoven to interpret it.

Every night Wong would change into a kimono and seat himself at the long wooden table that ran between our bunks. From within the colourful folds of his garment he would produce a stick of black Chinese ink, and a little bowl, into which he would put a little water. After grinding the ink in it to the right consistency, he commenced his letter to his wife, starting at the bottom of the right-hand corner and working upwards, with a delicate sable brush. This occupation was sometimes disturbed by Seton coming in to see how we were getting on.

One day I was in the Jeep with Wong at the beginning of the Road, when we met a Chinese lorry in front, carrying on in the usual erratic fashion and covering us with dust. I had discovered that the only way to pass a Chinese lorry was to take out my Luger and fire a few shots past the cab window. The driver normally thereupon hastily drew up or disappeared over the sheer incline

The Burma Road between Lashio and Loiwing

leading to the twisting river and trees many feet below. A horn was useless, merely encouraging the driver to make further speed and dust.

This time, whatever I tried, I could not pass, and failed to use my normal method successfully. By then we were both becoming frustrated and angry, when the lorry suddenly pulled off alongside a ramshackle hut selling Coke and similar goodies. I drew up alongside it and let rip; as it was perforce in English, the driver merely smiled. Wong climbed out of the jeep, and walked towards the driver, drawing his revolver as he did so. Horrified, I leapt out and arrested Wong's right arm as it seemed he was about to fire the weapon at the driver's head. I shouted at him: "What in the bloody hell are you trying to do, Wong? Get me hung for murder?"

Wong, replacing his revolver in its holster, gave me an aggrieved look.

"I was only threatening to shoot him for preventing an officer from doing his duty."

Soon after, we moved to Loiwing, where the mess was again an empty Roman Catholic mission, in which I placed all my pilots, with the other ranks in the surrounding buildings. It was just inside the Burmese border, with the aerodrome about 2 miles away in China.

Loiwing, besides housing a squadron of the American Volunteer Group, was also a staging post for the Chinese National Airlines operating across the Hump into India. A few Blenheims on sorties from India and the Arakan also used it for refuelling. It was situated on a plateau surrounded by mountains, bamboo groves and pine forests. The airfield was commanded by a Colonel Wang, who apparently came under a General Wong – no relation to my excellent liaison officer – which was rather confusing. Indeed, I found the Chinese altogether perplexing. Their palpable dislike and mistrust of all foreigners reminded me somewhat of the Cornish attitude. I think my Captain Wong was the exception rather than the rule.

On my arrival, I had to report to Colonel Wang, so decided to take Wong, who briefed me on the social ethics, which were rigid. Wong told me on no account would a breach of etiquette on my part be countenanced. I am sure Ronnie Barker could have made much out of the situation. I drove to the colonel's office in a state of trepidation, since Wong had told me that, at first, tea would be served, and there was a strict rule that the guest should raise the lid from the cup of tea before the host. Conversation should be general at first, and only lead gradually towards the matter in hand.

We arrived at the colonel's office, and were ushered in by a nondescript individual carrying a rifle with a fixed bayonet. The office was monastic, the boarded walls relieved by a few pinned maps and a framed photograph of the Generalissimo. The furniture consisted of a table surrounded by a few unstable-looking chairs, upon one of which sat a small figure, painting on one of the papers that littered the bare table.

We entered and saluted smartly, and for a moment he gazed at us while Wong, in Chinese, told him who I was – I supposed. Still expressionless he rose, shook hands, and indicated two chairs opposite with a commanding wave of his hand. When seated, he clapped his hands, and in came the dreaded tea, in beautiful small china cups, delicate and out of context with our rigid surroundings.

By then I felt like a farm labourer invited to dinner by the lord of the manor. I glanced appealingly at Wong, and followed the ritual like a ventriloquist's dummy. By then I had forgotten the order of ceremony. All appeared to go well, however, and I was given a dispersal and facilities for my four remaining Hurricanes.

I was destined to meet Colonel Wang once again a little later, under a stranger circumstance. I was told coldly that my Hurricanes were not to fly again. The airfield was being constantly bombed by the enemy, and finding this order strange, I enquired why. I was told that General Wong had given orders to this effect. I dispersed the few aircraft among bamboo thickets as far as possible from the main aerodrome. I never discovered the reason for this extraordinary order.

Just prior to this, I had been away, and, on my return, Alan Carvel, my flight commander, told me that they had been scrambled with the American Volunteer Group because of an air raid on the field. They had run into some Japanese Zeroes – the first time we had seen them. He said that the Hurricanes could do nothing with them, as they had met at about the same height, 20,000 feet.

In the process, Lieutenant Pieters, our South African, received a burst of cannon fire and dived out of control into a nearby pine forest. Alan reckoned that he must have gone in at about 400 miles an hour; surely nothing could survive such a crash. When the rescue team arrived they found a swathe of fallen pine trees, cut as with a scythe, 300 yards long, with bits of Hurricane – wings, tail and engine – littering the forest floor. Fifty yards on was Pieters, strapped to his armour-plated seat, suffering from shock and concussion, but with not a scratch on him. He was flown out to Calcutta at the end of April 1942. In late 1947, when I reached Johannesburg from Cornwall, he was the first person I met in Dawson's Hotel, where my wife and I were staying for the night.

Back at our quarters, our troops, with their usual adaptability, had made a football field and found their own way of entertaining themselves. We all fed quite well, which had not always been the case. An idea had come to me previously one night, when I was taken with a bad case of dysentry which had left me staggering to and from our loo. This consisted of a plank, on which one perched over an open 12-foot trench, into which I had shone my torch to observe thousands of maggots seething beneath. Their blowfly offspring obviously transferring disease all over the camp.

The next morning I said to the Padre, who was a good fellow: "Padre, I do not think that God can do much for us right now about malnutrition and contaminated food. Would you be willing to undertake an additional duty to increase our rations?"

"Certainly, sir."

So every morning I sent him off in a jeep, with the sergeant in charge of messing, armed with suitable currency, which consisted of rifles and rounds of .303 ammunition. He was outstanding in this job, returning from over the Chinese border, often late at night, with suckling pig, fowl, eggs and other delicacies which none of us had tasted for many a year. Indeed, our few days at this far distant part of the globe provided more varied surprises than most tour operators could produce today.

I could not see that we were contributing anything to the war effort sitting and consuming suckling pig on the Chinese border, so I decided to fly to Calcutta. Adjutant took me to Lashio in a jeep, and I got a lift to Calcutta in a returning Blenheim.

I went to see Old Boy the following morning. He appeared particularly affable, so I asked him if I could have some more Hurricanes and continue on to Chungking. I was informed that this was impossible, as the chiefs of staff had ordered that all British forces were to be withdrawn to India. This appeared reasonable, but he added that there was no need for me to return to my squadron in Burma, and that he could arrange to get me a job on his staff, which would mean promotion. I did not like this idea at all, because I knew that the retreat to Myitkyina via Bhamo was going to be extremely difficult, but I said nothing. He thereupon led me to the French windows, opening onto a lawn, and put his hand on my shoulder. I wondered what was coming next.

"Stone," he said, "I have read your reports and the others from Magwe. I don't quite understand the part about Group Captain Seton Broughall. I was wondering if your report is quite correct. Will you think about rewriting it?"

So that was it. I knew he did not like Seton much. I replied that my report had been written the day after the bombing, so I had nothing to add to it. (The sequel to this I came across after we had returned to India and I was adjutant to Seton, and found, by mistake, a letter on his desk recommending a bar to my DFC. Across it, in Old Boy's handwriting, was "Not Recommended".)

I left HQ as soon as possible and returned to Dum Dum. I booked a seat on a Chinese National Airlines Dakota for Lashio. The crew were all Chinese. In the plane, a very nice Dutch girl sat next to me. She worked in the Dutch Legation at Chungking. The monsoon was about to break, and as we approached the mountains, I could see the cumulus clouds building up ahead. They were slightly broken, but dead ahead there was an ugly mountain of dark cumulus towering over us, reaching up to easily 30,000 feet. The pilot continued on his course.

"Surely the clot isn't going into that one," I thought. As we touched the fingers of broken cloud, the aircraft began to shudder as the engines changed their synchronisation. I told the girl to fasten her seat belt, while I rapidly did the same. As we plunged deeper into the cumulus, our altitude began to change at an alarming rate. One moment we rose on the crest of an updraught, to then fall 300 to 400 feet to a sudden halt, as the whole aircraft shuddered. My eyes became glued to the wingtips, which were flexing like a bird's. Of course, I had flown in bad cumulus, especially in Scotland, but then I was in a Hurricane.

As we flew into the centre of this maelstrom, we hit a really bad downdraught, dropping 2,000 to 3,000 feet, to come to an awful halt. The whole aircraft shuddered from end to end, and the two fat Chinese businessmen who were sitting in front of us, having failed to fasten their seat belts before the downdraught, had become weightless and sailed to the ceiling, only to crash on their backs in the alleyway, where they lay groaning. Thinking we would break up at any moment, I put my hand on my companion's forearm, she nervously clutching the arm of her seat. This momentary human contact seemed infinitely reassuring. A few minutes later we broke into a clear valley of cloud, and the pilot turned back.

The next day I arrived at Lashio, and took a lift in a Blenheim bound for Loiwing. As we followed the Burma Road, the clouds came down, and the young officer pilot flew into one. I noticed that instead of transferring his gaze onto the instrument panel, he was looking out of the port window. When the turn-and-bank indicator showed that we were in a vertical dive to starboard, I could stand it no longer; tapping him on the shoulder, I pointed to the instrument panel and shouted: "Why don't you look at your bloody instruments?"

But, too late, we broke cloud about 20 feet away from a sheer mountainside. I told him to return to Lashio by following the Burma Road beneath the cloud base. On landing, we nearly overshot the runway, and ended up in a spectacular ground-loop. I got out, thanked him, and departed hastily to the watch office. I rang Loiwing and asked for someone to come and fetch me by jeep. I have disliked being flown by anybody else ever since. I think most single-seater pilots tend towards this feeling.

We were by now getting ready to move away from Loiwing, when one morning we heard a dreadful racket going on at the aerodrome; curious, we leapt into my jeep and drove towards the field. As we got closer we could see dozens of aircraft diving and zooming at zero feet, and heard cannon and machine-gun fire. There were about thirty Japanese Zeroes shooting at anything they could see.

I came to a halt behind a clump of bamboo, on the perimeter of the field, and got out to watch the fun. A moment later, we distinguished the whine of diving aircraft approaching from high up – the American Volunteer Group. With their height and speed, they made mincemeat of the Zeroes. I finally counted at least eleven wreckages burning on or around the aerodrome. At one time, a Zero passed about 20 feet over our heads, with a P40 close on his tail. The P40's bullets kicked up spurts of dust around us, and the Zero ended up in a ball of flame and dust 500 yards behind us. Gradually the battle drifted off towards the mountains to the east. It was the best show from the stalls that I have ever witnessed. The American Volunteer Group claimed fourteen Zeroes shot down. One P40 had one bullet hole in it.

I had met the US General "Pappy" Greenlaw several times at Loiwing. He was an engaging character, and beneath his humorous, slaphappy exterior, he was efficient, and knew how to command the respect of the Chinese. He told me that, properly trained, the Chinese made excellent mechanics and were great workers. One day he showed me around the maintenance factory he had installed when the American Volunteer Group were sent to Rangoon after Pearl Harbour. It was contained in a long, *basha*-type shed, with all the lathes and tools operated from belts and a countershaft, powered by a couple of diesel engines. After we had gone around, he told me he was moving the factory further north. On the following day the factory had disappeared overnight – not by motor transport, but on mules and by foot – a very impressive achievement.

Soon after, Pappy was giving us a briefing about the road to Bhamo and that part of north-western Burma. There was a frightful row of a battle going on overhead when, to our astonishment, a bejewelled goddess appeared through the door, looking as if she had just stepped from a New York or Paris salon. It was Pappy's wife. He just went on with his briefing, on which we found it hard to concentrate.

A month or so later I was in Calcutta, when someone told me Pappy was staying at a suite in the Grand Hotel. I went to see him, to find Pappy sitting despondently by a window, hurling bread out of the fourth-floor window to kite hawks which wheeled outside to collect it. The door opened and a bearer brought in a tray. Pappy pointed to a door: "Take it in there ... better knock."

The waiter did as he was bid. I could hear the distinct sound of a key turning in the lock. The tray was snatched from the man's hands, and the door slammed in his face.

I asked Pappy what was going on.

"Guess we had a kinda little difference of opinion ... have a drink."

I left Pappy still feeding the kite hawks.

A few days later we were on our final retreat. By now I had learnt never to be surprised at anything. We received our final instructions to get the squadron to the airfield at Myitkyina, where they were to be flown out by Dakota to Assam, in north-eastern India. The road from Loiwing to Bhamo, if it could be called that, was a single track, pursuing its way through dense jungle and forest on either side.

It was opened twelve hours one way and twelve the other to avoid congestion, since, if a vehicle broke down, it took considerable time to fell enough trees and undergrowth to get it out of the way, as we were to find when we lost our only vehicle since the retreat from Rangoon – a Ford truck with a burnt-out coil. It took three-quarters of an hour's hard work to remove it and allow the rest of the convoy to pass. Luckily, the adjutant had managed to obtain most of the hours of daylight for our passage.

It was an interesting journey, overshadowed, however, by the knowledge that the Japanese were not far behind us; we knew nothing of their whereabouts, nor were we trained for this form of warfare. Fortunately, we possessed plenty of rifles, Tommy guns, aircraft Browning machine-guns and ammunition. We set forth with close to thirty motor vehicles at about 6 o'clock one day at the end of March. I had given the heavy aircraft loader to Pappy, since I no longer had any use for it; the few remaining Hurricanes having gone to India just previously, with Carvel.

That part of Burma was intersected by many tributaries of the Irrawaddy and Chindwin rivers, which were usually spanned by rather flimsy bamboo bridges. To cross them entailed the tedious process of unloading the 3-tonners on one side of the stream and reloading them on the other, or ferrying them, unloaded, across on barges.

This is how we crossed some of the rivers between Loiwing and Bhamo

We also had to repair six bridges. The troop's morale, however, was high – even festive on occasions. During the whole Burma campaign, not one airman was brought before me on a charge of misconduct. In the evenings, I used to proceed ahead to find a suitable campsite for the night and take one or two of the boys, armed with shotguns, to find something for the pot. The green parakeets used to appear low over the trees to roost, iridescent in the evening sunlight. I have to admit that we shot a few of them, for they were excellent eating. It was strange how little wildlife we met in our progress. One of the sergeants said that a leopard jumped over him one evening. I was told that yellow fever, and a particularly virulent and usually fatal form of malaria, abounded in that part of the world, but I did not hear of anyone suffering subsequently, although we used to be badly bitten by mosquitos at night.

I worked out that during this part of the journey we averaged about 5 to 10 miles a day, which would hardly have won the Monte Carlo rally. We eventually arrived on the banks of the Irrawaddy opposite Myitkyina. There was no bridge and no apparent means of crossing it. Adjutant and I toured the banks north and south, until we found a sizeable vessel with a smokestack, drawn up on the riverbank opposite a small village. On further enquiry, I found that it belonged to a Sikh, whom we eventually traced.

The medical officer's ambulance becomes stuck during the retreat to Myitkyina

An RAF DC3 Dakota aircraft at Myitkyina, taking squadron personnel aboard to fly them back over the Hump to Dibrugah, in India. The bitter end [photo by Ken Hemingway]

I asked him if he would use his boat to ferry my troops across the river. He told me that the boat could not move. I offered him many rupees. He was adamant. The engine was not working and, from his description, would disappear altogether if placed in its natural environment in the stream. I had learned to play poker from my Canadian flight commander many years before. I told the Sikh I had many rifles and ammunition. His interest awakened, and in the end, after hard bargaining, his boat came alive at the cost of thirty rifles and 3,000 rounds of ammunition, so we all arrived safely on the other side.

In my elation, and in the context of the time, it was as good as two dozen oysters, a cold bottle of champagne and a large cigar – though it was years before I could actually indulge in them.

Unfortunately, we had to leave all of our motor transport on the other side, not knowing the situation ahead. We marched about 5 miles to the aerodrome, where, on the following morning, a hard-worked squadron of Dakotas flew us to Dibrugah in Assam, over the Hump.

The first man to greet me at Myitkyina was Count Czernin. He was, at that time, the commanding officer of a squadron of Curtiss Mohawks, which he sent that day to destroy all of my MT at the river.

The Gods laugh. But I am pleased I do not live on Mount Olympus.

AFTERWORD BY THE EDITOR

In my first edition of *Hurricanes over Burma*, chapter three in part two was devoted to some of Bunny's letters to me concerning the end of the first campaign, and also extracts from Slim's *Defeat into Victory*. I believe that these are worth printing as a sequel to Bunny's memoirs.

FROM SLIM'S *DEFEAT INTO VICTORY*

The R.A.F. are finished in Burma:

Some hard things were said by the angry soldiery when the Air Force disappeared, especially about the speed and disorder of the abandonment of Magwe. But they would have done well to remember that this same small Anglo-American force had already destroyed 233 Japanese machines in the air and 58 on the ground, of which total the A.V.G. accounted for 217 and the R.A.F. 74, at a cost to us of 46 in the air and 51 on the ground, or a ratio in the air of five-to-one in our favour. Even on the ground, with all the odds of range and warning against them, they had destroyed plane for plane.

General Wavell had decided that the only sound course was to retain in India such air forces as he could scrape together, so as to build up something capable of defending that country when the time came. To commit his pathetically meagre resources on the Burma front, without a warning organization and against overwhelmingly superior strength, would inevitably be to destroy them. The Army in Burma must struggle on without an Air Force. There is no doubt that this was the right decision.

On the 25th April, General Alexander and I met Stilwell, just returned from the taking of Taunggyi, at Kyaukse, twenty-five miles south of Mandalay. The complete disappearance of the VI Chinese Army and the rapidly spreading disintegration of the other two Chinese armies were the dominating facts of a grim situation. There was no longer any chance of staging a counter-offensive; the Japanese were about to seize Lashio and with it would go our hopes of holding Northern Burma. With the Chinese rapidly passing out of the picture, realism demanded that we should now decide to get out of Burma as intact as we could, with as much as we could.

The Post Mortem:

I had now an opportunity for a few days to sit down and think out what had happened during the last crowded months and why it had happened. The outstanding and incontrovertible fact was that we had taken a thorough beating. We, the Allies, had been outmaneuvered, outfought and outgeneraled. It was easy, of course, as it always is, to find excuses for our failure, but excuses are of no use for the next time; what is wanted are causes and remedies.

There were certain basic causes for our defeat. The first and over-riding one was lack of preparation. Until a few weeks before it happened, no higher authority, civil or military, had expected an invasion of Burma. They were all grievously pressed in other quarters, and what was held to be the comparatively minor responsibility of the defense of Burma was tossed from one to another, so that no one held it long enough to plan and provide over an adequate period. The two great errors that grew from this were the military separation of Burma from India and the division of operational from administrative control. An army whose plan of campaign is founded on fundamental errors in organization cannot hope for success unless it has vast superiority over the enemy in numbers and material. Another fatal omission, springing from the same cause, was that until too late no serious attempt was made to connect India and Burma by road, so that when Rangoon fell the army in Burma was for all practical purposes isolated.

A most obvious instance of the lack of preparation was the smallness and unsuitability of the forces provided to defend Burma. Two ill-found, hurriedly collected, and inexperienced divisions, of which one had been trained and equipped for desert warfare and the other, which contained a large proportion of raw and unreliable Burmese troops, were tragically insufficient to meet superior Japanese forces in a country of the size and topography of Burma. The arrival of the Chinese adjusted the numerical balance in favour of the Allies, and, if they could have been got up to the front in strength before Rangoon fell, they might, in spite of their lack of almost all the necessities of a modern army, have changed the result. It is perhaps doubtful if, with the transport and supply resources available, their forward concentration could have been achieved; the pity is that it was not tried. Even if it had been, the refusal of the Chinese to obey Stilwell's orders would probably have ensured defeat.

The completely inadequate air forces and their total elimination in the campaign were most grievous disadvantages to the Army.

The extreme inefficiency of our whole intelligence system in Burma was probably our greatest single handicap.

BUNNY STONE HAS THE LAST WORD

All records of the first Burma campaign were lost, but I believe that, as far as the Air Force was concerned, I was the only pilot who went through with it from first to last. Like Singapore, the whole campaign was a vast cock-up, but it was most certainly *not* our fault.

Slim had it somewhat wrong as far as our attack on Mingaladon was concerned. I guess he was briefed by Old Boy, who would have exaggerated. We did not claim to have destroyed the number of Japanese he reported (eleven in the air and sixteen on the ground), nor were there any Navy Zero fighters there – only Army 97s. He also had it wrong to say that our aircraft were unguarded at Magwe at his arrival on 12 March. It was the job of the Burma Rifles to guard the aerodrome, and, according to my ground crews, they certainly did their job successfully and well when we were there, and no aircraft were sabotaged or lost. What went on before that I am not certain, but I completely reject the intimation by Louis Allen, in his book *Burma, the Longest Retreat*, that the RAF failed in their duty in any way. His remarks are typical of one who was not at Magwe at that time.*

It was most unfair of Slim to comment that the evacuation of Magwe by the RAF was speedy and disorderly. Again, he had obviously been ill-advised by some excuse-maker in the Army. They had stuffed up the whole campaign well before, and after, they prematurely blew the Sittang river bridge; no doubt any scapegoat was welcome to them.

---

* EDITOR'S NOTE: Slim had mentioned the air attack on Mingaladon and the guarding of Magwe earlier in his book, and the above comment concerns this.

Magwe *had* to be abandoned for one reason – no warning system. Our retirement to Loiwing at least brought us under the AVG warning system. You cannot maintain a proper fighter force without it, something which was never understood by the Old Boy.

EDITOR'S COMMENT ON ALL THE ABOVE

To me, the saddest thing about the whole campaign was the failure to reward Bunny Stone for the absolutely magnificent job he did as the senior fighter squadron commander of the RAF forces in Burma. The fact that in Burma he had been credited with two confirmed and two damaged enemy aircraft in the air, destroyed two of their bombers on the ground, led the unit which sank the troop ship, and took part in numerous ground strafing sorties (particularly the one on Mingaladon) was, in itself, worthy of the addition of a bar to his DFC (won in the Battle of Britain).

His total refusal to give up the struggle until the very last; his deep sense of responsibility towards his squadron personnel – pilots and ground crew; his turning away from the temptation to compromise his integrity; and his love of those traditions which made the RAF such a superb fighting force were his guiding principles. It was quite shameful that they were never recognised by his own service's higher command at that time. His squadron could at least rightly share in the recognition by Sir William Slim, who said in his book: "Rarely can so small an Air Force have battled so gallantly and so effectively against comparable odds."

FINALLY

At the time of his departure from the India-Burma theatre in 1944 (actual date unknown), Bunny was the Wing Commander Air of 221 Group in Colombo, Ceylon. He was scheduled to fly back to Cairo, via Karachi, in an Avro Tudor – which was a civil version of the famous Lancaster bomber.

At this time, No. 17 squadron had been re-equipped with Spitfire 8s (which we all considered the best fighter ever produced, but were sad we did not have it well before) and was stationed under my command at an aerodrome at Vavuniya, in central Ceylon, where I handed the unit over to Squadron Leader E.A. Pevreal, of the Royal New Zealand Air Force, on my posting back to Australia on 23 July 1944. He led a flight of Spitfire 8s over Colombo to bid Bunny farewell.

Unfortunately, Squadron Leader Pevreal was later killed in an aircraft accident, and the unit then came under the charge of Squadron Leader "Ginger" Lacey, DFM and bar, AFM, on 23 November 1944.

Bunny finished the war lecturing young officers at a training college in the UK, where he completed his drawings but did not start on his memoirs until the late 1970s, after numerous attempts at earning a living as a portrait painter in South Africa and England.

His untimely death was a sad ending to a life in which he knew little or nothing of what went on in civilian life, and its patterns of behaviour outside service in the Air Force – which he had joined before the war. This was a problem which confounded many young men when the war finished.

His country was lucky indeed to have had so many like him who gave their lives for it on service, or after the war had spoiled them for peace.

APPENDIX A: THE FIRST FORTY

This list comprises the names, final ranks and destinies of the first forty Empire Air Training Scheme airmen to embark for overseas in 1940:

407071	Sgt	Barrett	R.L.	†
407072	F/O	Bishop	J.M.	Cas.
400024	Flt/Lt	Breheny	T.R.	
408000	P/O	Briggs	G..M.	†
400025	F/O	Campbell	R.B.	†
406004	Flt/Lt	Clark	S.M.	DFC
407041	Sqn/Ldr	Cotton	M.C.C.	DFC, Cas.
400051	W/O	Damman	R.G.	POW
407018	W/O	Davies	R.L.	
402000	Sgt	Drummond	F.A.V.M.	†
400054	Sgt	Field	P.	†
402002	Flt/Lt	Hall	C.M.	POW
408012	F/O	Harbottle	P.F.	†
406027	P/O	Hicks	K.M.	†
406012	W/O	Kerr	A.Mc.B.	POW (Esc.), Cas.
407077	F/O	Kinnane	J.	† MID
402018	W/O	Lloyd	G.S.	
402004	Sgt	McCullough	J.M.	†
400044	Flt/Lt	McKechnie	J.P.	POW, DFC
404007	P/O	McLeod	E.W.	†

402005	Sqn/Ldr	McSweyn	A.F.	POW (Esc.), MC, AFC
408001	Flt/Lt	Maxwell	M.M.	
407078	Flt/Lt	Milne	I.A.L.	POW
400045	P/O	Oak-Rhind	D.K.	†
400030	Flt/Lt	O'Neill	E.H.	DSO, DFC
400029	Sgt	Orbuck	L.D.	†
407079	P/O	Phillips	W.R.	†
402007	Flt/Lt	Roberts	A.C.	POW (Esc.), MID
400031	Sqn/Ldr	Robinson	K.E.	DFC, AFC, PFB
407019	Sgt	Ross	M.R.	†
402008	Flt/Sgt	Schwager	A.C.	†
402041	Flt/Lt	Scott	T.W.	
407021	Flt/Lt	Sheppard	F.G.	
400032	P/O	Shirtcliffe	W.J.	†
402009	Flt/Lt	Tainton	E.B.	
402011	Sgt	Uhrig	R.J.	†
400033	Flt/Lt	Walliker	E.V.	
400048	Flt/Lt	Wilson	P.	
407023	F/O	Wood	F.A.	Cas.
408003	Flt/Sgt	Woolnough	J.S.R.	†

Key to Symbols and Abbreviations

†	Killed		Sgt	Sergeant
Cas.	Casualty		Flt/Sgt	Flight Sergeant
POW	Prisoner of War		W/O	Warrant Officer
(Esc.)	Escaped		P/O	Pilot Officer
DFC	Distinguished Flying Cross		F/O	Flying Officer
DSO	Distinguished Service Order		Flt/Lt	Flight Lieutenant
AFC	Air Force Cross		S/Ldr	Squadron Leader
MID	Mentioned in dispatches			
PFB	Polish Flying Badge			

It is interesting to note that the casualty rate for the First Forty (including those killed, wounded and prisoner of war) is twenty-nine out of forty, which is 72 per cent. At the time of this publication there were only nine survivors.

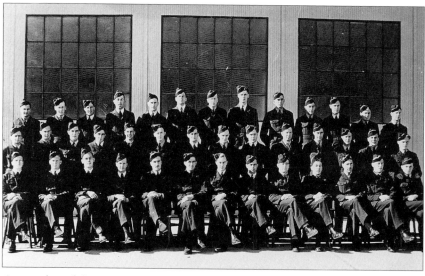

A group photo of the First Forty in Canada

BACK ROW: Woolnough, Oak-Rhind, O'Neill, Cotton, Damman, Hall, Wood, Maxwell, McLeod, McSweyn, Barrett, Bishop, Drummond
MIDDLE ROW: Roberts, Sheppard, Briggs, Orbuck, Tainton, Robinson, Kerr, Schwager, Hicks, Field, Ross, Kinnane, Uhrig, Lloyd
FRONT ROW: Wilson, Clark, Shirtcliffe, Walliker, McKechnie, Milne, Harbottle, Phillips, McCulloch, Davies, Breheney, Campbell, Scott

APPENDIX B: HISTORIES OF NUMBER 43 AND NUMBER 17 SQUADRONS

NUMBER 43 SQUADRON

Badge: *A gamecock.*

Motto: Gloria Finis *(Glory the aim)*

The gamecock badge commemorates the first postwar fighter, the Gloucester Gamecock, with which the squadron was equipped in 1926.

Number 43 Squadron's gestation period was unduly lengthy owing to delays in aircraft and crew supply. It was formed at Stirling on 15 April 1916 from No. 18 Reserve Squadron, and moved south to Nether Avon in August, expecting to go overseas shortly after. It was not until January 1917, however, that the squadron at last went to France, equipped with Sopwith $1\frac{1}{2}$ Strutters in the scout role. By now, however, this type was already obsolescent as a fighter, and most of No. 43's work comprised recconnaissance and photography, with some line patrols as well. In May, however, the squadron was used on the Scarpe to machine-gun the massed German troops and to strafe trenches and transport. This was one of the earliest uses of scouts for ground attack, and its success resulted in much wider use of fighters in this role, in the Battle of the Marne,

a month later, and subsequently. The squadron began to re-equip with Camels in September but was not fully equipped until a month later.

With these it was able to enter into the air battles of the period, and was mostly employed on offensive patrols and ground attack. The latter role was again to the fore in the German offensive in the spring of 1918, when No. 43 was heavily committed to its old task of low-level strafing. As the summer wore on, however, the squadron became more and more involved in the big air battles over the trenches. The record score in combat, for numbers of aircraft scored in one day, had been secured by a No. 43 Squadron pilot, Captain J.L. Trollope, on 24 March, when he destroyed six German aircraft, and on 12 April this was equalled by another No. 43 pilot, Captain H.W. Woolett. In September the Camels were replaced by Snipes, No. 43 being the first Snipe squadron, and these were used mainly on bomber-escort flights, but by now the air war was all but over. The squadron remained on the Continent for another year, as part of the Army of Occupation, then returned to Spittlegate and was disbanded three months later on 31 December 1919.

Number 43 reformed as a Home Defence fighter squadron at Henlow on 1 July 1925, and was again equipped with the Snipe. This was not for long, for the following spring the squadron began to receive Gloucester Gamecocks and these formed the foundation for No. 43's aerobatic prowess, which came to its height with Hawker Furies in the 1930s.

In December 1926, the squadron moved to Tangmere, where it remained as a rival to No. 1 Squadron until World War II. It retained the Furies, having been the first squadron to fly them, until November 1938, when most of the other fighter squadrons had already been converted to more modern but less enjoyable fighters.

Hurricanes now became No. 43's mount, and on the outbreak of war, when their rivals, No. 1 Squadron, went to France, No. 43 retired, in November, to Newcastle, where it flew convoy patrols in the main. First victory came on 30 January, when Flight Lieutenant Hull and Sergeant Carey shot down a Heinkel 111 while on convoy patrol. Two more He111s were destroyed in one action before No. 43 went further north for Scapa Flow defence. Here activity was livelier, and on 8 April two attacks were met in which three He111s were shot down and two damaged, one of which landed on Wick airfield.

On 1 June, No. 43 returned to Tangmere and went straight into patrols over the Dunkirk beaches. Although the score mounted, so did the losses, and the squadron went temporarily nonoperational during the month, owing to depletion of pilots. July was more varied, with escort sorties with Blenheim bombers and some night-flying, as well as air battles by day over the Channel. With an influx of new pilots, time had to be given to training, but in August the squadron was fully committed to the heavy fighting over the Channel and along the south coast in what is now known as the Battle of Britain. On 8 September, the squadron again flew north, this time for a rest.

During the remainder of 1940 and all of 1941, the squadron remained in the north, which period is covered within this book. Number 43 was now a day-and-night-fighter squadron, having increased its night-flying and managed to destroy several aircraft by night during these raids. Another year was to pass in this way before the squadron returned to much action. This was back at Tangmere in June 1942, when the squadron joined its old stablemate, No. 1, on intruder patrols over France. It was in on the Dieppe raids, flying low-level strafing attacks, then in September it became nonoperational to prepare for overseas.

It spent until August 1944 in support of the Allied armies in the Mediterranean theatre, and then moved to France to cover the landings in the south before returning to Italy, where it stayed for the rest of the war in an army-support role.

Commanding Officers of Number 43 Squadron

Apr. 1916-May 1917	Major W. Sholto Douglas, MC
May 1917-Nov. 1917	Major A.S.W. Dore
Nov. 1917-Jan. 1919	Major C.C. Miles, MC
Jan. 1919-Jun. 1919	Major R.S. Lucy
Jun. 1919-Aug. 1919	Major A.C.V. Parr
Aug. 1919-Sep. 1919	Major A.J. Capel
Jul. 1925-Jan. 1928	Squadron Leader A.F. Brooke
Jan. 1928-Nov. 1930	Squadron Leader C.N. Lowe, MC, DFC
Nov. 1930-Jan. 1932	Squadron Leader L.H. Slatter, OBE, DSO, DFC
Jan. 1932-Oct. 1934	Squadron Leader R.H. Hammer, MC
Oct. 1943-Apr. 1935	Squadron Leader F. Wright
Apr. 1935-Dec. 1935	Squadron Leader A.M. Wray, MC, DFC, AFC
Jan. 1936-Aug. 1936	Squadron Leader B.V. Reynolds
Aug. 1936-Feb. 1937	Flight Lieutenant R.I.G. McDougal
Feb. 1937-Oct. 1939	Squadron Leader R.E. Bain
Oct. 1939-Jul. 1940	Squadron Leader C.G. Lott, DSO
Jul. 1940-Sep. 1940	Squadron Leader J.V. Badger, DFC
Sep. 1940-Jan. 1942	Squadron Leader T.F.D. Morgan, DSO, DFC and two bars, Croix de Guerre.
Jan. 1942-Sep. 1942	Squadron Leader Le Roy du Vivier, DFC

Number 43 Squadron Aircraft

Sopwith 1½ Strutter	1916-1919
Sopwith F1 Camel	1916-1919
Sopwith 7F1 Snipe	1916-1919
Gloster Gamecock	March 1926
A.W. Siskin IIIa	June 1928
Hawker Fury	May 1931
Hawker Hurricane 1	November 1938
Hawker Hurricane 2b	April 1941
Hawker Hurricane 2c	November 1942

NUMBER 17 SQUADRON

Badge: *A gauntlet*

Motto: Excellere contende *(Strive to excel)*

The badge symbolises armed strength, and also commemorates the type of aircraft, the Gloucester Gauntlet, the squadron was flying when the badge was awarded.

The Standard of Battle Honours was presented to No. 17 Squadron at Wildrenath, Germany, on 12 July 1960 by Marshal of the Royal Air Force Sir Dermot A. Boyle, GCB, KCVO, KBE, AFC, an original pilot officer of 17 Squadron in 1926. The standard was created by His late Majesty King George VI to mark the twenty-fifth anniversary of the Royal Air Force in 1943. It was awarded only to squadrons of twenty-five years' standing, or with a history of special outstanding operations. Her Majesty the Queen affirmed her father's decision, and gives personal approval to each standard created.

The standard consists of a fringed and tasselled, blue silken banner mounted on a pike crowned by a golden eagle. Eight selected battle honours in scroll surround the squadron badge, and the decorative border contains the rose, leek, thistle and shamrock, embroidered in gold.

The Battle Honours of Number 17 Squadron

Egypt	1915-1916
Palestine	1916
Macedonia	1916-1918
France and the Low Countries	1940
Dunkirk	1940
Battle of Britain	1940
Burma	1942
Burma	1944-1945

During World War II, No. 17 Squadron destroyed 111 enemy aircraft and claimed further fifty-one probably destroyed, a total of 162 enemy aircraft shot down in air battles. Eighty-one of these were destroyed in the Battle of Britain.

This book deals with the activities of the squadron from the time I joined them during their rest period, up in Scotland, in October 1941, until I left them in July 1944.

At the end of the war, the squadron remained in Japan until disbanded in February 1948, and in February 1949 was reformed at Chivenor in Fighter Command as an Army Anti-Aircraft Co-Operation Unit, disbanding once more in March 1951.

In June 1956 the squadron reformed at RAF Whan, as a Photographic Reconnaissance Squadron, equipped with Canberra PR7 aircraft, later moving to Wildrenath, Germany, where it was based until in 1972, when it was re-equipped with McDonnell Douglas Phantoms and stationed at the strategic NATO base at Bruggen in West Germany (where I visited them in that year).

Number 17 Squadron served in the Gulf War under the command of Wing Commander Nigel Elsdon, son of Jimmy Elsdon who figures in this book. Sadly, Nigel was killed in action in the Gulf campaign, and was later commemorated at a funeral service in Westminster Abbey.

Commanding Officers of No. 17 Squadron

1 Dec. 1915	Major E.N. Fuller
19 Dec. 1916	Captain F. Hudson
4 Dec. 1917	Major J.H. Herring
2 Apr. 1918	Major S.G. Hodges
1 Jun. 1924	Squadron Leader J. Leacroft, MC

1 Apr. 1928	Squadron Leader A.R. Arnold, DSO, DFC
1 May 1930	Squadron Leader R. Harrison, DFC
1 Nov. 1931	Squadron Leader A.L. Fiddament
20 Nov. 1932	Squadron Leader F.J. Vincent
16 Aug. 1934	Squadron Leader H.S. Broughall, MC, DFC
31 Oct. 1935	Squadron Leader D. de H. Humphreys
9 Jan. 1937	Squadron Leader C. Walter
3 Nov. 1939	Squadron Leader A.C. Tomlinson
19 May 1940	Squadron Leader J.H. Edwardes-Jones
23 May 1940	Squadron Leader G.D. Emms
8 Jun. 1940	Squadron Leader R.I.G. McDougall
18 Jul. 1940	Squadron Leader C.W. Williams
29 Aug. 1940	Squadron Leader A.G. Miller
28 Jul. 1941	Squadron Leader C.A.C. Stone, DFC
1 Jun. 1942	Squadron Leader J.H. Iremonger
9 Dec. 1942	Squadron Leader M.C.C. Cotton, DFC, RAAF
23 Jul. 1944	Squadron Leader E.A. Pevreal, RNZAF
23 Nov. 1944	Squadron Leader J.H. Lacey, DFM Bar, AFM

Number 17 Squadron Aircraft

BE2c, BE2d, BE2e, BE12, BE12a Bristol Scout, DH7 Nieuport Scout, AW SE5a, Spad, Camel, DH9	December 1915 to November 1918
Snipe	April 1924
Woodcock	March 1926
Siskin	September 1928
Bulldog	October 1929
Hart	December 1935
Bulldog	March 1936
Gauntlet	August 1936
Hurricane 1, 2, 2b, 2c	June 1939 to April 1944
Spitfire 8	April 1944
Spitfire 14E	June 1945
Spitfire 14E, 18, 19	September 1945

APPENDIX C: EXTRACTS FROM CHRIS SHORES' BOOK ACES HIGH

BARRICK, John Frederick   Flight Lieutenant

"Tex" Barrick was born in Sweetwater, Texas, on 12 May 1918. He joined the RCAF in Ontario late in 1940, training in Canada before being sent to the UK, where he attended 55 OTU. He was posted to 17 Squadron in September 1941 just before this unit was ordered to the Middle East. Diverted to Burma after the Japanese attack in December, he saw action throughout the retreat, ending up at Loiwing in China during April 1942. During his last engagement on 10 April he shot down one Ki43 – identified as a Zero at the time – and circled to watch it crash. Three more attacked him, one of which he managed to damage, but the other two shot him down and he crash-landed, striking his face on the gunsight. He leapt from the cockpit and ran to cover just before his attackers strafed his stricken Hurricane. Meanwhile some AVG Tomahawks had arrived, the pilots of these shooting down the aircraft he had just damaged, and driving off the others. Initially Barrick was aided by missionary doctors, who got him to Colonel Chennault's HQ where he remained for two weeks before being flown out to India in a C-47. He subsequently rejoined the squadron, also now back in India, and in August was awarded a DFM and promoted from Flight Sergeant to Warrant Officer. In November 1942 he was commissioned, becoming a flight commander in May 1943. During June and July of that year he was involved in some ground attack sorties over the Arakan, but in August the unit moved to Ceylon. He finally ended his tour in December 1943, and returned to England. He was sent from there to Canada where he became an instructor at 1 OTU, Bagotville. In October 1944 he was posted to 135 Squadron,

RCAF, at Patricia Bay, British Columbia, remaining with this unit until his demobilisation on 2 October 1945. At the time of writing he was living in retirement in Alabama, USA.

Total Victories:　　5 destroyed, 2 damaged, 2 destroyed on the ground.

CAREY, Frank Reginald　　　Group Captain

Born in Brixton, South London, on 7 May 1912, Frank Carey became an RAF apprentice at Halton at the age of 15. On completion of his apprenticeship, he joined 43 Squadron as a Metal Rigger, where he spent the next three years. After promotion to LAC he went on a year's conversion course back at Halton to become a Fitter I. Service with 7 and 58 (Bomber) Squadrons at Worthy Down followed. Meanwhile he applied for pilot training, for which he was accepted in 1935, training at 6 FTS, Netheravon. In September 1936 he returned to 43 Squadron at Tangmere as a Sergeant Pilot, and was still present in this rank when the unit moved north to Acklington on the outbreak of war. Involved in patrols over the North Sea, he took part in three early victories against He111 shipping raiders, for which on 21 February 1940 he received the award of a DFM. In April he was commissioned and posted to 3 Squadron, accompanying that unit to France on 10 May at the outbreak of the "Blitzkrieg". He was to claim the squadron's first confirmed successes later that same day, when he reported shooting down three He111s during his first patrol, and a fourth just before dusk. Early on the 14th, after several more engagements, he was shot down by the rear gunner of a Do17 south of Louvain. He crash-landed in No Man's Land, and was rescued by a Belgian contact patrol, being taken to a local hospital with a leg wound. He then became caught up in the Army hospital system, being evacuated to England about 7 June, where he found that he had been listed "Missing, believed killed". He also discovered that he had been awarded both a DFC and Bar, both gazetted on 31 May. He was posted back to 43 Squadron, which was in action early in July, but in a fight with six Bf110s on 9th, lost the commanding officer, who was badly wounded. Heavy fighting in mid August brought Carey four confirmed and four probable victories against German bombers in a period of six days, but on 18th, just as he had shot down a Ju87 dive-bomber, which he saw go down vertically, streaming flames, his Hurricane R4109 was hit and he was wounded in the right knee; he crashed on landing, and was again despatched to hospital. He returned to the unit in September, now based in the North, remaining until February 1941 when he was posted to 52 OTU as an instructor. He returned to operations in July 1941, joining 245 Squadron at Aldergrove in Northern Ireland, as a flight commander. The following month he was posted to form and command 135 Squadron at Honiley. In November this unit sailed for the Middle East, but was diverted to the Far East when the Japanese launched their attack there in December, arriving at Rangoon, Burma, via India. He was quickly in action against Japanese raiders over the city. On 12 February he was promoted Wing Commander, taking over 267 Wing of which 135 Squadron formed a part. After one further victory, he led two successful attacks on Moulmein airfield in South Burma. The award of a Second Bar to his DFC followed on 24 March. Following the retreat from Burma into India, he was posted to command RAF Alipore. At the end of 1942 he joined Air HQ, Bengal, and then in February 1943 formed the Air Fighting Training Unit at Amarda Road, where he successfully provided aerial gunnery training to both RAF and USAAF units which were to operate over Burma. In November 1944 he moved to command 73 OTU at Fayid, Egypt, as Group Captain. He was to receive an AFC for his work in India; he was also awarded a US Silver Star after the end of the war. In July 1945 he returned at last to England, where after a spell as Group Captain (Tactics) at Central Fighter Establishment in 1945, he attended Army Staff College following which he was granted a Permanent Commission. Reverting to the rank of Wing Commander, he became Wing Leader of 135 Wing, 2nd Tactical Air Force, in Germany in August 1947, flying Tempest II fighters with this unit until February 1949. Following conversion to jet aircraft, he served as Wing Commander Flying at Gütersloh. After holding various staff appointments, he became Air Adviser to the British High Commission in Australia in 1958. Retiring from the RAF on 2 June 1960, having again become a Group Captain in 1956, he was made a CBE and joined Rolls-Royce Aero Division as their representative in Australia. He subsequently retired and returned to the UK, where he was living on the south coast at the time of writing.

Total Victories: 25 and 3 shared destroyed, 4 unconfirmed destroyed, 3 probables, 1 "possible", 8 damaged.

DALTON-MORGAN, Thomas Frederick   Group Captain

Born on 23 March 1917 in Cardiff, Thomas Dalton-Morgan joined the RAF on a short service commission in August 1935. In November 1936, on conclusion of his training, he was posted to 22 Squadron on Vildebeeste torpedo-bombers.

At the end of May 1939 he joined the staff of the Directorate of Training at the Air Ministry. Here he worked on a committee planning the handover of equipment to the new Fleet Air Arm, and took part in the initial flying training of Naval personnel. On completion of this task, he applied to return to operational flying and in June 1940 was posted to command "B" Flight of 43 Squadron. In action over the English Channel over the next month, he was hit by crossfire by He111s on 13 August, baling out of Hurricane P3972 with slight wounds. On recovery, he was soon back in action, but on 6 September was again wounded, this time in the knee, whilst in combat with Bf109s; he was obliged to crash-land at Tangmere. He was awarded a DFC and on 16th was promoted to command the squadron following the loss of Squadron Leader Caesar Hull. The unit then withdrew north the rest, having suffered heavy casualties. He was to gain several night victories off the Northumbrian coast during the first half of 1941, receiving a Bar to his DFC for these actions on 30 May. After sharing in the destruction of a day raider on 24 July, however, his engine failed and he came down in the sea, losing two front teeth against the gunsight in doing so. He was picked up by HMS *Ludlow*. He left the squadron in January 1942 to become a controller at Turnhouse until November, when he was promoted and became Wing Commander Operations at 13 Group. He subsequently became Wing Leader at Middle Wallop, which was then expanded to become the Ibsley Wing, when he had four Spitfire, two Whirlwind and two Canadian Mustang fighter reconnaissance squadrons under his control. On 25 May 1943 he was awarded a DSO, which recorded his victories at 17 by this time. Due to his experience of maximum-range escort operations whilst with the Wing, he was attached briefly to the 4th Fighter Group of the US 8th Air Force, which was just beginning long-range bomber escort work. Promotion to Group Captain followed early in 1944, and he served as Operation Officer, first with 11 Group, Fighter Command, and then in 2nd TAF, moving to the European mainland with this organisation following the Normandy Invasion. He stayed on in Germany with 2nd TAF for nine months after the end of the war, receiving an OBE in June 1945. Attendance at the Staff College, Bracknell, followed, upon graduation from which he became Chief Instructor with the Offensive Support Wing at the School of Land/Air Warfare at Old Sarum. He was then sent to France on special duties with the Western Union Defence Organisation, the predecessor of NATO. Following this he returned to Germany to take over leadership of the Gütersloh Vampire Wing from Peter Wickham, leading this for the next two years. He then became a Group Captain again, and station commander at Wunstorf. He left the RAF in November 1952 to join the

UK/Australian Joint Project, involving the testing of missiles and other scientific projects at the Woomera Ranges in Australia. He remained with this body until his retirement in 1982. He still resides in Australia but he and his wife visit England frequently to see some of the family that have returned.

Total Victories: 14 and 3 shared destroyed, 1 probable, 4 damaged.

DOLL, John Christopher Shaboe   Flight Lieutenant

Chris Doll, a native of Horsham, was posted to 258 Squadron as a Pilot Officer in 1941 on the completion of training. In August he moved to 610 Squadron and a year later became a flight commander in 131 Squadron. During his second tour he served as a flight commander in 91 Squadron in September 1943, flying Griffon-engined Spitfire XIIs on low-level interceptions of Luftwaffe "hit and run" raiders, and sweeps over France. With this unit he claimed four victories, three of them during September 1943, for which he was awarded a DFC the following month. He left the unit in May 1944 and little else is known regarding this pilot save that he survived the war.

Total Victories: 4 destroyed, 1 shared probable, 1 damaged.

DU VIVIER, Daniel Albert Raymond Georges Leroy   Wing Commander

Leroy du Vivier was born on 13 January 1915 in Amersfoort, Belgium. He undertook military service in the Guides, transferring to the Aeronautique Militaire in 1937, and gained his wings in March 1938. He was commissioned on 1 March 1940, serving with 4/II Groupe on Fiat CR42s and Fairey Fireflies. He was shot down in a Firefly by Belgian AA on 11 May and baled out, being taken prisoner as a suspected German paratrooper! Four days later he undertook a virtual suicide mission with two other pilots, for which he later received a Citation of Belgian Military Aviation. Next day, 16th, the unit withdrew with its remaining aircraft to Chartres in France, and from here on 27 June he escaped to England, arriving by sea at Liverpool on 7 July, having been posted as a deserter by the French. In August 1940, he was posted as a Pilot Officer to 43 Squadron, but after his initial action, he was shot down by Bf109s on 2 September, baling out of Hurricane P3903, wounded. On recovery later that month he was posted to 229 Squadron, but was to rejoin 43 Squadron at the end of the year, becoming a flight commander in April 1941. He was awarded a Croix de Guerre Belge on 21 July 1941, and on 15 January 1942, became commanding officer of 43 Squadron, the first non-British Commonwealth pilot to command an RAF unit. He received a DFC at the end of January and a Bar to this in September 1942, following the Dieppe operation, leaving the unit that month for HQ, 13 Group, where he was promoted Wing Commander. In April 1943 he was posted to the Mediterranean, becoming Wing Leader of 239 Wing from 19 July. He then attended the RAF staff college at Haifa, Palestine, rejoining the Wing in December. He returned to the UK in July 1944 and became commanding officer of 53 OTU. In April 1946 he took command of 160 Belgian Wing in Germany, but left the air force in September to join Shell Aviation. He later became representative for Sabena Airline in New York, but was killed here in a motorcycling accident on 2 September 1981.

Total Victories: 3 and 2 shared destroyed, 1 and 1 shared probable, 1 damaged.

ELSDON, Thomas Arthur Francis   Wing Commander

Born on 22 January 1917 in Broughty Ferry, Dundee, "Jimmie" Elsdon attended the RAF College at Cranwell in 1936, being commissioned in December 1937. He was posted to 72 Squadron, where he was serving at the outbreak of war; he was engaged in some of the early interceptions off the north-east coast. During the Battle of Britain his Spitfire was shot down over the Thames by a Bf110 on 7 September and he baled out, severely wounded in the knee and shoulder. A DFC followed early in October, recording eight victories, six after 31 August, but it was to be mid-July 1941 before he was again fit to fly opera-tionally. He then joined 257 Squadron, but during an engagement on 24th, he was again slightly wounded. On 25 August he was appointed commanding officer of 136 Squadron which was just forming, and at the end of the year he prepared the unit for service in the Middle East. On the way, the Japanese attack in the Far East occurred, and the unit was directed to Burma, where he was to arrive during January 1942 with one of the first Hurricanes. After the retreat from Burma into India, he was appointed Wing Commander Flying 165 Wing, at Dum Dum on 8 September 1942, moving to 293 Wing in October and to command 169 Wing in February 1943, followed by 185 Wing. Finally in October 1943, he returned to 165 Wing, leading it to the Arakan Front in late November. In July 1944 he was posted to the staff of HQ, Eastern Air Command, in Calcutta, and returned to the UK in September 1944. He then served with Transport Command in April 1945, becoming commander of RAF Boreham. He was awarded OBE in January 1945. He remained in the RAF after the war, becoming a Wing Commander again in 1949, and retired as an Acting Group Captain in October 1959. Subsequently his daughter was decorated for her work as an RAF Nursing Sister during the Falklands War, but his son Nigel, who had become a Wing Commander Tornado pilot at RAF Marham, was killed in action when his GR1 was shot down during the Gulf War on 20 January 1991. "Jimmie" Elsdon was living in retirement in Cambridgeshire at the time of writing.

Total Victories: 7 destroyed, 1 destroyed unconfirmed, 2 damaged.

FORBES, Athol Stanhope   Wing Commander

Athol Forbes was born in Hanover Square, London, in 1912. He joined the RAF in November 1935 on a short service commission, attending the School of Army Co-operation at Old Sarum, following which he was retained on the School's staff in August 1937. When 303 (Polish) Squadron was formed in August 1940, he was posted as one of the British flight commanders. His introduction to action was quite traumatic. On 6 September, having claimed a Bf109 shot down, his own aircraft was damaged and he crashed on landing at Northolt, having suffered a slight wound. Next day, having enjoyed another successful engagement, he was again hit by Bf109s, and this time was obliged to force-land in Essex, once more being slightly wounded. On 11th he was hit yet again, this time landing his damaged Hurricane at Heston, having been wounded for a third time. On 17 October he was posted to command 66 Squadron, being awarded a DFC a few days later, followed at the end of the year by a Virtuti Militari, 5th Class, from the Poles. He remained with 66 until October 1941, when he was posted to a staff job at HQ, to Group, the award of a Bar to his DFC following in November. Promoted Wing Commander in July 1943, he was posted out to India, serving with 165 Wing in 222 Group. Awarded an OBE in June 1948, he moved in August to HQ, 221 Group, as SASO. He left the RAF in 1948 as a Group Captain, and died in 1981.

Total Victories: 7 and 2 shared destroyed, 1 probable.

HALLOWES, Herbert James Lampriere   Wing Commander

Jim "Darkie" Hallowes was born in Lambeth, London, on 17 April 1912. He lived for three years in the Falkland Islands as a boy, where his father was a medical officer. In January 1929 he joined the RAF Apprentice Scheme, training at Hatton as a metal rigger, passing out in 1932. Two years later he volunteered for pilot training, becoming a Sergeant Pilot in August 1936, and being posted to 43 Squadron. He saw early action over the north of the UK in 1940, while during the fighting over the French coastal area on 7 June his Hurricane was set on fire by an attacking Bf109E. This overshot as he was about to bale out and he remained in his cockpit long enough to claim its destruction, before baling out and suffering a dislocated shoulder. Soldiers who picked him up, confirmed having seen the Messerschmitt crash. He was awarded both a DFM and Bar on 6 September and was commissioned during that month. In November he was posted to 65 Squadron as a flight commander, but was rested soon afterwards. Early in 1942, he began a second tour as a flight commander in 122 Squadron, but in July was given command of 222 Squadron. A month later he moved to lead 165 Squadron, with which unit he made his final claims, and was awarded a DFC in June 1943. He had been rested again in March, but in October 1943 commenced a fourth tour at the head of 504 Squadron, which he led until March 1944. He was then promoted Acting Wing Commander and became airfield commander at RAF Dunsfold. He remained in the RAF after the war in the Secretarial Branch, retiring in July 1956 as a Wing Commander. He then worked for the Ministry of Transport until his retirement, and died on 20 October 1987.

Total Victories: 17 and 2 shared destroyed, 4 probables, 8 damaged.

HARRIES, Raymond Hiley   Wing Commander

Born in South Wales in 1916, Ray Harries was a medical student at Guys Hospital when war broke out. He joined the RAF, and on completion of training was posted to 43 Squadron in Scotland. He had one night encounter with a German bomber here, but was then posted to 52 OTU at Debden as an instructor. He returned to operations in February 1942 with a posting to 131 Squadron as a flight commander, remaining with this unit until December, when he was given command of 91 Squadron, which in April 1943 received the first of the new Griffon-engined Spitfire XIIs. In June he was awarded a Bar to the DFC which he had received in August 1942. At the time the squadron moved to Westhampnett to join 41 Squadron in forming a Spitfire XII Wing. Victories mounted up fast, bringing a promotion to Wing Leader of the Westhampnett Wing in August, a second Bar to the DFC the following month, and then a DSO in November. At the end of the year he accompanied Bill Crawford-Compton to the USA to lecture on tactics. Returning to the UK in spring 1944, he became Wing Leader of 135 Wing in 2nd TAF, operating over France. In January 1945 he underwent a conversion course on Tempests at Predannack, as the Wing was to convert to these aircraft. He was then given command of the Wing, but shortly afterwards was posted to Wing Commander Training at 84 Group, 2nd TAF, until the war ended. He was subsequently awarded a Bar to his DSO and Croix de Guerre by both the French and Belgian governments. He remained in the RAF after the war, becoming commanding officer of 92 Squadron in November 1949. On 14 May 1950 he became lost in bad weather over Liverpool Bay and was killed whilst attempting to bale out of his Meteor.

Total Victories: 15 and 3 shared destroyed, 2 probables, 5 and 1 shared damaged.

HAY, Ronald Cuthbert   Lieutenant Colonel

Ronnie Hay was born in Perth, Scotland, on 4 October 1916. He sought to join the Royal Navy in 1935, but was already too old for a cadetship, so joined the Royal Marines instead. After training on shore duty, he undertook a spell aboard HMS *Devonshire* in the Mediterranean. Early in 1938 he volunteered for the Fleet Air Arm, returning to UK for training at Netheravon and Eastleigh. In December 1939 he was sent to Hyeres in Southern France for deck landing training, returning to the UK in 1940. Initially selected for the new 806 Squadron by Charles Evans, but was posted instead to 801 Squadron on *Ark Royal* for the Norwegian operations of April 1940, claiming his first victory on his first operational sortie. He was then posted to Lee-on-Solent to fly Swordfish float planes prior to operating Roc float planes from the fjords. The fall of Norway led instead to a posting to Detling to fly Skuas and Rocs over Channel convoys and then the Dunkirk beaches. A posting to Wick followed, where he joined 808 Squadron, receiving Fulmars, and in November 1940 this unit joined HMS *Ark Royal* and sailed for Gibraltar to join Force "H". Although his log book was lost subsequently when the carrier was sunk, he recalled a number of victories prior to the availability of unit records, and noted these in his replacement log book. These covered the period December 1940-February 1941. He remained active in the Mediterranean throughout 1941, claiming seven individual or shared victories here until the loss of *Ark Royal* on 13 November, and was awarded a DSC. Returning to the UK aboard HMS *Nelson*, he was posted to 759

Squadron at Yeovilton and then commanded 761 Squadron for six months, both being training units. He then prepared to form 897 Squadron, but instead was given command of 809 Squadron, a Fulmar unit which was training for the Army Co-operation role during the forthcoming invasion of French North-West Africa. In the event, the unit did not go and he then spent four months preparing a Naval Air Tactical Memorandum. He then attended the RAF Wing Leaders' course at Charmey Down, following which he returned to the Mediterranean as Air Group Tactics Officer, instructing on raid escort and fighter tactics. In November 1943 he moved to Ceylon, where he became Commander Flying at China Bay, and then of 6 Wing at Minneriya, charged with the defence of Southern India. In August 1944 he became Wing Leader of 47 Naval Wing aboard HMS *Victorious* on Corsairs, and led attacks on Palembang in January 1945 as Air Co-ordinator, his aircraft fitted with oblique and vertical cameras, and accompanied by three wingmen. During the two raids here, he claimed for victories over Japanese fighters, two of them shared. Awarded a DSO in May 1945 and a Bar to his DSC in July, he remained with the British Pacific Fleet until the end of June, and then travelled back to the UK via Ceylon, arriving in September. In October he became Naval Member of the Tactical Research Centre at CFE, West Raynham, but a bad crash put him out of action for a year and a half. In February 1948 he returned to the Marines as a Captain, seeing service with 40 Commando in Malta, Cyprus, Hong Kong and Malaya until 1951, when he was transferred to the Navy, becoming Lieutenant Commander Flying at Lee-on-Solent. He flew Fireflies here until 1953, and then Sea Furies. In 1954 he became President of the Plans Division and in 1955, promoted Commander, CO of RNAS Stretton on Vampires. In 1957 he commanded 700 Squadron at Ford, training pilots on Sea Hawks, following which he attended 17 Course at the Joint Services Staff College before becoming Naval Commander at Old Sarum. His final posting was to the Sultan of Ismir, Turkey (a NATO appointment), investigating aircraft failure rates. On leaving the service, he undertook boat charter work in the Mediterranean for 12 years, before retiring to Wiltshire, where he was living at the time of writing.

Total Victories: 4 (approx.) and 9 (approx.) shared destroyed, 3 shared damaged.

KILMARTIN, John Ignatius   Wing Commander

"Killy" Kilmartin was born in Dundalk, Eire, on 8 July 1913, the son of a forester and one of eight children. His father died when he was nine years old and he was shipped out to Australia under a scheme known as "Big Brother". As soon as he was old enough, he obtained a job on a cattle station in New South Wales, where he remained for nearly five years during the Great Depression of the Thirties, then joining an aunt in Shanghai, China. Here he worked as a clerk in the accounts department of the Shanghai Gas Works for over two years until he saw an advertisement for short service commission applicants in the RAF during 1936. Applying, he received a reply in about three months and set out on the Trans-Siberian railway in company with a group of Japanese sumo wrestlers heading for the Berlin Olympics. He was taught to fly at a civilian school in Perthshire, Scotland, and was then accepted by the RAF in February 1937, completing his training at 6 FTS, Netheravon, and joining 43 Squadron late in the year. He had been appointed adjutant at the outbreak of war, but when the opportunity arose to join 1 Squadron in France at the start of November 1939, he took it, becoming involved in several of the unit's early actions and then during the heavy fighting of the "Blitzkrieg" of May 1940. On return to the UK at the end of the month, he was posted as an instructor at 5 OTU until August, when he returned to 43 Squadron as a flight commander. Here he immediately claimed two further victories before the unit was withdrawn to the north to rest, receiving the award of a DFC on 8 October. In April 1941 he was posted to command 602 Squadron for a short period, but within a month went as a supernumerary to help form 313, the third Czech fighter squadron. In June he was posted out to West Africa, where he was to command 128 Squadron from March to August 1942. He returned to the UK late that year and was posted as a supernumerary to 504 Squadron, becoming commanding officer in January 1943. At the end of March he was promoted to Wing Commander and led the Hornchurch Wing during May. He then returned to 5 OTU for a spell of instruction, before going to HQ, 84 Group, in the new 2nd TAF as Wing Commander Op. During 1944 he was given command of 136 Wing, which was equipped with Typhoons, taking this unit to Normandy after the Invasion. When the Wing was disbanded later in June, he went to HQ, 2nd TAF, as Wing Commander Fighter Operations, where he remained until the end of the European war. In June 1945 he was sent out to Burma as Wing Leader, 910 Wing, on Thunderbolts until the end of the Far Eastern War, when he was sent to AHQ, East Indies, in Indonesia for nine months, after which he commanded Medan airfield in Sumatra. In mid-1946 he returned to the UK to undertake a long course at the Empire Flying School at Hullavington, before going out to Iraq to reform and command 249 Squadron at Habbaniyah on Tempest VIs for 18 months. He again returned to England to attend Staff

College at Bracknell, following which he was posted to Air Ministry on the staff of the Deputy Chief of Air Staff Training (Ops Training) on the fighter side until 1952. A spell as Wing Commander Admin. at Wunstorf in 83 Group, 2nd TAF, followed, and then he was seconded to NATO, Southern Europe HQ, on the Intelligence Staff in Naples for two years. A return to the UK brought a role as Wing Commander Ops at Turnhouse in the Fighter Command Caledonian Sector, followed by a move to the Western Sector. Finally early in 1957 he went to command a control and reporting station at Borgentreich in Germany until July 1958, when he retired from the service. Getting married, he settled in Devon where he ran a chicken farm for 15 years, before selling this and going abroad to various parts of Europe for ten years, 1974-1984. He then returned to Devon, where he was living in retirement at the time of writing.

Total Victories: 12 or 13 and 2 shared destroyed, 1 damaged.

STONE, Cedric Arthur Cuthbert   Wing Commander

"Bunny" Stone was born in Amritsar, India, on 8 December 1916, receiving his nickname at birth since he was covered in fluffy black hair. His father, a subaltern in Rattray's Scouts, was killed in Mesopotamia during the First World War. After a year at the College of Aero-Engineering in Chelsea, Stone attended Selwyn College, Cambridge, where he joined the University Air Squadron. In November 1936 he joined the RAF on a short service commission, being posted to 3 Squadron in February 1938. The unit was sent out to France at the start of the "Blitzkrieg" in May 1940, where he gained three victories and shared in two others, receiving a DFC on 31st of the month. On 10 June he was posted to 263 Squadron on its return from Norway, but on 13 July went to 245 Squadron in the north as a flight commander. In December he was posted to 607 Squadron, remaining with this unit until July 1941, when he became commanding officer of 17 Squadron. Late in the year the unit was posted to the Middle East as part of a wing due to operate on the southern Russian front, but the outbreak of the Pacific War led to the unit being sent to Burma instead. Over Rangoon he was to destroy two Japanese bombers, one at night, before the squadron was forced to withdraw. In action until the end of the retreat into India, he received a Bar to his DFC on 10 April 1942. After a spell off operations, he commanded 135 Squadron from November 1943 to March 1944, later being promoted Wing Commander and serving with 222 Group in Ceylon. He left the RAF in 1946 to become and artist, and in 1947 flew out to Cape Town,

South Africa, in an Auster with his wife. He lived there until the early 1960s, when he returned to England following a divorce. Here he lived at Yattendon on Lord Hiffe's estate until his death in 1990.

Total Victories: 5 and 2 shared destroyed, 1 unconfirmed destroyed, 2 damaged, 2 destroyed on the ground.

STOREY, William John   Squadron Leader

"Jack" Storey was born in Sale, Victoria, on 15 November 1915, becoming a local school teacher there before the war. Joining the RAAF in 1940, he attended EFTS in New South Wales and 5 FTS in Canada, subsequently arriving in the UK, where, after operational training, he joined 135 Squadron in September 1941. Shortly afterwards this squadron departed for overseas, its destination reportedly the Caucasus, in the Soviet Union. The Japanese attack in the Pacific caused the destination to be changed, personnel eventually disembarking in India. On 18 January 1942, he was one of the first members of the unit to reach Mingaladon airfield, near Rangoon, Burma. Here on 29 January on his first flight in two months, and his first operational sortie, he shot down a Nakajima Ki27 "Nate" fighter. In a big fight over Mingaladon on 6 February he was to claim two more and two probables, while later in the month he added a fourth success, being promoted flight commander shortly afterwards, directly from the rank of Pilot Officer, due to his proven ability as a skilful leader in combat. When the retreat from Burma ended, he had flown 60 hours in 28 days. A year later, still with the squadron, he led six Hurricanes over Akyab Island from a forward strip near the frontier, and here he claimed a Ki43 "Oscar" shot down during a fierce dogfight. That same afternoon, after escorting a VIP's aircraft away from the area, he returned to Akyab with his section to have "another look". Three sections each of three Ki43s were seen, the highest trio finally attempted to intercept, and all were claimed shot down, two of them by Storey. He was awarded a DFC on 9 April and on 3 May intercepted a formation of Ki43s returning from a sweep over the Arakan. He claimed one shot down, which he saw crash into jungle on the southern slopes of Mount Victoria. This was not confirmed until some time later when the wreckage was found by an army patrol. He was to see no further aerial action before leaving the unit in August 1943 to become an instructor at 1572 Gunnery Flight in India, having also been Mentioned in Despatches. In 1944 he returned to Australia, where he was promoted Squadron Leader and became Commanding Officer of Flying and Chief Instructor at the RAAF's Central Gunnery School at Cressy, near Geelong, Victoria. He left the RAAF at the end of the war to complete he BA degree at the University of Melbourne. Returning to teaching, he became a secondary school principal until his retirement in 1976. He then acquired a small property near Melbourne to set up a Connemara Pony Stud as a hobby. He was still so engaged at the time of writing.

Total Victories: 8 destroyed, 2 probables.

SUTTON, Fraser Barry   Wing Commander

Barry Sutton was born in Witney, Oxfordshire, on 28 January 1919. He worked as a journalist on an evening newspaper in Northampton before the war, joining the RAFVR in 1937. In February 1939 he entered the RAF on a short service commission, being posted to 56 Squadron in September, just as the war broke out. Detached to operate in France during the May 1940 "Blitzkrieg", he was attacked by a Bf109 just after taking off on 18th, and was wounded in one foot, force-landing successfully. On 28 August, during the Battle of Britain, he was shot down again (he believed by a Spitfire in error), baling out of Hurricane R4198, but suffering severe burns which were to keep him in hospital for a year. During this time he wrote *Way of a Pilot*, recounting his experiences. Posted to the Middle East on release from hospital, he was then sent to Burma as a flight commander in 136 Squadron, then becoming commanding officer of 135 Squadron in February 1942. In mid-April he was posted to Air HQ, Bengal, as a staff officer. Early in 1943 he went to the Air Fighting Training Unit at Amarda Road as CFI and then to HQ, Delhi, as Chief Tactics Officer. In April 1944 he was made Wing Leader of a Spitfire Wing in Bengal, and at the end of June moved to another Wing in the Imphal Valley. He returned to the UK in 1945, where on 17 August he was awarded a DFC. He also wrote a second book, *Jungle Pilot* (MacMillan, 1946). With the conclusion of the war he spent three years as Personal Air Secretary to the Secretary of State for Air, then commanding Aston Down. A period on the staff at the RAF Staff College, Andover, followed, and in 1957 he took command of North Weald airfield, followed in 1958 by Horsham St Faith. A spell in Cyprus was followed by a posting to Australia as an RAF Liaison Officer. Finally in 1965 he commanded RAF Bassingbourne until his retirement from the service in April 1966. He died on 16 March 1988.

Total Victories: 4 and 1 shared destroyed, 2 probables, 1 damaged.

WEST, Ronald   Squadron Leader

Ron West joined 43 Squadron as a Pilot Officer in the latter part of 1941, but shortly afterwards was posted as a reinforcement to Malta. Here he served with 126 Squadron early in 1942, and by March had been promoted Flying Officer. On 10 March his Hurricane was attacked by a Bf109F of III/JG53 as he went in to land and he had to make a crash-landing. He was transferred to 249 Squadron on 6 April to fly Spitfires and on 30th was promoted Flight Lieutenant, being flown to Gibraltar to help lead in a further reinforcement flight. This he did on 9 May, flying off USS *Wasp*. As he approached Luqa, he attempted to formate on what proved to be a formation of Bf109s and he was attacked, his aircraft being damaged, although he was able to force-land safely. By the end of May he had claimed six victories and was recommended for a DFC, then posted to 185 Squadron. After one further claim, he was recommended for a Bar to his decoration, both awards arriving close together in July. Shortly after this his tour ended and he returned to the UK. After a rest he was posted to 131 Squadron at Bolt Head in 1943. Soon after his arrival he was taking off with a 45 gallon "slipper" tank fitted to his aircraft, when he discovered that the undercarriage would not retract fully. He attempted to land at once, but it refused to extend again, and he belly-landed on the metal PSP surface, whereupon the tank blew up and he was killed.

Total Victories: 8 destroyed, 3 probables, 8 and 1 shared damaged.

APPENDIX D: NUMBER 17 SQUADRON RAF – SUMMARY OF FIGHTER TACTICS AND SQUADRON FORMATIONS

This summary of squadron tactics and formations supersedes and thus cancels all previous tracts on the subject. The reason for the change in tactics and formations will be obvious now that our Hurricanes have been replaced by the Spitfire VIIIs, thus giving us, for the first time in two years, a machine which is definitely superior to any enemy fighter. Because of this superiority you will notice that the following "Gen" is of a much more offensive nature than formerly, but that does not mean that you can fly around the sky just gazing through the reflector sight.

Spend as much of your time as possible in searching, especially behind and in the sun.

SQUADRON FORMATIONS

Divisions Line Astern

Before we go any further. You will notice that we now have only three colours in the squadron. Not only does this simplify matters considerably from the R/T point of view, but since the colour of the Starboard division is always Green and the colour of the Port division is always Red, then there should be no difficulty in remembering your colour should your division have to change sides, i.e. as in a cross-over turn.

A simple rule to determine your colour is to consider the divisions as navigation lights, i.e., White in the Middle, Green on the Starboard and Red on the Port.

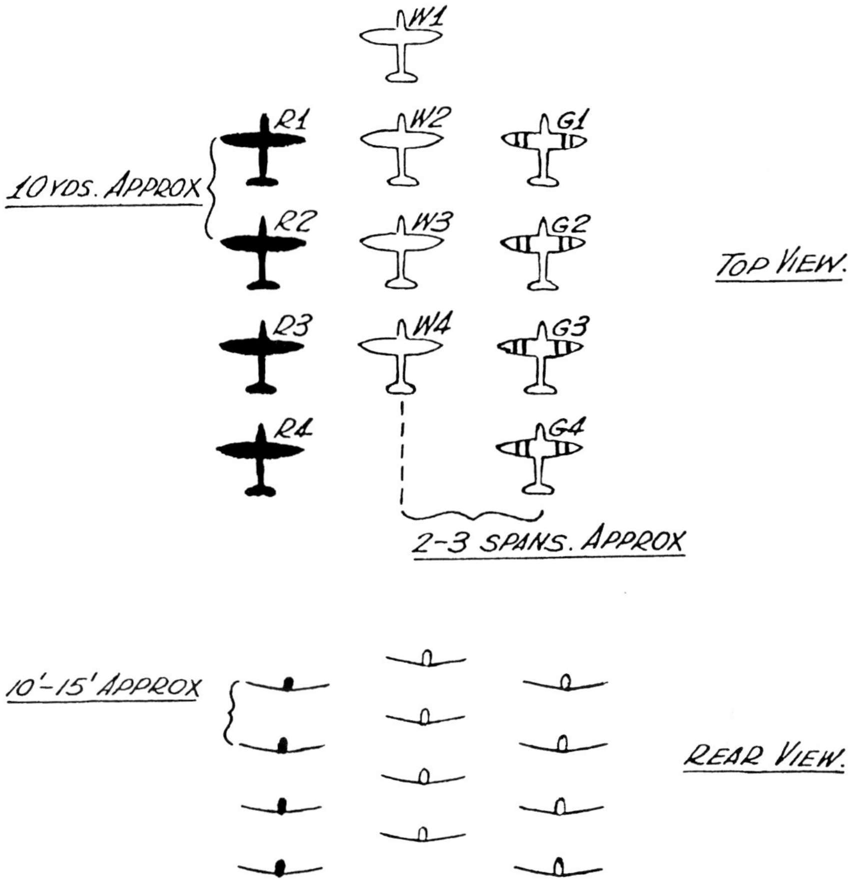

W1
R1
W2
G1
10 YDS. APPROX
R2
W3
G2
TOP VIEW.
R3
W4
G3
R4
G4
2-3 SPANS. APPROX
10'-15' APPROX
REAR VIEW.

During practise flying, to help you remember your colour, you may be asked at intervals by the Squadron Commander to "Check In". On receipt of the above order you will answer as follows: "White 2, Roger", "White 3, Roger", "White 4, Roger", "Green 1 Roger" and so on through the Green division and lastly Red division, ending up always with "Red 4 Roger". In any case you will be asked this after take-off on all flights where R/T silence is not essential. It ensures that your R/T is in working order. If it is not, see action to be taken under the heading, "Action in event of R/T failure".

The above formation will be used for joining up immediately after take-off, for climbing turns in gaining height over base and for quick manoeuvring onto vectors during interception work. It will also be used for orbiting while waiting for bombers to rendezvous and, in this latter case, may be flown with the divisions even more strung out in line astern than shown above. It will be appreciated that this formation is very vulnerable from the rear and thus it will be only used when there is little likelihood of imminent attack by enemy aircraft. It is a good formation for the dirty type of monsoon weather, which we will doubtless experience again, for it permits fairly violent weaving in and out of cloud banks and between rain storms.

As soon as weather (or the fact that a straight course can be flown for a reasonable length of time on a vector during an interception) permits, then the following formation will be adopted:

Search Formation

To go from "Divisions Line Astern" to "Search", the leader may signal by pitching his aircraft up and down in the looping plane, or use the R/T. (To return from "Search" to "Line Astern" he may rock his aircraft, quickly, from side to side in the rolling plane).

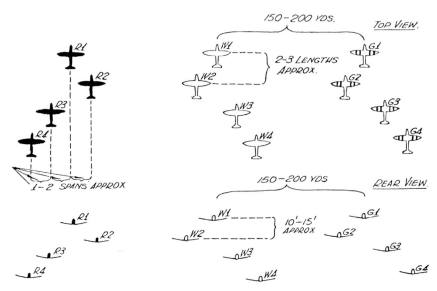

You can see from the above lay-out that we have retained to a small extent the cross-cover search by flying the divisions in a slight echelon. However, since we still want to retain maximum manoeuvrability, then, if a division begins to turn you should slip straight back into line astern.

The squadron turn will be done by the outside divisions crossing over and above the centre division in the usual manner unless the order "Break Turn" is given (see, "R/T, use of") and then the divisions will do their turns inside one another (but not so violently as the "Break Turn" from "Battle" formation). The No's 2, 3 and 4 in this case will follow their leader around in a tight line astern.

Thus it will be seen that this formation is still very manoeuvrable in both 90° and 180° turns and, at the same time, it is sufficiently opened out to allow individuals to search sideways and also will allow a slight amount of "jinking" while searching. Further to this, the leader of each division can see each man in his formation by inclining his head slightly, one way or the other.

The respective Division Commanders of the Port and Starboard Divisions will use their own discretion for stepping up or down sun. They will normally only do this when the sun is well on the one beam and makes formation keeping difficult.

By the way. All No. 3's are Section Leaders. Therefore No. 4's are just as much responsible for sticking to them, as they are, to the whole division.

The next formation we go into is:

Battle Formation

If you are flying in a division and you get the above order, or if the Squadron Commander does a pitching movement and the Division Leaders also start pitching then this is what happens:

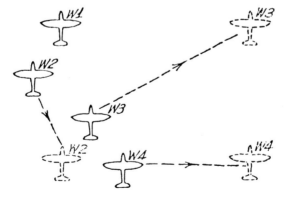

After each division has completed the above manoeuvre (except Red Division which does opposite to the other two) then this is how the whole formation should look:

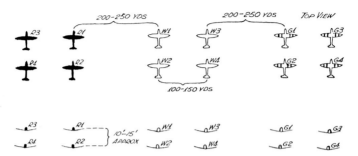

This formation gives exceptionally good cross-cover protection of the rear without weaving and it permits maximum use of the 180° "Break Turn". In this manoeuvre the wing men (No. 2's and No. 4's) follow their leaders around in close line astern. To be effective the No. 1's and 3's must always keep well forward in true line abreast.

No doubt you are wondering what is going to happen if the Squadron has to do a 90°, or less than 180°, turn. Here's the gen:

Turn to Starboard:

White 1 starts around and White 3 dives under and joins back into line astern as the turn lengthens and he falls back.

Green 1 starts around and by diving under (as in normal cross-over) he aims to finish up with his division on the Port side of White division (therefore he also turns a bit slower). Green 3, of course, dives under and comes into line astern (see figure below).

Red 1 turns fairly sharply, to cross-over behind and above White division and finish on his Starboard side, and this automatically causes Red 3 to fall back into line astern.

This is how it looks half-way through the turn:

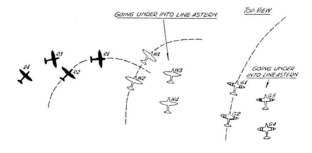

This is how it will look when nearly completed (we hope):

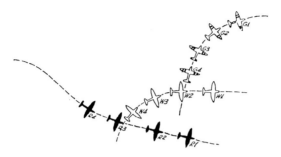

What is wrong with this picture? You're quite right. We shall now have to remember that the colours have changed. Try to remember this as soon as the turn has finished and don't let all this confuse you because it always looks difficult at first. Practise will make you perfect and we shall see that you get plenty of it.

Again, for your information we have:

Turn to Port:

White 1 starts around normally and White 3 falls automatically into line astern.

Green 1 starts around fairly quickly because he aims to cross-over and finish inside (Port side) of White division, Green 3 falls into line astern so damn quick that it isn't even funny.

Red 1 starts his turn a bit more slowly (while diving under the front of White division with the intention of finishing with his division on the Starboard side of White division) and Red 3 goes down and under in the prescribed fashion, in order to eventually finish up in line astern. Here's how it should look half-way through the turn:

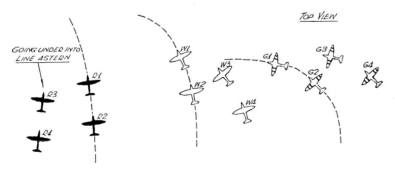

And here is how it should be when the turn is nearing completion:

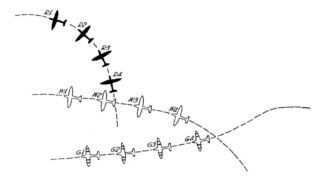

All you have to do to finish it off is to automatically change colour. Any comments about "b----y chameleons" you can keep to yourself.

Having arrived in the line astern position, any continuation of the Squadron turn will be taken care of by further normal cross-overs as in "Search Formation". As soon as a straight course is being flown then the original Battle Formation can be easily resumed, or otherwise, as ordered.

If, while in "Battle Formation", the Squadron Commander rocks his aircraft violently in the rolling plane, then this is the signal for immediate return to "Search" formation. Remember these visual signals because you must learn to do all these manoeuvres with an absolute minimum of R/T.

The "Break-Down"

This manoeuvre simply consists of the whole squadron, or any one specified division, or even section, flicking smartly over onto their backs and completing the half-roll and pull-out in formation. Not only can it be used if a division or section are hopelessly outnumbered by attacks from above, but it is a good fast way of attacking enemy aircraft which may have passed underneath the squadron head-on. In any case the occasion may well arise when it can be used and the R/T orders must be clear as to which side the half-roll must be done. This brings us to:

R/T. "Use Of"

This will naturally be used as sparingly as is humanly possible. All normal turns can easily be done without it as No. 1's and No. 3's are always formating on their Squadron and Division commanders, respectively.

a) For break turns the following will always be used:

To "Break" to the right:

"HELLO NITWITS! RIGHT RIGHT – BREAK!"

To "Break" to the left:

"HELLO NITWITS! LEFT – BREAK!"

The power to "Break" the squadron will rest with the Section, Division and Squadron Leaders only, until further notice.

b) To "Break" one division to the right and two to the left (in event of being attacked from both sides) the drill will be as follows:

"HELLO NITWITS! RED DIVISION LEFT, REMAINDER RIGHT RIGHT BREAK – GO!" or vice-versa:

"HELLO NITWITS! GREEN DIVISION RIGHT, REMAINDER LEFT BREAK – GO!"

c) To "Break Down" the following will be used:

"HELLO NITWITS! BREAK DOWN RIGHT RIGHT – GO!" or:

"HELLO NITWITS! BREAK DOWN LEFT – GO!"

If the unit to be "Broken Down" is smaller then it can be designated after the "NITWITS".

The power to "Break Down" the whole Squadron will rest with the Squadron Commander only, until further notice.

Action in the Event of R/T Failure:

The pilot concerned will rock his machine slowly in the rolling plane.

If the Squadron Commander's R/T packs it in, then the next senior Division Commander will swing his flight into the middle and take over the lead of the squadron. The C.O.'s section will fall back into the No. 3 and 4 positions in his own division and the original Nos 3 and 4 will take over as the leading section in that division.

If a Division Leader's R/T fails he will fall back and his section will become the last in that division.

Except during an interception there should be no need to return to the aerodrome because of R/T failure.

Cloud Flying

By now you should know which types of cloud you can and cannot fly through. Under certain conditions it is sometimes necessary to fly the whole squadron formation through cloud. Here is how it will be done:

a) From the "Line Astern" formation the order will be given:

"PREPARE FOR CLOUD FLYING."

b) On receipt of this information the division leaders will set compasses and gyros and note the A.S.I. and rate of climb, or descent.

c) When they have done this they will swing away to about 100 yards and allow No.'s 2, 3 and 4 to come forward into close "VIC" from their normal "Search Formation" stations.
   Thus:

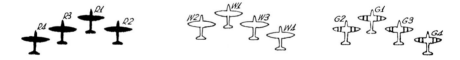

d) When the Squadron Commander sees that everybody is all set he will give the following order:

"ENTERING CLOUD, DIVISIONS MOVE OUT"

e) On receipt of this order Red 1 and Green 1 will swing off to Port and Starboard respectively, on a new vector of 5° for three minutes. They will then straighten out and continue on the original vector at the same A.S.I. and rate of ascent or descent.

f) On breaking cloud they must immediately look inwards for the centre division and, upon contact, reform in their original stations unless told otherwise. (On coming out above cloud be prepared to go straight into "Battle Formation" because you could be a sitting shot).

g)   There may come a time when the formation is inside cloud and it will have to turn back and descend. The order will be:

"HELLO NITWITS, TURNING BACK – TURNING BACK GO!"

After acknowledging this order, Red and Green divisions will turn outwards to Port and Starboard respectively and do a rate 1 turn for 180°. White Leader will fly straight ahead for two minutes and turn back in whichever direction he chooses. The whole formation will let down at 500 feet per minute and 250 miles per hour.

This may well mean that the whole formation may be split up, but this is better than flying gaily into a thunder-storm and splitting up the kite itself.

Flying in the "G" Suit

With this suit on you must still maintain your formation and your team-work up to the very last minute. Once you have split up and it has developed into a case of "Every man for himself" then you must still endeavour to attack only when you have the height on the Jap.

There comes a time however, in the life of every pilot when he has everything, including the kitchen sink, thrown at him and this may be the time when a sticky position can be reversed into a treacherous trap for the lecherous Jap. With plenty of altitude in hand (go home quickly if you haven't got this) do a flick half-roll onto your back and, after you have built up sufficient speed in an aileron turn, then convert this into a powered spiral and hold a constant 6 "G" minimum.

After praying fervently that your opponent is not wearing an "Anti-G" device you may well find that he has been silly enough to follow you down. If he has, then you've got him by the short and curlies. If he has not then don't hang around because he may still follow you down later on.

You have got a good tactical defensive device against enemy fighters. Use it as such and don't at the same time be led into dog-fighting at speeds lower than 250 m.p.h., or "G" lower than 5, or a height lower than 15,000 feet.

Lastly

Your Spitfire has to be flown above the enemy to be really useful so, in a scrap, always regain height as soon as possible when the squadron splits up. By doing this you may have a chance to protect one of your own aircraft underneath from being jumped.

Remember always: but especially when alone:

"WATCH AND WEAVE, FOR THE KINGDOM
OF HEAVEN IS AT HAND"

AUTHOR'S NOTE: The above paper was produced by me, after I had left 17 Squadron, to illustrate to other squadrons the methods we used, both before and after receiving the Spitfires, to ensure that we could operate our twelve machines in the air almost as one. It simply sets out in more readable form the various notes we had on the subject. I had the time to do this while on the RAAF test-flying unit in Australia.

The main aim was to arrive over the target area (be it on bomber escort or interception of an incoming raid) in a cohesive group without having the "Tail-end Charlie" problems that beset squadrons in the Battle of Britain, thus allowing any out-of-formation stragglers to be easily picked off by the enemy. It was a foregone conclusion that the squadron would be split up into small units if large numbers of enemy were encountered, but they were at least in reasonably close proximity to one another for mutual support.

Sadly, although we could fly all the above patterns really well after practice, they were never able to be used by the squadron in combat, as the Spitfires became mainly ground-support aircraft in the final retaking of Burma in 1945, due to the Japanese being almost entirely without air support. The squadron shot down only seven confirmed (and two probably destroyed) Japanese aircraft in the whole of that campaign.

APPENDIX E: GLOSSARY OF AUSTRALIAN AND AIR FORCE TERMS

ASI: Airspeed indicator.

blue: A misbehaviour.
brawl: A fight or melee, generally with more than two antagonists.
browned off: Bored; dissatisfied; fed-up.
bunds: The low earthen banks in rice fields to contain water.
buckboard: Generally a four-seater car with the rear seats removed and replaced with an open tray, often without sides. Used on farms as a carry-all.

chooks: Domestic egg-laying hens.
clapped out: Worn out.
cooee: Australian way of calling "Ahoy", "Halloo", "Yoo Hoo".
Cranwellian: A wordplay on the RAF Officer Training College at Cranwell.

Dakota Douglas DC2, twin-engine transport aircraft.
DSC: Distinguished Service Cross (Navy).

emus: A genus of large wingless birds peculiar to the Australian continent – closely related to the cassowary.

fête champêtre: Open air fair.
fitters: Ground staff who maintained the various components of an aircraft to ensure it was operational; that is, airframe, engine, radio, armaments.
flap: A panic, mad rush, sudden alarm, or such.

gen: Information, lowdown, good oil, and so on.
Götterdämmerung: Literally "twilight of the gods" (German).
Gp/Capt.:   Group Captain.

hobble: A leather strap to go around the pastern of a horse. Normally one on each front leg, connected by a short rope or chain to allow enough freedom to graze but not to stray too far from camp.
Hurricane 2c: Hurricane equipped with four 20-millimetre cannons, as opposed to the normal Hurricane 2b, which had eight .303-inch machine-guns.

jumped: Attacked by an unseen aircraft.

kangaroo dog: A cross between the Australian kelpie sheepdog and the greyhound. Used in the early days, before the kangaroo was protected, for hunting them down.
kite: Any aircraft.
kud: A ditch with a side bank.

line: Any statement or action with a connotation of boasting or bragging.
laissez-aller: French for carelessness.

mallee: A bushy Australian eucalypt tree, 4 to 6 metres tall.
MT: Motor transport.

natter: Talk.

OAM: Order of Australia Medal.
OBE: Order of the British Empire.

paddy: Rice field contained within a bund.
panga: A large-bladed knife for hacking through jungle.
pastern: That part of a horse's foot between the fetlock (ankle) and the hoof.
prang: A term originally coined by the RAF to mean an aircraft accident.
PR: Photographic Reconnaissance.

readiness: A fighter ready to take off at a moment's notice.
remounts: Horses trained in military methods.

rhubarb: A flight over enemy territory (generally at low level) seeking targets of opportunity.

RT: Radio Telephony.

sheep station: A sheep ranch, often hundreds of square miles in area. There is one in Australia as big as the whole of England.

sprogs: Nonoperational pilots under training.

stall: The angle reached by an aircraft wing at which the airflow over it is no longer smooth and it loses its capacity to lift.

tea-tree, ti-tree: *Leptospermum* species. Multistemmed, bushy, decorative shrubs, 3 to 5 metres tall.

VIP: Very important person.

wallah: A headman or leader (oriental use mainly).

INDEX